ABIA NAZIM

HOW ADAPTIVE ARE CHILDREN?

Exploring Various Factors

Abstract

The present research aimed to assess the adaptive skills of children and to explore their relationship with various personal, social and familial variables. To achieve this purpose, two main phases were designed. Phase- I aimed to develop an indigenous scale of adaptive functioning and to establish its psychometric properties. The final scale comprised 206 items and four factors namely daily living skills, social skills, self care skills and home living skills, collectively accounted for 64.23 % variance in factor analysis. The results of phase-I supported the newly developed scale as having strong psychometric characteristics through adequate evidences to support reliability indices along with good construct, content and criterion validity. The main objective of phase – II was to assess adaptive skills and the degree to which different psychosocial factors relate and predict adaptive functioning in children. The sample of main study consisted of 436 participants divided into three developmental groups, children with intellectual disabilities (n=105), ASD (n=92) and typical development (n=239). The joint family system, negative affectivity temperament, family income, single parent family and behavioral problems observed to have inverse correlation with adaptive skills scores. The results revealed that three developmental groups differed significantly from each other when compared on intellectual functioning, adaptive functioning and temperament. IQ and disability severity emerged as two strong predictors of adaptive behaviors in children. Whereas, gender and family income failed to predict adaptive behavior scores significantly. The findings of present research have significant implications for both clinical and educational settings.

CONTENTS

Page No

Acknowledgements ……………………………………………………………… i

Abstract ……………………………………………………………………….. ii

Table of Content……………………………………………………………..…iii

List of Tables ……………………………………………………………….....vi

List of Figures ………………………………………………………………. xii

List of Appendices ………………………………………………………… xiii

CHAPTER – I: INTRODUCTION………………………………...…………....…....…... 1

Background of Adaptive Skills Concept ………………………………………….…..3

Structure of Adaptive Skills Construct....……………………………………………...6

Dimensions of Adaptive Skills …………………………………………...………..7

Factors that Influence Adaptive Functioning……………………………………………9

Assessment of Adaptive Skills …..……………………………………………………..24

Psychometric Concerns in Using Adaptive Skills Scales……………...……………...25

Adaptive Behavior Scales with Well-Known Properties…………………………………28

Selection and Use of Adaptive Skills Scales in General Clinical Practice...…………31

Cultural Sensitivity of Adaptive Skills Scales…………………………….…...……….32

Adaptive Skills and Pakistani Culture …………………………………...…………....33

Assessment of Adaptive Skills in Pakistan………………………………………...35

CHAPTER-II: REVIEW OF LITERATURE…………………………………...37

Adaptive Skills Construct and Measures ………………………………...…………37

Adaptive Skills and IQ……………………………………………………………42

Adaptive Skills and Developmental Psychopathologies 46

Correlates and Predictors of Adaptive Skills......... 54

Culture and Disability 56

Culture and Adaptive Skills..... 66

Adaptive Skills in Pakistan...75

Summary 78

Purpose of the Present Research 79

CHAPTER – III : RESEARCH DESIGN **84**

CHAPTER – IV: PHASE – I..**91**

Study – I : Substantive Validity Phase...92

CHAPTER- V: STRUCTURAL VALIDITY PHASE....................................**102**

Study –II. Establishing Content Validity...102

Study – III. Determining Construct Validity 109

Study – III. Determining Construct Validity....................................138

Step IV – Establishing Reliability and Cut off Scores...........................147

CHAPTER – VI: PHASE – II..**163**

Study – I. Translation of Children Behavior Questionnaire – Teacher

Short Form...163

Study – II . Translation and Adaptation of Temperament in Middle

Childhood Questionnaire...183

Study – III. Assessment of Psychosocial Correlates and Predictors of Adaptive Skills in

Children with Intellectual Disability, ASD and Typical Development.................199

GENERAL SUMMARY..**267**

Conclusion..279

Limitations and Recommendations..279

Implications...281

REFERENCES..**283**

APPENDICES..**339**

12

LIST OF TABLES

Table 1   Frequently used Temperament scales………………………………….......20

Table 2   Summary of AB Measures Reviewed…………………………….…......30

Table 3   General Response Rate of Participants…………………………..…...95

Table 4   General Response Rate of Experts for Content Validity Rating……. 104

Table 5   Number of Items in Sub-domains Before and After Expert ICV-I

Ratings…..107

Table 6   Demographic Characteristics of the Sample – A (N = 800)……….... 111

Table 7   Demographic Characteristics of the Sample – B (N = 186)……....…112

Table 8   Item Loadings for Exploratory Factor Analysis With Promax Rotation

of Adaptive Behavior Scale ………………………………………...…120

Table 9   Eigen Values and Variance Explained by Factors of Adaptive

Behavior Scale…………………………………………………….....133

Table 10   Inter Scale Correlation of Adaptive Behavior Subscales…………...135

Table 11   Item to Total Correlation of Adaptive Behavior Scale……………...136

Table 12   Mean, Standard deviation and Mean Difference Values for Subscales

of AB Scale…………...142

Table 13   Correlation between Scores of AB Scale and CABS……………......144

Table 14   Mean Scores of Clinical and Non- Clinical Groups on AB Scale..…145

Table 15   Correlation between Scores of Adaptive Behavior Scale and

CBCL…………………………………………………………….146

Table 16   Internal Consistency of Adaptive Behavior Scale…………………..149

Table 17   Intra Class Correlation Coefficient for First and Second Administration

Scores...150

Table 18   Summary of ROC Analysis Findings for Adaptive Behavior

Scale...150

Table 19   Mean and Standard Deviation of Scale Scores For CBQ–T Scale

Urdu...171

Table 20   Internal Consistency of CBQ – T Urdu and CBQ – T...................172

Table 21   Test Re Test Reliability of CBQ – T Urdu...............................173

Table 22   Correlation Coefficients of Scale Scores of CBQ – Teacher Form

Urdu Version..175

Table 23   Correlation of Items to Subscale Total of CBQ – T Urdu 176

Table 24   Intra Class Correlations between Parent and Teacher Scores...........177

Table 25   Correlation between Scores of CABS and Urdu CBQ-T................178

Table 26   Mean and Standard Deviation of Scale Scores for TMCQ Scale

Urdu...187

Table 27   Mean and Standard Deviation of TMCQ Original and TMCQ

Urdu...188

Table 28   Internal Consistency of TMCQ Urdu and TMCQ Original............189

Table 29   Test Re Test Reliability of TMCQ Urdu..................................190

Table 30   Correlation Coefficients for Subscales of TMCQ Urdu.................191

Table 31   Correlation of Item to Subscale Scores of TMCQ Urdu................193

Table 32   Intra Class Correlations between Parent and Teacher Scores...........194

Table 33   Correlation between Scores of IQ and TMCQ Urdu....................195

Table 34   Personal Demographic Characteristics of the Sample 206

Table 35   Family Demographic Characteristics of Sample (N = 436)..........207

Table 36   Education and Occupation of Fathers Across Group..................209

Table 37   Education and Occupation of Mothers Across Group..................210

Table 38   Correlation between Domains of Adaptive Behavior Score and

Behavioral Problems 211

Table 39   Correlation between Domains of Adaptive Behavior Score and

Family System 212

Table 40   Correlation between Adaptive Behavior Score and Family

Income..213

Table 41   Correlation between Domains of Adaptive Behavior Score and

Number of Siblings (N=436)..................................214

Table 42   Correlation between Domains of Adaptive Behavior Score and

Parental Education and Age................................... 215

Table 43   Correlation between Domains of Adaptive Behavior Score and

Parental Marital Status..216

Table 44   Means, Standard Deviations and F value of Composite Adaptive

Behavior Score for Three Groups (N =436).....................217

Table 45   Mean, SD and t values of Adaptive Behavior Scores for ID and ASD

Groups...218

Table 46   Correlation between Domains of Adaptive Behavior Scale,

Temperament and IQ (N= 436) 220

Table 47   Correlation between Scores of Adaptive Behavior Scale and IQ

Across Groups……………………………………………………...221

Table 48   MANOVA Results of Adaptive Behavior Domains by

Exceptionality………………………...…………………………..222

Table 49   Difference Between Adaptive Behavior Domain Scores Across

Groups…………………………………..…………………….…..222

Table 50   Means, Standard Deviations and F value of Composite Adaptive

Behavior for IQ Categories in ID Group…………………...……….224

Table 51   Means, Standard Deviations and F value of Composite Adaptive

Behavior for IQ Categories in ASD Group………….…………...…225

Table 52   Means, Standard Deviations and F value of Composite Adaptive

Behavior for IQ Categories in TD Group…………………………...226

Table 53   Correlation between Domains of Adaptive Scale and Age among

Three Groups …………………………………………...………..228

Table 54   Mean and Standard Deviation of ABS for Three Groups…..……...…229

Table 55   Means, Standard Deviations and F value of Composite Adaptive

Behavior Scores……………………………………….……………231

Table 56   Tukey's – HSD Post Hoc Comparison on ABS Across Age Groups232

Table 57   Means, Standard Deviations and F value of Daily Living Skills domain

of Adaptive Behavior for Age Groups……………..……………..233

Table 58   Means, Standard Deviations and F value of Social Skills Domain of Adaptive

Skills for Sample…………………………………..………...234

Table 59   Means, Standard Deviations and F value of Self Care domain of

Adaptive Skills for Sample…………..……………………………235

Table 60   Means, Standard Deviations and F value of Home Living Domain of Adaptive

Behavior……………………………………………………………..……..236

Table 61   MANOVA Results of Gender on Adaptive behavior for Combined

Sample(N= 436) ……………………………………………………..……237

Table 62   Mean and SD of Subscales of Adaptive behavior for ID Group….….239

Table 63   Gender Differences in Mean Scores of Adaptive Behavior Subscales

for ASD Group…..……………………………………………………......240

Table 64   Gender Differences in Mean Scores of Adaptive Behavior Subscales

for TD Group…..………………………………………………………...…241

Table 65   Correlation of Three Domains of Temperament and Adaptive Scale

for the Sample (N=436)………..………………………………………….242

Table 66   Correlation of Surgency and Domains of Adaptive Scale for the

Three Groups (N=436)…..…………………………………………….243

Table 67   Correlation of Effortful Control and Domains of Adaptive Scale for

the Three Groups (N=436)……..…………………………………...243

Table 68   Correlation of Negative Affectivity and Domains of Adaptive Scale

for the Three Groups (N=436)……………………………………...244

Table 69   Correlation between Daily Living Skills and Temperament Domains

for the Three Groups…….……………………………………………...245

Table 70   Correlation between Social Skills and Temperament Domains for the Three

Groups…………………………………………………………..………..246

Table 71   Correlation between Self Care and Temperament Domains for the

Three Groups…………………………………………………………….247

Table 72   Correlation between Home Living and Temperament Domains for the Three

Groups…………………………………………………………..249

Table 73   Mean and Standard Deviations of Scores on Three Main Domains of

Temperament For Sample……………………………………….250

Table 74   Gender Differences in Mean Scores of Temperament Subscales for TD

Group…………………………………………………………..252

Table 75   Multiple Linear Regression Analysis for Family Income, Age and IQ

as Predictors of Adaptive Behavior Scores….…………………......253

Table 76   Multiple Linear Regression Analysis for Diagnosis, Family System

and Gender as Predictors of Adaptive Behavior Scores……………..254

Table 77   Multiple Linear Regression Analysis for Surgency, Effortful Control

and Negative Affectivity as Predictors of Adaptive Behavior Composite

Scores………………………………………………………….......255

18

LIST OF FIGURES

Figure 1   Flow chart of present research project................................85

Figure 2   Conceptual Model of Phase-I based on Loevinger's Model of Scale

                     Development... 91

Figure 3   Flow chart showing details of response rate of participants 105

Figure 4   Comparison of number of items in each scale before and after the

                     ICVI calculation...108

Figure 5   Flow Chart of Sample 115

Figure 6   Selection of items at different stages of scale development...........143

Figure 7   Flow chart of studies of phase-II..164

Figure 8   Pattern of adaptive behavior scores across three groups...............219

Figure 9   Mean adaptive behavior scores across age groups.....................230

Figure 10   Mean differences in adaptive behavior scores across gender..........238

Figure 11   Mean scores of three groups on surgency, effortful control and

                     negative affectivity dimensions of temperament........................251

LIST OF APPENDICES

Appendix – A	Letter to generate items for Adaptive Behavior Scale	339
Appendix – B	Brief explanation of domains of Adaptive Behavior Scale	340
Appendix – C	Supplementary booklet for Adaptive Behavior Scale	342
Appendix – D	Consent Letter	353
Appendix – E	Reinforcers	354
Appendix – F	Sample pictures of mazes	356
Appendix – G	Instructions for CVI Raters	358
G.1	List of items sent for content validity review	361
G.2	Sample of ICVI rating charts	367
G.3	Details of ICVI Ratings of Items	369
Appendix – H	List of items deleted or changed after ICVI	372
Appendix – I	Demographic Form	378
Appendix – J	Adaptive Behavior Scale Response Sheet	379
Appendix – K	Permission Letters to Collect data	380
Appendix – L	List of Adaptive Behavior Items	385
Appendix – M	List of Items Placed in Each Factor after Factor Analysis	395
Appendix – N	Adaptive Behavior Score and Corresponding ROC Values	402
Appendix – O	CBQ T and TMCQ Questionnaires	405
Appendix – P	Permission to translate CBQ – T and TMCQ	416
Appendix – Q	Instructions for Translating CBQ-T and TMCQ into Urdu	417
Appendix – R	Permission to Change Items of CBQ-T and TMCQ	418
Appendix – R-1	CBQ –T Final Urdu Translation	420

Appendix – R-2   TMCQ Final Urdu Translation 424

Appendix – S   Details of Sample D, Second Study Phase-II.........................430

Appendix – T   Characteristics of Sample Representing ID Group.................431

Appendix – U   Characteristics of Sample Representing ASD Group..............434

Appendix – V   Characteristics of Sample Representing TD Group...................437

Appendix – W   Final Urdu Version of Indigenous Adaptive Behavior Scale......440

Appendix – X   Response Sheet of Indigenous Adaptive Behavior Scale...........446

Appendix – Y   Report Turnitin Review...448

Appendix – Z   List of Articles Published from thesis...450

CHAPTER- I

Introduction

Human's ability to evolve and adapt is the most distinct feature of its history. This is a continuous process which provides an index of differentiation between the individual's capacities and potential. The process of adaptation entails many diverse abilities of the individual be it intellectual, emotional or physical. Therefore, it seems pertinent that when an evaluation of individual's potential is made his abilities to adapt are observed as well. Adaptation is a process that ensures the survival and growth of the species and enables them to become effective unit of their community. A related developmental phenomenon is adaptive skills that help individuals to effectively meet the demands of their daily lives. The adaptive skills may provide analysis of patterns of an individual's usual performance in familiar settings like home and school and the individual's ability to generalize learned tasks across settings. Adaptive skills can provide an estimate of the degree to which the individual can meet the demands of personal life and whether he or she can respond appropriately to larger environmental or social demands. The concept may also be helpful in targeting areas for different skill acquisition.

As adaptive behaviors are comprised of various skills that are significant to normal functioning, assessment of this area cannot be underscored. Adaptive skills are sensitive to behavioral standards accepted as norms in a given culture. As adaptive skills are culture specific, clinicians emphasize the need to develop and use culturally relevant tools to assess adaptive functioning. Since long adaptive functioning has remained one of the most significant parameter to assess human functioning (Oakland, & Harrison, 2008). Initially, the adaptive construct was used to assess general mental ability or intelligence. Later, with the refinement of theories of general mental ability, adaptive skills were recognized as an independent construct reflecting significant dimensions of human functioning.

The present research project was an attempt to explore the adaptive skills of Pakistani children. Assessment of adaptive skills was believed to be important for both children following typical development and children with some significant clinical problems, therefore, present project attempted to explore the adaptive functioning of children in both these groups. In literature and clinical practice developmental patterns are categorized in three broad states, that is, delayed, deviant and typical (Levy, 2018). Children with delayed and deviant developmental pattern follow atypical pattern of development and have significant symptoms that warrant clinical attention. Intellectual disability and autism spectrum disorders are two most prevalent developmental problems that result in delayed or deviant development (CDC, 2017; Walters, 2010). Whereas, children and adolescents who achieve all developmental milestones age appropriately and maintain at least average level of functioning are believed to follow the typical developmental pattern. The current project followed this distinction and included both children following typical development and those with ID or ASD. As literature also signified the relationship of various factors with adaptive skills to better understand this construct. Therefore, a secondary aim was to study the relationship of adaptive skills with different psychosocial factors.

The chapter one of this thesis provides a brief introduction of adaptive behaviors and factors significantly associated with it. The second chapter discusses different researches related to the aim of the thesis. As the literature reveals absence of culturally relevant scales, therefore, it was decided to construct scale of adaptive behaviors and translate and adapt two relevant measures. Chapter 4, 5 and 6 describe the process of scale construction and translation. The final section of the thesis covers the assessment of main aims and discussion of the results.

Background of Adaptive Skills Concept

Throughout the long history of mental retardation adaptive functioning has remained an integral part of its definition. During 19th century the diagnosis of mental retardation primarily depends on appraisal of multiple factors such as one's ability to understand and being aware of the surroundings, to get engaged in regular social and economic activities, ability to ensure safety and maintaining health etc. (Brockley, 1999). Even at the end of 19th century, intelligence assessment was largely dependent on ability to practically apply academic skills and evaluation of "moral behaviors". The moral behaviors are characteristic components that constitute current social competence constructs. All these academic, social and personal roles and tasks are now representing adaptive skills. During this time, the absence of standardized procedures increased reliance on subjective assessment of general motor coordination, age, physiognomy and lag in school performance (Scheerenberger, 1983). This made many experts show their dissatisfaction and raised serious concerns on ignoring the past history and present social and cultural conditions of the client (Oakland, & Harrison, 2008; Jacobson et al., 2005).

At the start of 20th century many professionals presented several measures to supplement intellectual functioning instruments. During 1920s Edger Doll and his colleagues expressed their strong disagreement towards using mental age as the defining feature of mental retardation. They rejected the sole reliance of definition of mental retardation on mental age and instead highlighted the equal role of adaptive functioning which was then referred as social competence. Doll Highlighted that low intelligence can result in social inadequacy which is a pertinent feature indicating mental retardation. By developing a new measure Vineland Social Maturity Scale (VSMS) Doll presented himself as a leader in adaptive skills instruments development. The VSMS aimed to assess performance related to everyday activities and this 117 items tool maintained the position of one of the most often used adaptive functioning instruments for decades. This tool also led to the development of many contemporary adaptive functioning instruments. Despite the vast popularity of VSMS, it is also criticized for lacking adult norms, as the norms only cover children and adolescents (Scheerenberger, 1983).

The publication of manual of American Association of Mental Deficiency in 1959 is marked as a significant event in history of adaptive skills. The assessment of functioning was included as a formal criterion of diagnostic nomenclature for mental retardation for the first time. The manual was published in 1961 and discussed adaptive functioning in relation to general learning, social adjustment and maturation (Heber, 1961). These two significant developments paved the way for development and publication of a large variety of adaptive skills instruments (Allen, Cortazzo, & Adamo 1970).

1970s highlighted the significance of adaptive skills in clinical decision making as a result of normalization movement in which serious actions were taken to mainstream the institutionalized individuals. The clinicians find the adaptive skills construct and measuring instruments useful in identifying social development outside the academic domain and facilitated fair placement decisions. Therefore, experts identified this construct as a facilitator to the normalizing movement which resulted in rapid growth of new adaptive skills tools (Walls & Werner, 1977). Even the measures developed during 1960s were updated their scoring and psychometric features (Sparrow & Cicchetti, 1985). In connection to this movement, clinicians found adaptive instruments particularly useful in making fair decisions regarding placement of deinstitutionalized individuals and assessing their development outside traditional academic domains.

Years 1990s and 2000s had witnessed the refinement of structure and basic parameters of adaptive skills measures (McGrew & Bruininks, 1990) through employing large representative samples (Siperstein, & Leffert, 1997). The traditional conceptual frameworks of adaptive skills were modified and endorsed (Jacobson & Mulick, 1996), while several new conceptual frameworks were proposed to elaborate the construct of adaptive skills during this time period (American Association on Mental Retardation, 1992). This time era also acknowledged the influence of diverse cultural practices over adaptive skills and explored new avenues for applications of adaptive skills measures.

Presence of a clear definition of the construct of interest is commonly believed to ensure successful assessment at all levels. Most relevant in this connection is a recent definition of adaptive skills by American Association on Intellectual and Developmental Disabilities (AAIDD) states that a set of practical, conceptual and social skills people learned to function adequately in their daily lives (AAIDD, 2014). AAIDD proposes three core categories of skills each with several subcategories. The three main clusters include including the basic educational concepts acquired by an individual over time; *practical skills,* consisting of day to day life skills that individuals engage in over a life span; and *social skills,* encompassing the social communications and interpersonal relationships which one develops and experiences over time (AAMR, 2002).

Structure of Adaptive Skills Construct

There is a long standing debate about the nature of the construct throughout the history of adaptive skills concept. Meyers, Nihira and Zetlin (1979) conducted a thorough review of literature of factor analytic studies related to adaptive skills construct. They concluded that the construct of adaptive functioning was definitely multidimensional in nature and therefore the use of a composite score to indicate a general level of adaptation would be inappropriate and misleading.

Thompson, McGrew and Bruininks (1999) and McGrew and Bruininks (1989) analyzed the researches that conducted factor analysis on adaptive skills construct and presented one of the most comprehensive review of adaptive skills construct. They concluded that adaptive skills construct is multidimensional in nature and identified three general categories namely social responsibility, personal independence and cognitive / academic as most frequently reported dimensions. Whereas, vocational/community and physical /developmental dimensions were identified as less commonly reported dimensions. Finally, Thompson et al. (1999) concluded that no single measure presented factor structure including all the domains of adaptive functioning as different instruments focused attention on different domains of adaptive functioning.

Widaman and McGrew (1996) and Widaman, Stacy and Borthwick-Duffy (1993) also made a noteworthy contribution in term of refining the structure of adaptive skills construct. They reported strong evidences supporting the hierarchical model of adaptive skills comprising four discrete domains namely 1) conceptual intelligence, cognitive competence or communication; 2) social intelligence or social competence; 3) practical intelligence, daily living skills or independent living and 4) physical or motor competence.

They also suggested that a consensus on adaptive skills structure can be achieved by establishing common terms for adaptive domains Widaman and McGrew (1996).

Dimensions of Adaptive Skills

Although, there have been many attempts to define the concept of adaptive skills, there is still no single definition that can define the concept comprehensively. Even the domains of the adaptive skills are not yet clear, different adaptive skills instruments assign relative importance to different domains. According to researchers a considerable variation exists in the content of different adaptive skills measure depending on target age group, assessment context and purpose of instrument (Holman & Bruininks, 1985; Thompson et al., 1999). As scales used to assess adaptive functioning of adults need not to include items on behaviors related to school, similarly instruments intended to be used in schools need not to included items representing work domain (Kamphaus, 1987). This incongruity at times makes experts infer that adaptive skills construct lacks a unifying theoretical base Zigler et al. (1984).

Like definition, researches define different domains of adaptive skills. The most commonly defined domains include personal independence, socialization, communication, motor and number skills (Mash & Terdal, 1997).

Personal independence evaluates skills that develop personal independence or efficacy in one's daily living activities. The skills included in this domain are independent functioning or self-help skills, self-direction etc. *Socialization* domain is comprised of different skills including participation in social activities, knowledge and understanding of social rules, conformity to social community norms or rules, cooperation in social or community activities etc. It also includes establishing and maintaining relationships in different social situations, acknowledging and understanding feelings of others. *Numerical skills* include ability to apply basic mathematical principles in daily living, using tools like calendar and clock, recognition of currency, basic money handling etc. *Motor skills* defined as controlled movements of muscle groups is another domain which is divided in two sub groups namely, fine motor skills and gross motor skills. Skills dependent on small muscle dexterity of feet, hands and head, for instance buttoning shirts, snipping, cutting, writing etc. are grouped as Fine motor skills. On the other hand, the arms, legs, muscles in back, abdomen and torso are generally involved in gross motor skills and include tasks like crawling, sitting, walking, running, hitting a bat throwing and catching a ball etc. *Communication* is consisted of receptive, expressive and written language skills. It assesses both semantic and pragmatic language skills. This domain includes communicating with others, carrying out reciprocal communication, using the phone, writing, reading etc. *Community use* is another domain exploring individual's ability to do shopping, utilizing community services such as traveling through public transport, going to doctor, reaching out for help in times of need. *Self- direction* involves skills like setting and achieving goals, managing time, effective decision making, seeking help in times of need and coping with the novel situation, etc. *Health and safety* is about illness recognition and seeking treatment, choosing right things to eat, staying away from health dangers. *Home living* includes budgeting and planning for shopping, maintenance of property, clothing care, and basic housekeeping skills, preparing and cooking food.

A broader adaptive skills perspective may also extend to skills related to school like academic skills, play skills or general involvement with social environment and or work materials. In recent years adaptive skills scales also include a subsection covering the maladaptive behaviors.

Although many newly adaptive skills measures have included the maladaptive or problem behavior component in past few decades, the correlation between maladaptive and adaptive components is generally reported to be below 0.25 in normal individuals and higher among individuals with severe developmental problems (Harrison, 1987). APA along with many theorists (Hill,1999) emphasized that even the presence of significant maladaptive behaviors should not be confused as the significant lack of adaptive skills (Jacobson, & Mulick, 1996).

Factors that Influence Adaptive Skills

There is a wide range of social and psychological factors which influences the defining features of adaptive skills. The adaptive skills have taken a central position in assessment for multiple spheres of behavioral and academic functioning. Researchers had identified many factors like culture, gender, age, social practices, nature of disability, severity of disability, cognitive functioning and family characteristics as some of the significant correlates of adaptive functioning.

Culture and Development of Adaptive Skills. With a wide array of research, the influence of culture on one's development is becoming more pronounced. As primary parenting, child rearing practices and developmental expectations are regulated by cultural attitudes and values (Rosenthal, 1999). The popular cultural beliefs assist parents generate and reshape the expectations for developmental outcomes and also make them provide the relevant social environmental settings to facilitate achievement of those developmental outcomes (Wise, & Sanson, 2000). These accepted cultural beliefs also define the primary criteria for adaptive or maladaptive and typical and Atypical behavioral expectations. For instance, since early childhood many educationists and parents assign more value to sharing, respect and compliance to authority, living in accord with others, altruistic course, developing strong emotional bonds among members, active social participation and other collective goals compared to Western societies reflecting individualized cultural scripts (Rosenthal 2000).

Developmental Psychopathologies. Although, previous studies have established an association between disability and adaptive functioning, there are few studies that comment on whether adaptive functioning varies across different developmental disabilities. The present research project selected two main most frequently occurring developmental psychopathologies, that is, intellectual disability and autism spectrum disorder to explore their relationship with adaptive skills.

Intellectual disability (ID) and autism spectrum disorders (ASD) are generally considered as two most common developmental disabilities. The American Association on Intellectual and Developmental Disabilities (AAIDD, 2002; Schalock et al., 2010) and major diagnostic classification systems define ID as significant deficits in intellectual and adaptive functioning emerging before 18 years of age (APA,2013; WHO,1992). Intellectual disability is divided into categories based on the intellectual functioning namely mild (IQ from 55 - 69), moderate (IQ from 40 - 54), severe (IQ from 25 - 39) and profound with IQ below 25 (McDermott, Durkin, Schupf & Stein, 2007). ID is considered to be one of the most frequently occurring developmental disability that even co-occur with many other developmental problems like ASD (APA, 2013) is believed to have enormous social cost as it influences not only the life of sufferers but also disrupts the functioning of a family and society in general (Katz, & Lazcano-Ponce, 2008). There are many factors that are considered responsible for causing ID some of which includes genetic, chromosomal abnormalities, metabolic problems, serious prenatal, peri and post-natal infections, family history, low parental education (He, Chen, Wang, Guo & Zheng, 2017; Huq, & Tasnim, 2008; Zheng et al., 2012) and lower socioeconomic level (Katz, & Lazcano-Ponce, 2008). The prevalence rates of ID vary considerably depending on its definition, age, assessment measures used and geographical regions etc. The DSM-5 reported a prevalence of 1 % in general population with an incident rate of 6 in 1000 individuals in USA (APA, 2013),14.3 per 1000 in Western Australia (Leonard, Petterson, Bower, & Sanders, 2003). Maulik, Mascarenhas, Mathers, Dua and Saxena (2011) conducted meta analysis of researches discussing prevalence of ID and reported that prevalence rates varied across countries depending on socioeconomic levels, criteria and assessment procedures being used for assessment and age groups. They concluded that the prevalence rate of ID was 10.37 per 1000, with 1 % across the world highest prevalence observed among children and adolescents and almost two times less in high income countries compared to low and middle income countries (Maulik et al., 2011). According to the 1998 census data the prevalence of intellectual disability was reported to be 6.4 percent and 55 % of disability cases were identified from Punjab (Shakil & Johar, 2014; Ibrahim & Bhutta, 2013). A study in Sindh reported a disability ratio of 5.5 per 1000 children but it included all developmental disabilities and 56 percent of identified cases were males in both urban and rural areas (Ibrahim & Bhutta, 2013).

Like intellectual disability, ASD is another rapidly growing developmental psychopathology. ASD is neurodevelopmental disorder that includes difficulties related to behaviors and communication. DSM-5 has combined all the separate conditions of pervasive developmental disorders into a broader category of ASD (APA, 2013).

The term autism was first coined by Kanner in 1943 describing a disorder presenting symptoms of obsessiveness, echolalia and stereotypical actions. Whereas, the concept of autism spectrum disorders was first proposed by Wing (1988) based on two case studies of Asperger's disorder and autism indicating that there is a strong overlay of symptoms between the two disorders and the differences between both conditions can best be described only by the severity of symptoms (Kita, & Hosokawa, 2011). The term 'Autism Spectrum Disorder" is not a diagnostic label but a commonly used category to include individuals who present significant qualitative deficits in social interactions, communication skills, and restricted, repetitive or stereotypic patterns of behavior, interests or activities. Autism Spectrum Disorders (ASD) is synonymous with Pervasive Developmental Disorder (PDD; Volkmar & Pauls, 2003) and encompasses autism (high and low functioning), Asperger syndrome, and Pervasive Developmental Disorder Not Otherwise Specified (PDD NOS). In the recent years ASD is ranked as the second most common developmental disorder after intellectual disability in USA and its prevalence has increased 10 folds in a decade, still most aspects including core etiological factors needs to be explored (Phillips, Minjarez, Mercier, Feinstein, & Hardan, 2011). There is not much known about the actual causes of ASD, but clinicians suggest to rule out general developmental delay, bad parenting, psychological trauma, physical abuse and separation anxiety (Steiner, 2011; Volkmar & Pauls, 2003) before making a formal ASD diagnosis. Most of the available research places speculation around the genetic components, neurochemistry and functioning of the brain specifically affecting cerebral functioning as a legitimate cause of ASD. Most clinicians and researchers agree that the causal factors have a neurological basis that (Volkmar & Pauls, 2003). Efforts to clearly explain the causes of

ASD are ongoing, the increased risk of having a child with autism in families with already one autistic child strongly support the genetic component as cause of ASD (Bailey, Palferman,Heavey, & Le Couteur, 1998; Baird et al., 2001). Many promising management programs are available to help families improve the quality of life of ASD children despite not knowing the exact causes of autism. There are several risk factors that are said to be attached with the development of ASDs, the most common of these include male gender, older parents and having a sibling with ASD. Experts historically define ASD as a heterogeneous disorder meaning no two individuals have identical symptom profiles, but symptoms do fall in the core domains that generally remain consistent over time (Lord, Cook, Leventhal, & Amaral, 2000). There is a wide array of symptom depicted in ASDs, conventionally symptoms included in ASD are repetitive restrictive behaviors like specific ritualistic acts, intense interest in certain objects and or activities; social difficulties include difficulty imitating and maintaining social relationships, problems with social emotional reciprocity etc. (Tonge & Brereton, 2011). Delayed and under developed communication skills are other common signs and many children with ASD also has sensory hypersensitivity or hyposensitivity towards multiple stimulus (The National Institute of Mental Health, 2016). The DMS-5 only considers deficits in two broad domains for diagnosis of ASD namely social communication and restrictive interests. The manual also recognizes the severity of autism symptoms relative to chronological age and developmental levels (APA, 2013). Clinicians usually divide ASD in high functioning autism (HFA) category and those who have autism and cognitive deficit (Klin, Pauls, Schultz, Volkmar, 2005; Songa, Kima, Chunb, & Kima,2014; Volkmar, & McPartland, 2014;). The expression of symptoms in HFA is usually less intense compared to children suffering from both autism and intellectual delay

(Feinstein, 2012). ASDs first appear in early infancy and diagnosis is made within the first three years of life and most of the children who suffer from ASDs also have intellectual delay along with problems related to socialization, motor activity, communication, symbolic play and sensory responsiveness (Lord et al., 2000). Most of these skills are considered key components of adaptive functioning. ASD in most cases is also accompanied by symptoms of developmental coordination disorders, anxiety disorders, inattention, hyperactivity, impulsivity and sleep problems. The prevalence of autism and related disorders is more common than perceived prevalence (Matson, Rivet, Fodstad, Dempsey, & Boisjoli, 2009). The reported prevalence rates range from 0.5 to 1 percent in school age children (Wing & Potter, 2000), ASDs are more frequent among boys than girls.

Other than psychopathologies, temperament is another important variable related to adaptive skills, the relationship between adaptive skills and temperament had attracted lots of attention in past few years as both these variables are considered pertinent to both the course and prognosis of developmental problems (Rothbart, 2007).

Temperament. The literature over past many years has placed lots of attention on temperament as this is considered to be one of the most significant intra personal factor influencing human functioning and development (Bates, 1986; Slabach, Morrow & Wachs, 1991). Many researchers had highlighted the key role temperament plays in the acquisition and strength of adaptive functioning of individuals (Gunnar, 1990). There is considerable variability in children's reactions to the environment since early infancy (Rothbart & Mauro, 1990;Strauss, & Rourke,1978) .

Rothbart and Derryberry (1981) described temperament as set of individual differences in attentional, motor and emotional reactivity measured by recovery of response, intensity, latency and self-regulation processes like effortful control that modulate reactivity (Rothbart & Bates, 2006). Further, Posner, Rothbart and Sheese (2007) added that these differences are biological in nature and linked to genetic endowment of an individual. Temperament's basic biological processes (Rothbart, & Posner, 1985; Eysenck & Eysenck, 1987; Gunnar, 1990; Gray, 1987) can be shared across cultures but outcomes may vary depending on the child's experiences and cultural values (Ahadi, Rothbart and Ye, 1993). Maturation of inhibitory regulation's brain system is the basis of temperamental difference in the early human ontogeny of individuals. Moreover, in the second half-year, new cognitive abilities of a child affect the dynamic behavioral features like fear of isolation from mother and fear of new people (Herschkowitz, Kagan & Zilles, 1997; Pribram, & McGuinness, 1992). EC strongly develops into the school years (Bohlin, Hagekull, & Lindhagen, 1981; Sanson, Prior, Garino, Oberklaid, & Sewell, 1987). Children show performance consistency across tasks by 30 months while significant stability is found afterward (Kochanska, Murray & Harlan, 2000).

Models of Temperament. Temperament refers to predispositions or traits for displaying particular behavioral predisposition. These tendencies are relatively stable and biological in nature (Bates, Wachs, & Emde, 1994). Galen presented early historical temperament theory with a combination of both emotional and physical characteristics explained as four humors or temperaments (Stelmack & Stalikas, 1991). Carl Jung (1921) identified two attitudes conceptualized as Introverted and Extroverted qualities as a continuum's opposite ends. In order to get better adjustment results, he proposed to develop a degree of balance in temperament qualities and emphasized enhancing either set of qualities. Four other basic psychological functions delineated in his theory are: Thinking/Feeling and

Sensation/Intuition. Further, Myers and Myers (1980) modified this theory by adding a fourth dimension, Judging/Perceiving.

The structure of temperament is consisted of nine dimensions primarily identified by Thomas and Chess in 1977 in their New York Longitudinal Study. These nine dimensions are threshold, distractibility, intensity, rhythmicity, adaptability, activity level, mood, attention span persistence and approach/withdrawal. Thomas and Chess (1977) conceptualized temperament as the stylistic component of behavior and they derived their list of temperament traits including nine dimensions mentioned earlier. According to Chess and Thomas (1990), there are three types of temperament: Easy or flexible (almost 40% of children), Difficult or Feisty (almost 10 % of children) and Slow-to-Warm-Up or Fearful Child (almost 15% of children). Typically, the easy child is adaptable, approachable, generally positive in mood of mild to medium intensity, shows deep feelings and regular in biological rhythms. The difficult child typically fusses at anything new, shows disagreeable or unpleasant mood, hard to get to sleep throughout the night, difficult to toilet train, changed nap schedules from day to day, and usually adapts slowly. The fearful child is often called shy. The shy child may have discomfort with the new things, express negative moods slowly, adapts slowly and may or may not be irregular in bowl elimination, sleep and feelings. The problem in this model is that conceptually it is not truly possible to distinguish children's style of behavior from the content of and motivation from their behavior and empirically their questionnaire does not yield nine distinct traits rather only irritability, activity level, social inhibition, sensory sensitivity and attention/persistence.

Rothbart, Ahadi, Hershey and Fisher (2001) identified three broad dimensions of temperament that are related to the Big Five personality factors of Neuroticism (negative affectivity), Extraversion (extraversion/surgency) and Conscientiousness (Effortful control) (Rothbart, Ahadi, & Evans, 2000; Ahadi, Rothbart & Ye,1993). The Agreeableness and Openness factors are related to adults' dimensions of affiliation and perceptual sensitivity (Evans & Rothbart, 2001). Mary Rothbart's theoretical model of temperament argues that temperament traits consist of "constitutional differences in reactivity and self-regulation, with 'constitutional' seen as the relatively enduring biological makeup of the organism influenced over time by heredity, maturation, and experience" (Rothbart & Derryberry, 1981, p. 37). According to this model, as children mature, new temperament traits emerge over. Child's reactive traits like affective tendencies reflect biological arousability while regulatory traits modulate child's reactivity. Rothbart and colleagues argued that temperament includes individual differences in self-regulation, activity, attention and affect (Rothbart & Bates, 2006). This model like the ancient Greek model emphasized individual differences in emotional processes including positive and negative emotions that reflect reactivity to the environment and unlike the Greek model equally highlights the importance of individual differences in regulation of reactive tendencies through self-regulation and attention. This view concludes that temperamental traits are closely linked with biological processes, emerge during childhood, are shaped by heredity and experiences and are organized hierarchically across the lifespan. Some behavioral descriptors tend to co-vary like not shy while meeting new people, expressive and talkative. These descriptors are lower-order traits and are narrow in focus like assertiveness and sociability. Some lower-order traits further co-vary that is accounted for with greater breadth by higher-order traits like extraversion. This hierarchical structure of traits manifests in infancy and early childhood (Rothbart, & Bates, 2006).

Each higher-order dimension is comprised of lower-order temperament traits (Rothbart & Bates, 2006). In Rothbart's model, self-regulation has a prominent place and is a core component of temperament. Effortful control develops during toddlerhood and it exerts brakes on motor activities and unregulated negative emotionality and enhances child's ability to adapt to environmental demands (Rothbart & Derryberry, 2002). Less negative emotional arousal is due to higher effortful control (Rothbart, 2007). The efficiency in regulating reactivity at the neural level is sub-served by the coupling of regulation and reactivity. The reciprocal and continued dynamic interactions between temperamental regulation and reactivity contribute to instability of temperament expression overtime (Pien & Rothbart, 1980; Rothbart, 2007).

The literature suggested scarcity of significant research on temperament in children and adolescents, though, significant work was found on temperament in adults. The little work that has been done studying the temperament was done on adolescents (Majeed & Malik, 2015) or infants rather than on children in middle childhood.

Measures of Temperament. Although lab observations help to explore valuable information regarding child's temperament, yet they consume time. For this reason, numerous paper-and-pencil measures are available to assess temperament in children like the *Temperament Survey for Children* (reliability ranges from 0.60 to 0.75) is a 20 items parental rating (Buss, & Plomin, 1984). It differentiates between various temperament dimensions consisting of four scales; emotionality scale (measures distress), the shyness (measures tension and inhibition), the activity scale (measures vigor and tempo) and the experimental sociability scale (measures preferences for being alone to being with others).

The Children's Behavior Questionnaire (CBQ), a parent-report measure of temperament (Rothbart, Ahadi & Hershey, 1994), provides a highly differentiated assessment of temperament in children through 195 items covering 15 domains. CBQ can be used to measure consistency in temperament, perceived competence, temperamental clusters in preschoolers, injury proneness and ability estimation, problem behaviors, ability to delay gratification, mental development, prosocial behavior, mothers' patterns of control and perceptions of power, social competence in peer interactions, physiological stress responses and parents' reactions to children's negative emotions (Goldsmith, Buss, & Lemery, 1997; Schaughency & Fagot, 1993; Silverman & Ippolito, 1995; Schwebel & Plumert, 1999).

Another tool *Temperament in Middle Childhood Questionnaire* (TMCQ) is an established valid and reliable self-report instrument of temperament in middle childhood (Simonds & Rothbart, 2006). The TMCQ assesses 17 domains, 11 out of 16 self-report scales indicate good internal consistency i.e. .60 while parent scale shows internal consistency ranges from .69 to .90.

Other measures such as *Short Temperament Scale for Children* (Prior, Sanson & Oberklaid, 1989) is helpful to measure temperamental anxiety proneness in children. This scale is a parent report questionnaire to evaluate children's temperamental characteristics for children of 3 to7 year. This scale is consisted of 30 items with four subscales measuring persistence, reactivity, rhythmicity and approach/withdrawal dimensions. The scale shows good reliability of .70. In order to examine behavioral problems in relation of temperament, the 100-items parental-report measure *Behavioral Style Questionnaire (*BSQ) of the *Carey Temperament Scales* (CTS; McDevitt & Carey, 1996) can be used. It offers scores on nine aspects of temperament proposed by Thomas, Chess, Birch, Hertzig, and Korn (1963) and modified by Thomas, Chess, and Birch (1968) and Chess and Thomas (1996). Some other scales to measure temperament are *Temperament Assessment Battery for Children-Revised*

(TABC –R; Martin & Bridger, 1999) , *Dimensions of Temperament Survey – Revised* (DOTS-R; Windle & Lerner, 1986) , *Early Adolescent Temperament Questionnaire* (EATQ) developed by Capaldi & Rothbart (1992).

Table 1

Some Frequently Used Temperament Measures

Authors	Measure	Developed in	Comment
Buss, & Plomin (1984)	Temperament Survey for Children (EAS). Can be used with children from 1 to 9 years of age	Developed and standardized in USA. Translated and adapted in other countries as well.	The instrument is available in English language. It has a restricted use in Pakistan as it can only be used with parents who can read and understands English language
Rothbart, Ahadi, Hershey, & Fisher (1997)	The Children's Behavior Questionnaire (CBQ). Used with children from 3 to 7 years	Developed and standardized in USA Translated and adapted in more than 20 languages	This was not available in Urdu and there were items that used examples/ linguistic expression that were culturally irrelevant
Rothbart (2001)	Temperament in Middle Childhood Questionnaire (TMCQ) to be used with 7 to 10 years old children	Developed and standardized in USA. Translated and adapted in 9 languages.	This was not available in Urdu and there were items that used examples/ linguistic expression that were culturally irrelevant
Prior, Sanson & Oberklaid (1989)	Short Temperament Scale for Children to be used with 3 to 7 years old children	Developed and standardized in USA.	The instrument is available in English language. It has a restricted use in Pakistan as it can only be used with parents who can read and understands English language.
McDevitt & Carey (1996)	Behavioral Style Questionnaire (BSQ) is used with children aged 3 to 7 years.	Developed and standardized in USA.	It mainly measures preschool temperament to assess school readiness and interpersonal competencies. The measure assesses constructs that do not match the aim of present research. It is only available in English language which makes its use restricted in Pakistan.

Temperament and Developmental Psychopathologies. Interaction occurs between child development and temperament traits. However, child behavior modifies as cognitive skills develop and nervous system matures (Shiner & Caspi, 2003) and temperamental differences can affect child's development, behavior and emotions including their learning and discovery processes (Rothbart & Jones, 1998).

Down's syndrome is a chromosomal disorder with the presence of intellectual impairment in children (Selikowitz, 1992). Children with Down's syndrome show many physical features and behavioral characteristics that make them readily identifiable. Experts pointed to many individual differences attributable to temperamental traits among these children (Benda, 1969; Benda, & Strassmann, 1965; Menolascino,1965). It was reported that children with Down's syndrome shows 15 percent incidence of emotional problems and concluded that these children becomes emotionally disturbed as normal children do. The intensity of overall reactivity is translated into the dampening of negative emotional responses in children with Down's syndrome and decreased sensitivity to novelty causes them to perseverate (Ganiban, Wagner, & Cicchetti, 1990) and lead them to longer duration of orientation and lower level of behavioral inhibition or fear. Children with down's syndrome are more persistent in orientation, less approaching, exhibit less laughter/smiling, vocal reactivity, fearful and having a lower threshold for stimulation (Rothbart & Hanson, 1983) while children aged four to eleven exhibit sadness, inhibitory control and decreased attentional focusing as compared to normal children (Nygaard, Smith, & Torgersen, 2002).

Children with intellectual disability are at greater risk of emotional disturbances. A higher proportion of behavior difficulties are reported in these children as compared to intellectually normal children. Temperament plays a significant role in etiology of behavior disorders (Koller, Richardson, Katz and McLaren (1983). The "difficult child" shows a specific cluster of temperamental attributes that constitutes vulnerability for stressful interactions (Chess & Korn, 1970). According to experts, intellectual disability in young children is associated with higher levels of motor activity and perpetual motion- fidgety, restlessness and always getting into things, seemingly acting without thinking and tends to be impulsive (Mulick, Hammer & Dura, 1991). Hyperactive children with ID show several aspects of temperament like persistence, attention span and distractibility problems that are subject to psychological influence (Osdol & Carlson, 1972; Lerner, 1976).

One of the most common childhood developmental disorder is Attention deficit hyperactivity disorder (ADHD), affecting 5-7% percent of population (Goldstein & Barkley, 1998). There is an established relationship between temperament and ADHD as temperament is defined as constitutionally based individual differences in reactivity and self-regulation (White, 1999). Temperament-relevant behavior may be observed for regulation of attention and emotion and motor activities (Vaughn & Bost, 1999). Children who are frequently diagnosed with ADHD have high emotional reactivity and activity and may be more impulsive and distractible. Another key factor in ADHD is temperamental differences in inhibition level that has been observed in infants and relatively remains stable throughout the life span (White, 1999).

In special population, the role of child temperament in the adaptation of children within past two decades has been increased. To date, the specific diagnostic categories such as Autism Spectrum Disorder (ASD) or fragile X syndrome in children are not empirically assessed (Konstantareas & Stewart, 2001; Leibowitz, 1991). The development of maladaptive behaviors, responsiveness of parents and parenting stress are related factors of temperament of children with ASD (Eaves, Ho, & Eaves, 1994; Konstantareas & Homatidis, 1989; Kasari & Sigman, 1997; Bristol & Schopler, 1984; Holroyd & MacArthur, 1976). Child temperament is also helpful to describe different manifestations of the behavioral phenotype like children with ASD present insistence on sameness, anxiety and intense fears that lead to conclude an anxious phenotypic subtype of the disorder (Hollander, 2004).

Intellectual Functioning and Adaptive Skills

The relationship between the constructs of intellectual functioning and adaptive skills is reported to be highly inconsistent. There are experts who consider the two constructs as similar yet others describe the constructs being distinct and free of influence from each other. Published studies reported almost no correlations to almost perfect correlation between intelligence and adaptive functioning (Reschly, Meyers & Hartel, 2009). Keith, Fehrmann, Harrison and Pottebaum (1987) conducted one of the most significant research on this topic and concluded that adaptive behavior and intellectual ability should be considered as separate, but related constructs. The literature also pointed that the strength of correlation should be considered while reviewing this association, whereas, age is a pertinent factor directly influencing this relationship. The relationship believed to be weak among early years and stronger in the later ages. Another important study was carried out by Ittenbach, Spiegel, McGrew and Bruininks (1992) who concluded that the findings of their study were in line with those found by Keith et al. (1987) research. They reported moderate association of .5 indicates that intelligence and adaptive functioning share almost 25 % common variance. According to McGrew (2012) relationship between intelligence and adaptive functioning is influenced by multiple factors like item content, floor and ceiling problems, sample inconsistencies and category of mental retardation.

Assessment of Adaptive Skills

Although experts suggest several ways to assess adaptive skills, a number of significant considerations regarding characteristic features and biases that directly influence the assessment procedure should be taken into account. Experts usually consider assessment of adaptive skills complex and stress considering quality, proficiency and level of adaptive functioning equally important as general competencies in specific domains. Sociocultural and psychometric biases are usually of significant concern of the experts in this context. Particularly experts who consider many features of adaptive skills as culturally determined are concerned about varied cross cultural, ethnic and racial practices (Boyle et al., 1996; Valdivia, 1999).

The adaptive skills in general is believed to be based on behavioral expectations that differ across cultures. Accordingly APA (2013), ICD (WHO, 1992) and AAIDD (2002) consider adaptive skills dependent on cultural practices and stress the need to assess it with reference to specific cultural context. The socio-cultural variations can deeply affect the assessment modes used to evaluate adaptive skills. Adaptive skills assessment generally rely on interviews conducted by trained professionals with the primary caregiver or someone who knows the assessee well, direct observation, caregiver self report checklists and self reports of the assessee. None of these exploration procedures is considered free of cultural biases. However, the interviews conducted by the trained professionals are considered to be most appropriate as the professional can modify the statements according to the comprehension level and cultural beliefs of the reporting person.

Psychometric Concerns in Using Adaptive Skills Scales

Many clinicians express their concerns about the robustness of adaptive skills measures because of its pertinent role in developmental assessment. Such concerns are generally focused around the basic structure and characteristics of instruments, procedures of information collection and standardization of these tools.

As adaptive skill covers a broad range of developmental facets, most of the adaptive skills tools are developed as being comprehensive and not cumbersome which requires to balance several elements to make the tools more adequate (Adams, 2000).

As most of the adaptive functioning instruments are specifically constructed to assess the behavioral development of individuals of 3 through 21 years of age consequently, scale selection, item development and norming samples is targeted at children and teens. It is important that the items of adaptive skills scale should cover all the developmental tasks and characteristics of particular age groups within the targeted range. The items included in scale should have appropriate floor and ceiling levels by having an adequate number of items in subscales.

In order to ensure inclusion of both limitations and strengths the scale must adequately represent all important dimensions of behavioral development represented through various descriptive categories and sufficient number of factors. The second major concern is related to item density, a good scale is believed to fairly maintain representation of various items adequately reflecting age typical functioning of a broad age range.

As the items of adaptive skills measures are based on age typical performance and thus are not suitable to be used with all age ranges, for instances, motor skills acquisition in childhood and items related to work or school setting are not relevant to all age groups.

These kinds of provisions can decrease the comparability of the associated skills measured from various adaptive skills instruments.

As most of the adaptive skills measures primarily rely on caregiver reports, the issue of reliability and validity of informant responses become an important concern for experts. In order to minimize the informant biases most adaptive skills tools encourage using multiple informants and giving clear and detail instructions to informants about the ratings (Bruininks, Woodcock, Weatherman, & Hill, 2000).

Because of the key role of adaptive skills measures in developmental assessment adequacy of the normative sample remains a significant psychometric concern. Though the normative sample of adaptive skills tools is smaller compared to most comprehensive intelligence tests, most adaptive skills measures are normed on groups that adequately represent the age range and other developmental characteristics of the population with which it is used.

Sociocultural Biases. Many experts view the adaptive skills culturally influenced, therefore, the issue of socio cultural biases influencing the adaptive skills assessment becomes important. These biases include a range of demographic factors such as race, gender, age, and ethnic membership directly attributed to distortions in adaptive functioning scores.

Many experts explain that the age norms of most of the psychological tests predominantly reflect white middle class child rearing practices, however, the developmental acquisitions are mostly affected by cultural standards (Valdivia, 1999). Hart (2000) pointed an important issue that differences in developmental attainments are related to availability of stimulation in socioeconomic class and parental educational level that results in different child rearing practices rather than some other socioeconomic or cultural factors. The studies (Bryant , Bryant, & Chamberlains, 1999) that compared performance of majority and minority children identified differing child rearing practices and language as factors that may result in differences in developmental trajectories. The linguistic concerns include translation of items and administering the tools in informant's primary language (Craig & Tasse, 1999).

The linguistic biases are generally reflected by language differences among examiners and examinees and inappropriate translations of items that can directly affect the validity of data collected its clinical interpretation. According to experts, adaptive skills assessment should be carried out in informant's primary language and the impact of cultural practices on adaptive functioning should also be taken under consideration.

Typical Performance Measurement and Adaptive Skills. One of the most significant issue in adaptive functioning assessment is the matter of typical and best performance. Best performance reflects one's mastery over a task and assessee is encouraged to perform to their maximum potential. Traditional intellectual functioning measures employ this strategy to estimate the intellectual potential of their assessees. On the other hand, typical performance assesses the usual or most frequently carried out activities. The best performance primarily relies on the examinees performance whereas typical performance evaluation also takes third party account into consideration (Cronbach, 1990).

Typical adaptive skills measures use a combination of these two approaches and investigate both the abilities of an individual and what he/she does generally. However, most of the instruments vary in their relative focus on assessing typical and best performance aspects related to adaptive skills (Adams, 2000; Sparrow, Balla & Cicchetti, 1984).

Adaptive Skills Scales with Well-Known Properties

The literature indicates more than 200 published adaptive skills tools used in clinical practice for research, diagnosis, treatment planning and program evaluation. Most of these scales are developed to serve a dual purpose of providing assistance in diagnostic process and establishing individualized treatment plans, however, some measure only fulfill one of these purposes. Generally selecting a specific adaptive skills depends on multiple factors like training of the assessor, age of the assessee, adequacy of the normative sample. The following section briefly reviews the most frequently and widely used adaptive skills instruments.

Vineland Adaptive Behavior Scales (VABS). Although VABS (Sparrow, Balla & Cicchetti, 2005) shares its conceptual roots with the Vineland Social Maturity Scale, overlap between the two scales is minimum (Kamphaus, 1987). The VABS is available in three forms including an extended, survey from and class room form employing interviews with caregivers or parents. VABS classroom edition is reported to be adequate to use with 3 to 12 years old children, whereas, norms of other forms are available from birth to 18 years of age. The norms are established on a standardized sample stratified by community size, age, gender, ethnicity and race consistent with US census data. An extensive research data provides impressive evidence of reliability and validity of the scales.

Scales of Independent Behavior (SIB-R). The Scales of Independent Behavior (Bruininks et al., 1996) is a part of the broader Woodcock-Johnson Psycho-Educational Battery and consists of 4 major clusters including 14 subscales. The SIB has established norms from infancy through more than 40 years of age. One of the strengths of SIB is that its manual discusses in detail the issues and factors that can affect the administration, scoring and interpretation of scores.

Battelle Developmental Inventory (BDI). Although BDI (Newborg et al., 1984) was intended to be used as a developmental scale, it is also used to evaluate adaptive skills for children from birth till 8 years of age (Spector, 1999). BDI offers adequate norms for this group based on a representative USA sample. Many studies reported well documented evidence of norms, validity and reliability of BDI representative of national sample (Harrington, 1985; Oehler-Stinnett, 1989), along with significant correlations with other tools of language, social, cognitive and adaptive skills (Bailey, Hatton & Skinner, 1998). One of the major strengths of BDI is that it provides adequate floor effects for children with younger ages which is generally not offered by other adaptive skills measures.

AAMR Adaptive Behavior Scales (ABS). Adaptive behavior scales are available in two versions that is, residential and community version (ABS-RC:2, Nihira, Leland, & Lambert, 1993) and ABS–a school version (ABS-S:2, Lambert , Nihira, & Leland, 1993). ABA scales are divided in two broad categories namely adaptive skills and maladaptive behaviors. ABS covers self care and social skills areas in detail, whereas, leisure, health and safety and homeliving have very few items to give reliable estimates of these domains. For ABS-S:2 percentile ranks, standardized scores and age equivalent scores are available for subscales and three factor scores from 3 to 21 years of age (Lambert et al., 1993). The community and residential version was constructed to be used with individuals through 79 years of age with developmental disabilities and doesn't not provide norm referenced scores for adults with typical functioning (AAMR, 1992). The standardization samples employed for ABS scales are reported to be excellent (Stinnett, 1997).

Adaptive Behavior Assessment System (ABAS). The ABAS by Harrison &

Oakland (2000) is considered to be a comparatively new instrument of adaptive skills

possessing sound psychometric properties. ABAS cover all 10 domains of adaptive skills

proposed by AAMR and is considered to adequately used with a wide age range starting

from children older than 5 years of age through adulthood. The norms are available for

infancy till adulthood. The adult forms can be filled with account of others or self report.

ABAS is known to have sound psychometric properties with average reliability coefficient

ranging from .86 to .97, for individuals with typical development majority of the coefficients

are above .90 and above .98 for individuals with atypical pattern of development. The key

points of all the above measures are summarized in the table below.

Table 2

Summary of Adaptive Skills Measures Reviewed

Authors	Name of Measure & Information	Country of	Comment
Sparrow, Balla & Cicchetti (2005)	Vineland Adaptive Behavior Scales (VABS). Age Range: from infancy- 90 years	Developed and standardized in USA	It has been translated in many languages and most of the researchers concluded that content of many items were not culturally relevant particularly for Asian, Middle eastern & African countries. Norms for Pakistani population are not available. Not available in Urdu Language and many items are not culturally relevant
Bruininks et al. (1996)	Scales of Independent Behavior (SIB-R) Age Range: 3 months -80 + years	Developed and standardized in USA.	A norm-referenced assessment of adaptive and maladaptive behavior. The instrument is available in English language. It has a restricted use in Pakistan as it can only be used with parents who can read and understands English language. Norms for Pakistani population are not available. Not available in Urdu

			Language and many items are not culturally relevant
Newborg (2005)	Battelle Developmental Inventory (BDI). Age range: from birth – 7/8 years	Developed and standardized in USA.	Measures a child's progress along the developmental continuum. Not available in Urdu Language and does not cover the full range of adaptive behaviors. Norms for Pakistani population are not available.
Harrison & Oakland (2000)	Adaptive behavior assessment system (ABAS) Age Range: 0 months - 89 years	Developed and standardized in USA.	Not available in Urdu Language and many items are not culturally relevant for Pakistani children. Norms for Pakistani population are not available.

All these measures of adaptive skills are developed in English language and represent standardized norms of urban middle class children of western countries. From time and again Pakistani clinicians have been sharing their serious concerns regarding content and linguistic biases involved in all these measures. Researchers from countries that share some significant religious, socio-cultural and other characteristics have also reported content biases and linguistic limitations when these measures are used in those countries (Nourani,1998; Goldberg, Dill, Shin & Nhan, 2008; Zhang, Wheeler, & Richey, 2006).

Selection and Use of Adaptive Skills Scales in General Clinical Practice

The researchers focusing on educational and school psychology reported that adaptive functioning instruments are amongst most frequently used measures and their need in clinical practice is still growing (Ochoa, Powell, & Robles-Pina, 1996). Archer, Maruish, Imhof & Piotowski (1991) pointed to two adaptive skills instruments among frequently used psychological assessment measures, however, another study that measured the use of different assessment tools in general clinical practice found that AB scales were not frequently used as component of regular assessment batteries (Watkins, Campbell, Nieberding, & Hallmark, 1995). Experts concluded that social competence and adaptive functioning are as important facets of academic adjustment as intelligence, highlighting the significance of this construct in practice (Forness, Keogh, macMillan, Kavale, & Greesham, 1998).

Cultural Sensitivity of Adaptive Skills Scales

Most of the popular adaptive skills assessment measures are not normed to address the varied cultural considerations and wide range of racial groups. This directs to the need for clinical practitioners to develop assessment tools and strategies ensuring that referred individuals are assessed fairly. The increased racial and ethnic diversity among assessment groups has highlighted the significant role of ethno-cultural factors in assessment. This has led to the need to evaluate the adequacy and use of tools developed concurrently (Allen-Meares, 2008).

Many experts have recognized different set of factors significantly affecting the pace and pattern of development among children. These factors include a range of informant's characteristics and client's age and gender. A significant developmental task of adaptive skills measures is to identify the extent to which the above factors interfere in the development by establishing adequate norms representative to groups based on age, gender and other characteristics (Achenbach, 2005).

At time of using standardized psychological assessment tools, clinicians conform to a basic assumption that each assessee is similar to individuals on which that tool is standardized; however, this assumption is violated when these tools are administered on clients coming from other cultures (Flanagan & Ortiz, 2001). The violation of this basic testing assumption can result in multiple serious issues like false diagnoses, under and over diagnoses by the inappropriate use of standardized measures with culturally diverse clients

(Hays, 2001). As clinicians are becoming more concerned about the adequacy of psychological measures they use and their psychometric characteristics, more research studies are being directed to study the factors influencing these measures and different cultural issues has emerged as focal area of these studies. Experts believe that general behavior can strongly get influenced by both environmental experiences and biological tendencies. In this context culture stands out as a significant factor using customized sets of beliefs, values and attitudes shared by large segment of population to shape behavior (Shiraev & Levy, 2010). And adaptive skills are considered to grew out of social cultural behavioral role expectations with reference to one's age and gender. Therefore, all major classification systems and a good number of experts assert the need to take cultural background into consideration while assessing adaptive skills.

Adaptive Skills and Pakistani Culture

In Pakistan, there are many subcultures and each subculture is not only influenced by the regional norms but socioeconomic levels as well. The nature of social expectations varies from one subculture to the other. Two main cultural contexts are the urban and rural cultures, where the child rearing practices, role expectations and exposure of children is totally different from one another. There is possibility that adaptive skills expectations may differ significantly across these different cultural groups.

In rural parts, children are expected to share domestic and agricultural responsibilities of their family even in their middle childhood. They are expected to take active part in domestic chores, looking after their cattle and helping in the fields particularly during harvesting season. The rural sub culture makes the children comparatively more social and independent compared to their urban counterparts.

Role expectation in urban culture varied across different socioeconomic classes. Children from lower SES are expected to fulfill similar role responsibilities as rural children. These children help in domestic responsibilities, baby sitting of younger siblings and sometimes they also share financial burdens by either doing odd jobs or helping their parents in their work/ jobs. Majority of the middle and upper class children in urban areas are only expected to develop good academic skills and attainment of nonacademic skills are mostly restricted to self-help skills.

Gender is another important factor that has strong influence on societal expectations in both rural and urban settings in Pakistani culture. As the role expectancies vary from one gender to other, female children are expected to be more involved in domestic chores and helping their mothers in looking after the younger siblings. On the other hand, the male children are less likely to be expected to take part in household chores. They are instead expected to be more active in social, community and economic domains. Children who belong to middle and upper SES have somewhat restricted exposure of scissors, knives and other sharp domestic tools or instruments have more exposure to electronic devices and gadgets than children in rural areas.

Urban children are trained to be somewhat dependent on adult relatives and servants, housemaids as compared to rural counterparts who are encouraged to be independent. Children who belong to rural areas are more independent in traveling alone from one place to another, this ranges from moving within the neighborhood to the nearby villages. The major reason is being their social set up that inculcate this behavior. As the schools are sometimes miles away from their home villages, and many at times they have to visit the nearest big village to buy routine goods like grocery.

Assessment of Adaptive Skills in Pakistan

Adaptive skills measures have been frequently used in Pakistan for both screening and treatment planning. Clinical psychologists frequently use these measures to screen out children with typical development from children who have mental retardation and other developmental disabilities. The VABS, Childhood adaptive behavior scale (CABS) and Portage guide for early education (PGEE) are the most commonly used adaptive skills assessment tools. However, the experts who have been using these scales often report multiple problems related to the use and interpretation of these measures.

One main problem is that all these scales are in English language which creates a language barrier that result in many complications. May at times the respondent and or child fail to understand and comprehend the language properly. As large majority of the Pakistani population particularly those who come to government hospitals are unfamiliar with this foreign language that is, English. Some clinicians translate the items into Urdu or other regional language during administration. While some experts use their own translated and adapted versions that are not properly standardized and even the basic psychometric properties of these translated versions are unknown. Thus, they violate the standard procedures for the item presentations and add variability that eventually affects the results and quality of administrations. Another related problem is that, the experts are assessing the Pakistani children on measures that are standardized on western children who have totally different level of exposure and societal expectancies from our culture. In this case, the validity and reliability of such administrations and interpretations remain highly questionable. This is a violation of one of the basic assumptions of psychological assessment theory that assessee is similar to population on whom the instrument was standardized (Flanagan & Ortiz, 2001).

Second problem is related to the item content and presentation, as some of the items are culturally biased such as picture cards used in CABS or middle childhood vocational items in VABS. These items must be relevant in western countries but are neither relevant to our culture nor our children relate with them. Our children are not either unfamiliar or get the late exposure to some of the materials used in the tasks of CABS and VABS. For instance, in western culture the child started using knife and fork at early age while in our culture the young children are usually not given exposure to these utensils. Above all, there is not much research that can provide any reliable information about the applicability of the adaptive skills measures developed in western countries with reference to Pakistan.

CHAPTER-II

Review of Literature

Adaptive skills scales have successfully attracted the attention of clinical practitioners not only because of the essential role they play in assessment but in clinical and placement decision making, treatment evaluation and prognosis of developmental psychopathologies. Consequently, many researchers developed their interest in studying the construct and carried out large array of researches in this area. Following section contains the review of researches related to the frequently used adaptive skills scales, their use in developmentally problems especially in intellectual disability and autism spectrum disorders disabilities, the cultural practices and adaptive skills, role of different factors in adaptive skills and the utility of adaptive skills scales in different cultures.

Adaptive Skills Construct and Measures

There are several adaptive skills measures that have been developed over the past few decades across the world. As discussed earlier, these measures are often used to determine the presence of adaptive skills deficits and to establish therapeutic goals. The following section contains the review of researches carried out to establish the psychometric characteristics of the frequently used adaptive skills scales.

The most recent and significant research on the adaptive skills structure is that of Thompson et al. (1999), who conducted a review on thirty-one factor analytical studies on adaptive skills. They concluded that the construct of adaptive skills is definitely multidimensional in nature. They broadly categorized three most commonly found domains as personal independence, getting along with others in social contexts or meeting expectations of others and academic or cognitive dimensions. Furthermore, they reported that maladaptive behavior factors generally fall into two broad categories of personal and social problem behaviors. They also found that no particular adaptive or maladaptive behavior tool completely measures the complete array of maladaptive or adaptive skills domains rather, different measures lay levels of emphasis on different domains.

According to Arias et al., (2013) although the presence of significant limitations in adaptive skills constitutes one of the three necessary criteria for diagnosing intellectual disability, adaptive skills structure has always been the subject of considerable controversy among researchers. They conducted a study to extend previous research results that provide further support to a multidimensional structure of conceptual, social, and practical skills compared to the unidimensional structure. One-factor and 3-correlated factors models as measured by 15 observable indicators were analyzed by means of confirmatory factor analysis (CFA), as well as their relationships with one second-order factor (i.e., adaptive behavior). To that end, 388 children with and without intellectual disabilities were assessed with the Diagnostic Adaptive Behavior Scale (DABS). Results of CFA indicated that the 3 first-order factors solution provides the best fit to the data. Reliability and validity of the multidimensional model were also analyzed through different methods such as the composite reliability and the average variance extracted.

Lambert, Nihira, & Leland (1993) developed the ABS-S:2 which has become one of the popular measures of adaptive skills. Watkins, Ravert and Crosby, (2002) pointed towards the serious concerns raised regarding structural validity of this scale in light of the findings based on exploratory factor analyses (EFA) carried out independently and serious methodological errors of confirmatory factor analysis reported in the manual raises concerns. Therefore, they carried out EFA using normative data of 3328 participants including 1254 individuals without intellectual disability and 2074 with intellectual disability. The considered 2 factor model as best fit by employing oblique rotation for principle axis factor extraction method. The Physical development and Social engagement domains reported comparatively low communalities, however. As these domains possibly function in a different way across groups of individuals without and with intellectual disability. These findings propose that the interpretation of ABSS:2 should be based on its two key conceptual components of social behavior and personal independence instead of 16 domains of five factors supported by its original authors. Likewise, as the score variation is described best by two common factors, they discouraged comparing the domain scores to identify weaknesses and strengths of adaptive skills.

Bildt, Kraiger, Sytema and Minderaa (2005) studied the psychometric properties of the Vineland Adaptive Behavior Scales Survey Form in a population of children and adolescents with MR, and in the specific levels of functioning (n=826, age 4–18 years). The participants were assigned to the four levels of mental retardation as defined by the DSM-IV-TR (APA, 2000) namely profound (IQ 0–20), severe (IQ 21–35), moderate (IQ 36–50) or mild (IQ 51–70). The original division into (sub) domains, as assigned by the authors, was replicated in the total population and in the mild and moderate levels of functioning. In the severe and profound levels of functioning the structure was less well recognized. The reliability of the instrument proved to be good in the total population and the subgroups. The construct validity was high in all groups. The authors reported strong evidence from this study for the applicability of the Vineland in the population with mental retardation, and stressed the need for supplementary norms for mentally retarded population.

Carter et al., (1998) developed the norms of VABS for a special group of 684 individuals with autism. The sample was divided into four groups including children younger than 10 years with few verbal skills at least, younger than 10 years mute children; 10 years or older children with few verbal skills at least; 10 years or older mute children. The sample was approached at 5 different university sites offering expert services in autism and the participants referred for autism/ PDD field trial study for DSM-IV. The researchers reported that the older children had lower scores compared to younger children on all domains of adaptive functioning. On daily living skills domain mute participants shad significantly lower scores compared to verbal participants within the same age range. Mute participants who were older than 10 years were found to have most impaired in terms of performance on communication domain, whereas, younger verbal participants were least impaired. Verbal participants older than 10 and younger mute children scored in the average range on this domain. The results also suggest relatively higher scores on daily living skills and relatively lower scores on socialization domain with reference to age but not standard scores. At the end, researchers highlighted the significance of using special population norms along with national norms of VABS while assessing individuals with autism and associated conditions.

Tasse´ et al., (2012) updates the current conceptualization, measurement, and use of the adaptive skills construct. Major sections of the article address an understanding of the construct, the current approaches to its measurement, four assessment issues and challenges related to using the adaptive skills information for intellectual disability diagnosis, and two future issues regarding the relations of adaptive skills with the distribution of adaptive skills scores and multidimensional models of personal competence. An understanding of the construct of adaptive skills and its measurement is critical to clinicians and practitioners in the field because of its role in understanding the phenomenon of intellectual functioning, identifying a person with intellectual disability, offering framework to person-referenced habilitation and education goals, and focusing on other significant dimensions of individual's functioning.

Mathias and Nettelbeck (1992) assessed the validity of the personal competence model of Greenspan (1979) which was a comprehensive attempt to define the structure of adaptive skills. This model divided personal competence into three major components of physical competence, adaptive intelligence and socio-emotional adaptation. Physical competence was not well defined in this model and includes such variables as strength, size and coordination. Adaptive intelligence drawn from Thorndike's and Guilford's models of intelligence is viewed to be comprised of three subcomponents. The first was similar to conventional concept of intelligence. Social intelligence was second component, which was described as an individual's skill to understand and effectively cope with interpersonal and social situations and objects. A concept very similar to present adaptive skills was presented as practical intelligence. This concept was based on skills that help dealing effectively with vocational and self-maintaining activities which are part of general mechanical and physical aspects of human functioning. Socio-emotional adaptation reflects a range of temperament and personality factors that offer explanation similar to maladaptive behaviors part of some adaptive skills instruments (Greenspan, 1979).

Meyers, Nihira and Zetlin (1979) reviewed the adaptive skills measurement literature from 1965 to 1979. Their work is not only probably the most comprehensive and research based attempt to elucidate the construct of adaptive skills but also contributed answers to a number of theoretical questions concerning the nature of the adaptive skills construct. Their extensive review of factor analytical studies suggests that adaptive behavior is defined in most available assessment instruments as two dimensional structure. The factors are interpreted as functional autonomy or self-sufficiency and a social responsibility dimension, and they considered these dimensions to be universal factors. Meyers et al (1979) defined a consistent two factor maladaptive structure as well. They suggest that two maladaptive factors are interpreted to represent the extra-intra dimensions (extra punitive, intra punitive; or extraversion, introversion) commonly used to describe personal adjustment.

Adaptive Behaviors and IQ

Although the construct of adaptive skills has got somewhat clear in the past few decades, the construct is still shadowed with many confusions and misconceptions, one of which is confusing it with other concepts such as intelligence, social skills etc.

Puig et al., (2013) stated that despite the cognitive potential of individuals with HFASD (high functioning autism spectrum disorder), adaptive limitations are frequently evident in their functioning. According to the researchers most of the researches in this area had focused on studying the association of adaptive skills with intellectual quotient (IQ) and had used correlation as a primary method to explore the relationships between these variables. There are limited number of researches that investigated cognitive factors other than intelligence quotient as likely predictors of adaptive skills in HF-ASD using regression methods. Puig and colleagues carried out research to investigate the effects of various cognitive factors on adaptive skills among 16 adolescents and children with HFASD from 7 to 17 years of age, the sample only included boys. Cognitive assessment consisted measures of general intelligence, verbal memory, visual memory, problem solving/flexibility and working memory tests. VABS was employed to evaluate adaptive skills. In order to determine the predictive ability of cognitive variables for each domain of adaptive skills linear regression models using stepwise methods were used. According to the reported results, IQ and verbal memory appeared as the main independent predictors for adaptive skills scores on VABS. IQ predicted 41% of the total variance in adaptive domain of communication. Verbal memory predicted the 35% of variance for daily living skills. Both these variables together predicted almost half of the variance (49 %) for domain of socialization. Adaptive skills scores was not found to be associated with any other cognitive function. The researchers finally highlighted the significant influence of verbal memory and IQ on adaptive skills of individuals with HF-ASD.

Platt, Kamphaus, Cole and Smity (1991) carried out a study to examine correlations between the VABS, WISC-R and Stanford-Binet Intelligence Scale. The sample included 5 to 19 years old 99 participants who were referred for clinical assessment of intellectual disabilities. The correlation between scores of intelligence and adaptive skills was found to be low to moderate. The researchers concluded that the results of their study confirm the findings of the previous researches conducted on this topic and support findings that intelligence and adaptive skills are related yet independent contrasts. They also recommended to include adaptive skills an evaluation procedure.

Bolte and Poustka (2002) investigated the relationship of adaptive skills with general cognitive functioning of individuals with autism or PDD-NOS without and with comorbid intellectual disability. They administered VABS and WISC on a group of 67 participants divided into two groups, having higher intellectual functioning (n=34) with IQ more than 70 and lower intellectual functioning (n=33) having an IQ lower than 70. The results revealed that in the lower intellectual functioning group the level of adaptive functioning and IQ were comparable among individuals with and without comorbid intellectual disability. However, on the other hand, the performances of two groups differ significantly on WISC and VABS. In non intellectual disabled participants, a higher correlation was revealed between single adaptive domain and IQ and communication domain emerged as having highest predictive power for single adaptive skills domain through regression analysis. The findings further suggested that the qualitative reduction of intelligence mediated the relationship between intellectual and adaptive skills among autistic children.

According to Schatz and Hamdan- Allen (1995) researchers have examined adaptive behavior in autism, but few studies have looked for different patterns of adaptive skills according to age and intelligence. The researchers studied the effects of age and IQ on adaptive behavior. Domain scores from the Vineland Adaptive Behavior Scale (VABS) were compared in relation to age and Performance IQ for 72 children and adolescents with autism and 37 non autistic children and adolescents with mental retardation. Age and IQ were positively related to each of the Vineland domains. Children with autism had lower scores in the socialization domain. An interaction was present between Performance IQ and group: With increasing IQ, children with autism showed smaller increases in social functioning than children with mental retardation. A similar trend was present for daily living skills. Results suggest that (a) the relationship between the two groups' adaptive skills scores is stable from preschool age through adolescence, and (b) increasing IQ is associated with less of an increase in certain adaptive skills for children with autism.

Tasse′ and Havercamp (2006) explored the relations among motivation, adaptive skills, and psychopathology. They also presented their concept of IQ–adaptive skills discrepancy and report on the preliminary results of a pilot study that explored this phenomenon. In total 14 children were included in the sample with the age ranged from 6 to 17 years. Two participants were girls; the 12 remaining participants were boys. The full scale IQ was 41 to 74 with 59 as a mean and 8 standard deviation. The Scales of Independent Behavior-R scores were 20 to 82 with 62 mean and 17 as standard deviation. Stanford-Binet–4th Ed, SIBehavior—R, EZ-Yale Personality Questionnaire and Nisonger Child Behavior Rating Form were used to measure IQ, adaptive skills, motivation, and psychopathology respectively. The results reveal a relatively strong inverse relationship between the individuals' motivation and the magnitude of an IQ–adaptive skills discrepancy. From the seven subscales of motivational scale, only one subscale ''Negative Reaction Tendency'' (r ¼ 0.23) and ''Positive Reaction Tendency'' (r ¼ 0.13) show positive correlations with IQ–adaptive skills discrepancy. All other correlation coefficients were negative, ranging from r ¼ 0.18 to r ¼ 0.52, indicating a relatively strong inverse relationship between the individuals' motivation and the magnitude of an IQ. None of these coefficients was large enough to achieve statistical significance. The magnitude of an individual's IQ–adaptive skills discrepancy is strongly related to the severity of the individual's psychopathology. The correlation coefficient between the severity of psychopathology and the magnitude of the IQ–adaptive skills discrepancy ranged from r ¼ 0.38 to r ¼ 0.72. In other words, the severity of the psychopathology resulted in greater magnitude of the adaptive skills and IQ discrepancy.

The researches reviewed in this section reveal that the construct of intelligence and adaptive skills are different yet strongly associated with each other. Both the constructs are pertinent in the field of developmental psychopathologies and their importance cannot be under estimated.

Adaptive Skills and Developmental Psychopathologies

Adaptive skills along with intellectual assessment is a critical part of evaluating children who have or are suspected of having any of the developmental psychopathologies. The following section provides an overview of researches that highlight the relationship of adaptive skills with developmental psychopathologies.

Pellicano (2012) Autism is a common and often highly debilitating neurodevelopmental condition, whose core behavioral features are believed to be rooted in disrupted neurocognitive processes, including especially "executive function." In this paper author identifies one potential source of symptoms variability, namely, autistic children's emerging "executive function" (EF), those higher-order processes, closely associated with the prefrontal cortex, which are necessary for regulating and controlling behavior. Specifically, it suggests that individual differences in the growth trajectories of autistic children's EF skills could explain some of the variability in children's functional outcomes, including their social awareness, real-life adaptive skills, and readiness to learn in school, both in the short term and in the long term. Researchers have predominantly focused upon understanding the putative causal relationship between difficulties in EF and autistic symptomatology. This paper suggests, however, that the effects of individual differences in EF should be more far-reaching, playing a significant part in the real-life outcomes of individuals with autism, including their social competence, everyday adaptive skills, and academic achievement. It further considers the nature of the EF-outcome relationship, including the possible determinants of individual differences in EF, and makes several recommendations for future research.

MacDonald, Lord, Ulrich (2013) explored the association between adaptive skills and motor skills in a groups of 159 children aged between 12 and 33 months. The sample was divided into three main groups, children with PDD NOS (n= 26), non-ASD developmental delay (n= 23) and ASD (n= 110) recruited from early intervention studies and clinical referrals. Developmental delay group was included to provide a range of scores indicted through calibrated autism severity. A trained clinician administered PLADOS and ADOS on all participants in order to get the diagnostic information. VABS-II and MSEL were also administered on all participants to assess adaptive skills and cognitive level respectively. The gross motor and fine motor scales of the MSEL were 18 used to assess motor skills (Mullen, 1995). Multiple regression analysis identified fine motor skills and calibrated autism severity as significant predictors of adapted skills composite (p < .001), daily living skills (p < .001), adaptive social skills (p < .05) and adaptive communicative skills (p < .001). Gross motor skills and calibrated autism severity were identified as predictors of daily living skills (p < .001). Calibrated autism severity and non-verbal problem solving were predictors of the adaptive skills composite, adaptive social communicative skills (p < .001). The researchers found that the calibrated autism severity was significantly predicted by the gross motor skills and fine motor skills. Participants having motor skills displayed higher levels of calibrated autism severity. The investigators suggested focusing more on and to explore creative ways to design and implement early rehabilitation and intervention programs for children with autism.

Doobay (2010) had conducted a research examining the assessment reports of gifted adolescents with and without ASD for domains of adaptive functioning, intellectual functioning, social skills and behavioral functioning. Empirical group study design was employed to assess a sample of 81 school going adolescents identified with intellectual giftedness. In total 41 participants did not fulfill criteria for any DSM –IV-TR psychological disorder, whereas, 40 participants fulfilled criteria of ASD. The researchers hypothesized that adolescents with ASD would show relatively poor performance on adaptive skills, processing speed and social skills having more behavioral concerns with equally strong non verbal and verbal intellectual abilities compared to adolescents without ASD. Adaptive skills was assessed by administering VABS-II and BASC-2 was used to evaluate behavior and self perception of participants. The data was analyzed through split-plots and independent sample t test. The findings revealed statistically significant differences in domain scores of adaptive skills, behavioral functioning, processing speed and social skills between adolescents with and without ASD regardless of comparable non verbal and verbal intellectual functioning. This research made a unique contribution in the absence of any study empirically comparing different characteristics of gifted adolescents with and without ASD. The research revealed important implications for individuals with ASD in providing empirical basis to build effective classroom management programs according to specific needs of ASD population.

Mordre and colleagues (2011) conducted a longitudinal investigation on 39 children having PDD-NOS and 74 children with autism for varied amount of time ranging from 17–38 years as part of a record linkage research. The groups were compared for marital status, rates of mortality, disability pension and criminality. The disability pension award emerged as the single outcome variable differing significantly between the two groups, that is, 72 percent for PDD-NOS and 89 percent for autistic group. Better psychosocial functioning among individuals with PDD-NOS predicted the low rates of disability pension. The researchers also supported the dimensional explanation of ASD with reference to then proposed DSM-5 by highlighting the lack of substantial differences in prognosis between the two groups.

Adaptive skills measures are used frequently to assess adaptive skills of children with HFASDs, though very little information is available on the efficacy of the adaptive skills instruments to give similar findings. Thomeer and colleagues (2013) carried out a study to assess the degree to which the mentioned tools offered comparable scores; to record the relative weaknesses and strengths on adaptive skills of 6 to 11 years old children with HFASD based on the ratings of their parent on BASC-2, VABS-II and ABAS-II; to finally evaluate the relative differences between adaptive skills and cognitive functioning across the instruments. The ABAS-II and VABS-II revealed relative strengths in skills related to academics and relative deficits in social skills with significant overall limitations among participants of the current study were observed. Significant differences in the definite scores magnitude was reported through cross instrument comparisons. Overall, ABAS-II and BASC-II showed significantly lower scores compared to VABS-II. The composite and domain scores across the three adaptive skills tools and average IQ score demonstrated significant discrepancies. Researchers reported adaptive social skills as a critical domain to assess in individuals with HFASDs and ABAS-II and VABS-II did not yield any significant differences in scores on this area.

Sadrossadat, Moghaddami, Sadrossadat (2010) compared adaptive skills of individuals with intellectual disability with normal individuals. The study consisted of 246 individuals with typical development and 74 individuals with intellectual disability aged 7 till 18 years from Tehran a city of Iran. ABS-RC2 including 18 behavioral domains was used to assess the adaptive skills. Researchers use standard procedure or back translation to adapt and translate the scale in Persian language. A significant relationship between general adaptive skills and mental status was found. Individuals with intellectual disability demonstrated significantly low scores on domains of number & time, economic activity, independent functioning, responsibility, self direction, socialization, prevocational /vocational activity, language development, social engagement, disturbed interpersonal behavior, trustworthiness, conformity and domestic activity compared to those with typical development. The two groups didn't differ significantly in their performance on sexual behaviors, hyperactive and stereotype behaviors, self abuse behavior and physical development domains. The researchers finally highlight the importance of early behavioral intervention to improve adaptive skills lags of individuals as individuals with intellectual disability performed significantly poor compared to their counterparts with typical development. They proposed that need based adaptive intervention plans can effectively help individuals with ID to improve their level of functioning in residential and general social environments.

Hauser-Cram (2001) studied the adaptive and cognitive development in developmentally disabled children, and adaptation of their parents in a longitudinal research spanning from infancy to middle childhood. The primary aim of the study was to develop and evaluate the conceptual models of family and child development. Sample comprised 183 children diagnosed with Down syndrome along with developmental and motor impairments. The families of these children were also included in the study. Researchers paid home visits to collect information at 5 different points in time since enrolment in early management around 3 years of age to 10th birthday. At each point, researchers interviewed mothers, assessed children and requested both parents to independently fill questionnaires.

Hierarchical linear models were made to analyze parental well being and developmental trajectories of children. The particular type of illness predicted developmental pattern in social skills, cognition and daily living skills. Children with Down syndrome revealed the weakest relationship between child's mental age and mother child interaction when compared to other disabilities. The type of disability also predicted changes in spouse related and child related stress in mothers. Child's self regulatory processes particularly mastery motivation and behavior problems and mother child interaction emerged as key predictors in both parental well being and child outcomes. Moreover, mother child interaction also observed to be the key predictor in adaptive skills domains of social skills and communication skills. The problem focused coping and social support available to parents also turned out to be a predictor of maternal and paternal stress respectively.

Sikora, et al., (2012) investigated the association of health related quality of life and adaptive functioning with ADHD symptoms in a group of children with ASD with comorbid ADHD symptoms. CBCL was used to assess ADHD symptoms, VABS employed to assess adaptive functioning, PQLI was used to explore quality of health of participants. The ratings of parents on CBCL scales were used to divide participants into two groups as having significant ADHD symptoms or not. Multivariate analysis was carried out to compare the scores of groups on quality of life and adaptive functioning scores. Almost 19 percent of the sample had elevated scores on both subscales of CBCL, whereas, 40 percent children had elevated score on only one scale. Children in ASD only group had higher scores on both PQLI and VABS-II scores compared to children in ASD and ADHD comorbid group. The researchers concluded poor health related quality of life and greater impairment in adaptive functioning in children with ASD and clinically significant ADHD symptoms compared to

ASD children with non significant or no ADHD symptoms. Finally, researchers suggested professionals to assess the symptoms of ADHD in children with ASD and incorporate management of these symptoms in treatment plans.

Ditterline, Banner, Oakland and Becto (2008) stated that conventionally the evaluation of adaptive functioning is associated with the screening of individuals with intellectual disability. The assessment of adaptive functioning is increasingly used for detailed evaluation, designing treatment plans and treatment evaluation for many disorders. According to researchers, the normative data of adaptive skills tools in USA offers information on adaptive behavior profiles of individuals with different disabilities, for instance, learning disabilities, autism, sensory deficits and autism. In this context, researchers review the adaptive skill profiles of individuals who fulfilled the eligibility criteria for special education services for diagnoses of emotional disturbances, learning disabilities, autism and specific learning disability with comorbid emotional disturbance. The findings reported that overall adaptive profiles and mean scores on sub domains differ significantly across groups. The adaptive skill scores were significantly lower among students with severe disabilities and comorbid conditions. Researchers stressed the need to use adaptive skill scores to develop better understanding of students suffering from different disabilities and to use these scores to increase effectiveness of management plans.

Wells, Condillac, Perry and Factor (2010) assessed the utility and construct validity of 3 frequently used adaptive functioning instruments including ABS-2, VABS-II, SIB-R. The study carried out a content review of case files of individuals from TRE-ADD program at Thistletown Regional Centre completed between 1993 and 2005. The study was focused around two main objectives, firstly to examine the relationship between severity of autism and cognitive levels of individuals. The second objective was to compare the associations between three instruments of adaptive functioning. The files of 50 participants were selected only if it contained assessment on SIB-R, VABS and ABS. Results indicated moderate negative correlations between adaptive scores on three measures and autism severity. However, adaptive functioning level on all measures found to have strong positive correlations with mental age. Mental age had slightly lower correlation with SIB-R compared to other two measures and ABS-S-2 had comparatively lower correlation with autism severity than other measures. VABS-II was strongly correlated with autism severity and mental age than other two measures. Researcher, however, suggested to prefer either ABS or SIB-R for the lower functioning autistic population as VABS-II essentially measured the developmental level instead of adaptive skills as a distinct construct.

It is concluded that adaptive behavior measures can be very helpful for professionals working with children with developmental psychopathologies. The studies indicate that the presentation of adaptive behavior is somewhat different and the score on different dimensions change from one problem to another. As children with mild developmental delay score highest on almost all dimensions of adaptive behavior as compared to other children and children with autism score less on communication and socialization etc. Age, level of intelligence and severity and type of developmental problem emerged as important factors that can mediate the score on adaptive behavior measures.

It is important to note that all of the researches mentioned above were conducted in western countries except one, which was carried out in Iran. Iran shares common religious and cultural values and practices with Pakistan. The studies highlight the importance of adaptive functioning assessment to improve the functioning of children in different cultural contexts.

Correlates and Predictors of Adaptive Skills

This section presents the review of correlational studies that particularly focused to study the relationship of adaptive behaviors with a variety of factors including personal, social and familial variables.

Hall (2008) examined the family support networks, parental coping and the relationships, their parental stress and adaptive skills of children with ASD. The researchers also explored the association of all these variables with each other and some other variables. The researcher selected a group of 75 primary caregivers of ASD children through purposive sampling for conducting a cross sectional, correlational descriptive study. The participants provided detailed information regarding the adaptive skills of children along with all other variables mentioned above. Multiple regression analysis and Pearson product moment correlation were used along with descriptive analysis to examine the data. Researchers found that parental behaviors focused to continue using and seeking social support, emotional strength and self respect were negatively associated with adaptive skills of children. Parental behaviors focused on teamwork, family adjustment and positive interpretation of situation were reported to be positively associated with parental perception of support received by their family. Authors also reported a significant trend between parental stress and adaptive behaviors of autistic children. Researchers highlighted the significance of early screening and extensive intervention to successfully overcome the limitations of adaptive functioning. The study further suggested to provide support to parents of children with autism to help them deal with special needs of their children and to improve their existing patterns of coping.

Kanne and colleagues (2011) examined the association of symptoms of autism with adaptive functioning. The sample included 1089 individuals with ASD with verbal ability present. The researchers examined the sample by IQ, adaptive skills and intensity of ASD symptomatology. Sample showed significant overall deficit in adaptive functioning. They found strong positive association of IQ and sub domains of adaptive skills. Age was found to be positively related with adaptive skills. When ASD intensity and age was controlled, IQ was found to have significant variance in adaptive skills which accounted for overall 55 percent variance. Adaptive skills observed to have negative association with autistic symptoms. IQ emerged as a strong predictor and the gap between adaptive skills and intelligence was found to be higher among older participants, while small gap was observed in lower functioning individuals with ASD.

Liss et al., (2001) examined a sample of children diagnosed with different developmental disorders. The objective of the study was to explore and compare the correlates and predictors of adaptive skills in children with developmental disorders. They selected a group of 30 children with HAD matched with 40 children with low functioning autism, 31 children and 17 children with low I, 9 years of age and assessed on VABS, all group were match on non-verbal memory and language, and autistic symptomatology. Findings revealed that children with LAD and HAD had significant impairments on daily living and socialization domains compared to children in matched groups. Children with HAD and LAD didn't show significant impairment on communication compared to children in LAD, HAD group showed autistic symptomatology showed significant association with adaptive skills only in children with ASD. Results also revealed that IQ strongly predicted adaptive skills in children with LAD and ID, whereas, verbal memory and language score emerged as a string predictor of adaptive skills in children with HAD. Finally, researchers concluded that although IQ emerged as a restricting factor for children with low functioning, the particular deficits were more pronounced in HAD children. The children with HAD had most significant impairments in language, autistic symptoms and verbal memory areas.

Culture and Disability

Cultural beliefs and standards not only influence the perception of symptoms as problematic but can also influence the process of assessment. Therefore, it is relevant to review the literature that explains the association between culture and disability.

Maulik and Darmstadt (2008) conducted a content analysis to gather information regarding present knowledge around childhood disability in middle and low income countries to recognize the existing gaps in knowledge of childhood disabilities. They carried out an extensive search on electronic data bases including Embase, PubMed and PsychInfo by using particular search terms pointing to childhood disability in developing countries. They also searched Cochrane library in order to screen out similar reviews. They selected 80 full text articles meeting the research criteria and generated information regarding screening instruments, disability related services, research methodology used, legislation, promotion and prevention activities and epidemiology. Researchers generated frequency distributions of all study parameters by collating both qualitative and quantitative information. In total 41 articles were representing low income countries and 66 researchers were epidemiologic in nature. From all studies, whereas cross-sectional studies made 60% of all researchers. The most commonly explored conditions were intellectual(26%) and hearing(26%) disabilities, and most frequently employed screening instrument was the Ten questionnaire. The researchers reported that the general quality of research was inappropriate and most researchers lack information about service utilization, legislation and particular interventions used. They also pointed that most studies particularly lack information about morbidities outcomes such as neonatal and early childhood illness and delivery complications. The researchers finally concluded that most studies did not include any conditions other than intellectual and hearing disabilities and most of the studies even epidemiologic researches had inadequate quality. Finally, they suggested that future studies should translate their findings into public health policy which may bring change in lives of disabled children in middle and low income countries instead of only addressing.

Durkin, Hasan and Hasan (1998) reported prevalence and related demographic factors of intellectual disability among children between 2 and 9 years of age in Karachi. They carried out a two phase population survey between 1988 and 1989. In phase I they assessed 617 children living in rural areas and 5748 children living in urban areas. They used the Ten Questions measure based on parental ratings to screen out disabilities among 6365 children from their cluster sample. In phase II, structured psychological and medical examination was conducted for 10 percent of children from initial sample who received negative disability results and all children who had positive results in disability screening. Psychological assessment was based on SBIT to assess intellectual level and adaptive behavior tool developed by the authors. The researchers did not mention psychometric details of these two instruments. Structured observation of participants, developmental history, ability to comprehend instructions, and observation of motor skills was carried out during physicians for evaluation of mental retardation. Psychologists classified level of mental retardation according to IQ. Researchers reported to had also used comprehensive medical, psychological, neurological evaluations in areas of hearing, seizures, motor and vision to investigate the intensity of disability. They used serious category of disability by combining severe and moderate disability groups. The researchers reported that the prevalence estimates of 65.3 per 1000 individuals for mental retardation with mild severity and 19.0 per 1000 as prevalence estimates for serious mental retardation. When compared to prevalence in other countries the data from industrialized countries and selected less developed countries reveal considerably lower prevalence rates. Finally researchers concluded that perinatal difficulties, traumatic brain injuries, neonatal infections, malnourishment and post natal brain infections were found to be significant correlates of intellectual disability in their sample. The maternal educated had strong correlation with prevalence of disability in both groups. Researchers stressed the need to conduct further research to find out other factors associated with prevalence of intellectual disabilities.

Hussein, Taha and Almanasef (2011) reported that there are very few studies conducted on autism in middle east despite the factor that autism has well explain discrete phenomenology. Supporting the biological nature of this disorder. Although, phenomenology and symptomatology of autism has attracted lots of attention in past decades, there still of lack of information on cultural information on characteristic symptoms and management. The researchers attempted to compare a group of Saudi children with a group of Egyptian children on symptoms of autism. The sample consisted of 48 children divided into two groups, including as Saudi children from a hospital in Dammam, Saudi Arabia and 20 Egyptian children contacted at an Institute of Psychiatry, Cairo. All children were administered VABS, GARS and SIBT for assessing their adaptive functioning, autism symptoms and their intensity and level of intelligence respectively. The researchers found that typical symptoms of autism were uncommon in both groups compared to typical symptoms of autism. They found that clinical factors like hyperactivity, regression, mental retardation and epilepsy did not differ significantly across groups. The children of Saudi Arabia showed significantly lower performance on all developmental milestones compared to Egyptian children. Egyptian children showed significantly delayed development on language than Saudi children. They finally concluded that culture influences both investigation and treatment of autism in many significant ways, like perception of perinatal developmental difficulties, age of noticing initial signs of abnormality, family's perception of the developmental difficulties and age of seeking intervention. All these factors are not only directly related with the autistic severity and symptomatology but prognosis as well.

Nihira, Webster, Tomiyasu and Oshio (1998) conducted a cross-cultural research to explore the characteristics of child environment associations in families of children with mild intellectual disability in America and Japan. Total 93 families in America and 90 families in Japan participated in this study, all families had a child with mild intellectual disability. To assess psychosocial adjustment and social competency of children ABS was administered on all children. Researchers used observations and interviews to develop understanding of home environments and child family interaction. The Family Environment Scale and the Henderson Environment Learning and Process Scale were used to understand the characteristics and dynamics of familial environment. The results suggested strong association between social competence of children and cognitive opportunities available at home and this relationship seem similar across the two cultures. On the other hand however, the relation between psychosocial adjustment of children and affective components of home environment turned out to be different in both cultures.

Govender (2002) studied the parental attitudes towards their children with intellectual disability in Zululand. The sample was approached at a hospital clinic and a special children's institute in rural area of Zululand. The results indicate a positive attitude of parents towards their children with intellectual disability. There was no significant difference in paternal and maternal attitudes, however family setups where both parents were living together showed relatively more positive attitudes than single parents. Although most parents shared feelings of embarrassment and disappointments on having a child with intellectual disability, parents accepted and loved their intellectually challenged children. Finally, researchers recommended holding more researches in this area with intensions of using this information for developing successful and effective intervention and rehabilitation programs for children with intellectual disabilities and their families.

According to Mirza, Tareen, Davidson and Rahman (2009) reported that Pakistan is amongst the countries having highest reported rates of intellectual disability in children. The estimates of prevalence vary from 65 per 1000 children for mild intellectual disability to 19 per 1000 children for serious intellectual disability. The researchers reported to conduct focus group and in-depth interviews of small groups of primary care givers and health professionals other than that they surveyed 100 caregivers of intellectually challenged children. The results suggest a significant delay of 2.92 years to 4.17 years in identification and care seeking of intellectual disabilities. The findings also revealed that the rural settings were particularly linked with significant delay in identification of intellectual disability. They also reported that social stigma about intellectual disability results in restricted participation of children and their families in community which may increases the burden of disease further. The findings also revealed lack of parental knowledge related to causes, early identification signs and availability of adequate intervention programs of intellectual disability. They also reported that lack of access to services offering identification and management and knowledge of prognosis and course of intellectual disability increases care giver stress. In the end researchers stressed to establish practical, community based and cost effective rehabilitation and intervention programs for children with learning disabilities and their care givers.

Blair and Peters (2003) explored neurocognitive and physiological correlates of adaptive behaviors in children attending Head Start program in USA. Researchers assessed neurocognitive functions through executive function tasks, in one task children were required to discontinue pre potent response and the other task required them to remember and execute rules of correct response set. Researchers examined the receptive language ability of children and collected information on negative emotionality of children particularly related to anger and fear from parents. The results reported that higher social competence was related to vagal increase during cognitive tasks, higher resting vagal tone and increased fearfulness. However, higher executive functioning, vagal suppression during cognitive tasks and lower resting vagal tone were correlated with higher rating of on-task behavior. Researchers reported that findings can particularly be helpful to understand the relationship of preschool adaptation, academic and social competence of individuals with autism.

Kelly, Sacker, Schoon and Nazroo, (2006) examined the cultural differences in achieving developmental skills by studying the pattern of developmental milestones of infants in different ethnic groups. They examined 15994 infants who participated in first phase of the Millennium Cohort Study, the mean age of sample was 9.2 months and included both female ($n = 7782$) and male infants ($n = 8212$). The results showed that White infants were more likely to show delay in achieving gross motor skills as compared to Black Caribbean, Indian and Black African infants. However, they reported that infants of Bangladeshi and Pakistani origin were more likely to experience delay in communicative gestures and other fine motor skills. The researchers reported that these developmental delays were influenced by different cultural practices and socioeconomic factors. The findings also suggested that unexplained ethnic and cultural variations were found to be influencing the achievement of gross motor skills in Black African, Black Caribbean and Indian infants. They finally concluded that when socioeconomic factors were controlled the higher likelihood of motor delay among Bangladeshi and Pakistani infants disappeared significantly. The researchers highlighted the need to take into account the ethno cultural variations affecting developmental processes while assessing individuals and stressed to control the environmental deprivation that may lead to long term behavioral and cognitive deficits.

Zhao et al., (2002) investigated the factors influencing social adaptive behavior of children. A group of six hundred 6 to 12 years old children comprised the sample whose adaptive functioning was assessed through AAMD-ABS (revised edition). Stepwise linear regression was used as a main statistical analysis to examine the data. The results revealed that parent's relationship, age and health state of mothers had a strong impact on social adaptive behaviors of children. The type of preschool fostering, social mood of the neighborhood also turned out to be strong predictors of social skills domain of adaptive behaviors. Researchers highlighted that supportive relationship between parents, a good fostering care for the child, strong health of mothers and healthy social environment not only enrich general development of adaptive behaviors but particularly help improving social domain of adaptive functioning.

Minshawi (2007) conducted a research to understand the nature of the association between adaptive functioning and problem behaviors in participants with intellectual disability (ID) through two experiments. The adaptive behaviors were measured through VABS and Problem Behavior Inventory (PBI) was used to assess problem behaviors. In first experiment the researcher found a negative relationship between adaptive functioning and problem behaviors. Researcher also noted the ability of the daily living skills, communication and socialization to predict adaptive functioning; it was found through multiple regression analyses that no individual domain could significantly predict adaptive functioning. The second experiment was conducted to assess whether adaptive behaviors were related to factors that maintain problem behaviors like availability of tangible items, social attention, nonsocial reinforcement, escape from situation and physical pain. The results revealed that participants who had non social reinforcement and physical pain had lower scores on socialization, communication and daily living skill domains compared to other participants.

Sigman and Ruskin (1999) conducted a longitudinal study aimed to assess the continuity and change in diagnosis, intelligence, and language skills in children with Down syndrome, autism and other developmental problems and to identify the limitations in language and social skills of these children. They also planned to recognize factors that can help preschool children acquire language skills and develop peer associations during mid-school period. The original sample included 93 children with Down syndrome, 70 children with autism and 59 children with developmental delays along with another group of 108 children with typical development. The children in first three groups were assessed during 2 to 6 years of age. Total 71 children with Down syndrome, 51 children with autism and 33 children with developmental delays were examined when they were between10 and 13 years of age. Researchers observed significant improvement in language and intellectual abilities with non significant change in symptoms of autism, however, this pattern was absent in children with Down syndrome. Children in down syndrome presented significant limitations in only language area, whereas children in autism group showed distinctive deficits in symbolic play, joint attention, initiating peer contact, emotional responsiveness towards others. Autistic children were observed to have very low social engagement with their peers compared to children in other groups, and this limitation was free of their general functioning level. Joint attention skills found to be related to linguistic skills across all groups and predicted later acquisition of expressive language among autistic children. The peer play initiation in children in Down syndrome group and peer association in children with autism was predicted by early play and nonverbal communication skills. On the basis of findings of this study, researchers recommended to focus on developing play and early communication skills to help children with developmental delays to acquire social competence and language skills later in life.

According to Gillespie-Lynch et al., (2012) longitudinal studies discussing the autistic issues in adult life is limited in number, therefore, they conducted a research to study the childhood factors that predict social competence in adults with ASD. The sample included 20 participants who were assessed through multiple evaluations from early childhood (mean = 3.9 years) to adulthood (mean = 26.6 years) unlike longitudinal evaluations of adult outcomes done in previous studies. During early childhood, participants were assessed for language, responsiveness to joint attention and intelligence. In adulthood, parents of all participants completed interviews for their children that assessed autistic symptomatology, adaptive functioning and global functioning. Composite score of adult independence and social functioning was predicted by language and responsiveness of joint attention acquired in early childhood. Autistics symptoms, social skills and adult non verbal communication were also predicted by responsiveness to joint attention. Intelligence and early childhood language skills predicted the adult adaptive functioning. Researchers concluded that autistic symptoms did not change with development but adaptive function did.

Calzada, Brotman, Huang, Bat-Chavae, and Kingston (2009) examined the socioemotional and behavioral functioning of preschool children and cultural adaptation of their parents in a group of unban families with diverse cultural background. This community sample included families of 130 children with 4.1 years mean age going to pre kindergarten public programs arranged in urban communities. Teachers rated children for classroom adaptive skills along with internalizing and externalizing problems. While parents rated their children for enculturation and acculturation on a cultural adaptation instrument. Results suggest that specific aspects of acculturation and retention of parental culture of origin were associated with positive outcomes in this particular group. Parents with low ethnic and American identity had children with higher levels of internalizing problems and lower levels of adaptive skills compared to children of bicultural parents. Researchers stressed the need to promote ethnic identity among parents to augment positive behavioral outcomes in children. The researches viewed above reveal interesting information regarding the link between developmental disabilities and culture. Most of the researches conclude that culture has strong impact on not only early identification and management of disability but the way disabilities are perceived, their causal attributions and their effect on family functioning. Since the role of cultural variations has been established through various researches, it had generated interests of experts in other related areas such as developmental assessment.

Culture and Adaptive Behaviors

Adaptive behavior scales become pertinent to use in developmental assessment. The importance of cultural influences over one's behavior and the assessor's perception cannot be under estimated, as the norms of even well standardized tools can vary across countries due to cultural disparity. The following section includes the review of some important researches that addressed the effects of differing cultural contexts on adaptive behavior performance.

Manohari, Raman, and Ashok (2013) describe their experience in using the Vineland adaptive behavior scale with children who has autism and illustrated difficulties encountered while administering VABS to children in India. Authors attributed these difficulties to cultural variability that influences the way a particular task is carried out and gender role expectations. Researchers attributed these difficulties to cultural variations particularly with reference to perceived gender roles and specific ways in which some tasks are carried out. They had administered the Vineland-II Survey Interview Form on a group of 20 children diagnosed with autism spectrum disorder, aged 4-8 years, and also used the caregiver/parent report form on 100 children. They pointed that some items of the scale were not applicable in their culture. They noted that 85% of the items of Vineland-II could be used in Indian setting without any difficulty. They reported that 11.7% items of the scale need modification and 3.3% items of the scale were difficult to modify.

Tan et al., (2011) formulated a study on assumption that the construct of adaptive functioning which is usually taken as universal actually has different manifestation in different cultural settings. They selected Zambian children to examine academic achievement and adaptive, functioning. They translated VABS-II in to Chitonga and many cultural adaptations were made in the scale. Due to concerns about construct validity, the writing section from the communication domain was completely omitted. During pilot study researchers observed that most of the children failed to demonstrate the writing skills primarily because even their parents lack literary skills. The researchers also evaluated the difficulty level and cultural relevance of other items. As soap is not available to all children all the time nor is used frequently to wash face in this region, the word soap was removed from the item in DLS personal section. Another item "uses savings or checking account responsibly" from community sub-scale section was omitted as it was not found to be culturally appropriate. In total 100 items were dropped in the process of adaptation. Finally, the adapted version was applied to a group of 114 school children with mean age of 12.94 in rural Southern province of Zambia. The association between academic achievement, adaptive functioning and indicators of cognitive ability were then compared with the findings observed in US samples. The results of Zambian children revealed no significant relationship between cognitive ability and adaptive functioning. However, the relationship between scores of reading instruments and adaptive functioning was observed to be significant. They also noted that the pattern of association between academic achievement and adaptive behaviors diverged from that observed in US sample.

Zhang, Wheeler and Richey (2006) conducted a study to investigate the characteristics of cultural validity of four assessment measures used with children with ASD in Chinese cultural context. The instruments used in their study were CARS, MCHAT, CHAT and VABS. They used CARS to provide clinical screening for absence or presence of autistic symptoms and the degree of severity. CHAT is a screening instrument consisting of child practitioner and parent observation questionnaire used to identify autistic symptoms in children uptill 2 years of age. The researchers pointed out items that could not be used as effective screening indicators of autism screening in Chinese Children. The authors pointed out that items assessing eye contact, making faces and pointing index finger were inappropriate for Chinese culture, as those were either not approved or seldom used cultural actions. Researchers pointed out that Chinese children were raised up in ways very different from Western world, therefore, many items of the VABS were noted to be inadequate in Chinese culture. They identified that item 23, 26, 30 and 34 of motor skill domain involving scissors is inappropriate for Chinese children as in order to keep children safe, Chinese adults avoid giving them scissors. Item 38 and 41 from daily living domain also found to be culturally inadequate as researchers mentioned that young children in China are not encouraged to participate I activities related to kitchen particularly tasks sharp and breakable utensils. Item 12 of DLS involves use of knife and fork during meal times, while both children and adults in China use chopsticks instead. They also pointed out that item 24 of DLS did not make sense in Chinese culture as people used boiled water instead of fresh tap water. The item 36 of motor domain was also reported to be inadequate as according to researchers most of the Chinese children ride tricycle instead of bicycle. Researchers argued that children should have exposure to particular tasks to practice mastery and adequate experiences are critical for this. And a child should only be labeled as having delayed development when the child does not have adequate exposure. And require practice to master the skills.

Wachs et al., (1993) explored the relationship of adaptive functioning in Egyptian toddlers with rearing environment. They formulated two main questions that whether association between adaptive skills and specific psychosocial environmental factors in toddlers observed in Western cultures matches the pattern present in non Western cultures.

And does the specific relations between performance and environment existing in Western cultures also function in a non-Western set-up. The sample included 18 to 30 months old 153 Egyptian toddlers and their primary caregivers. Measures of toddler functioning and caregivers behavior were completed by observing naturalistic interactions between toddlers and their primary caregivers twice a month. Canonical analysis revealed that physical contact stimulation and non-verbal vocalization responses were negatively associated, while toddler behavioral competence indices were positively associated with vocal stimulation of caregivers. The importance of sibling caregivers was also observed. During the age between 24 to 29 months particularly, toddler emotionality was uniquely associated with caregivers' response to distress, while measures of toddler vocalization were uniquely associated with measures of vocal stimulation of caregivers. The researchers finally concluded that the specific pattern of findings revealed in this research suggests at least some extent of cross-cultural generalizability of specific model of environmental influences and environmental development relations.

Hauser-Cram et al., (1999) explored the influences of family environment on adaptive development trajectories in young children diagnosed with Down Syndrome. The sample included families of 54 children with Down Syndrome. As a part of a longitudinal study, the development of these children was studied from infancy to 5 years of age. In order to estimate the parameters of hierarchical linear models were employed. Finding reveal that measures of family environment (like mother child interaction and family cohesion) predicted the growth in different domains of adaptive skills, that is, daily living skills, communicate and socialization above and beyond that predicted by predict changes in any of the domains of adaptive functioning.

Runtukahu and Nitko (2002) investigated the applicability of VABS in Indonesia. They wanted to investigate the cultural and social relevance of an adaptive behavior measure developed and standardized in western countries and establishes its utility in Indonesia. The main purpose of their research was to describe a detailed procedure for cross cultural translation, adaptation and standardization of adaptive functioning instrument. They also aimed to develop a measure relevant and sensitive to needs of Indonesian settings. The researchers reported using a standard back translation procedure and making some major changes in the wording and content presentation of the items of VABS to the instrument more relevant to Indonesian culture. They used a small sample size to validate the translated tool but reported that basic indicators of validity were found to be satisfactory. They stressed the need to assess the content relevance of measures borrowed from other culture and establishing basic psychometric characteristics and standardization before using such tools for educational evaluations and program planning.

Alonso et al., (2010) pointed to the lack of availability of standardized adaptive behavior scales in Spanish language to assess intellectually challenged children and adolescents. The authors selected ABS to create a valid translation of it to be used in Spain. The authors reported making few changes in the items and their wordings but the details are not mentioned in this article. The researchers reported sufficient evidences supporting the validity of translated version of ABS and reported that it could be used to assess children speaking Castilian Spanish. The sample comprised of 142 children with ID and 65 children without an ID in Burgos. The researchers hypothesized that development of adaptive behaviors is associated with intellectual functioning of children and the development of adaptive skills remains delayed and irregular among children with ID. Their results indicated that children with ID have strengths and limitations related to development of adaptive skills and the acquisition of adaptive behaviors remains restricted in presence of maladaptive behaviors. The findings also showed that of children with ID showed discontinuity in adaptive functioning with age and their adaptive functioning scores were significantly lower than the scores of children without ID.

Goldberg, Dill, Shin and Nhan (2008) assessed the psychometric characteristics of VABS adapted for Vietnamese culture. The VABS was translated and some cultural adaptations were made according to Vietnamese culture in 1987. In order to examine the newly adapted scale, mothers of 120 preschool children without disabilities attending kindergarten were interviewed to administer the scale. Researchers reported many changes in item content and presentation to make them more relevant to Vietnamese culture. The findings suggested that the Vietnamese version of VABS successfully discriminated children with IDs from children following typical developmental pattern. The scale had also shown to have acceptable levels of construct validity and internal consistency. The mean score of children were comparable to those of included in the normative group in USA.

Baghooli, Toeiserkani and Chavooshi (2009) evaluated 3 cases with intellectual disability and behavioral or emotional problems to determine the efficacy of VABS in clinical settings in Iran. The subjects were referred to take rehabilitative and psycho educational aids. The analyses of the obtained scores exhibit a powerful dimension of the VABS to discriminate weakness and strength adaptive behavior's components. The researchers found VABS to particularly useful in assessing children with developmental disabilities to screen out children with developmental handicaps from those without any developmental problem and progress monitoring during treatment. They also highlighted the use of VABS while designing individualized rehabilitative, educational and management programs for children with special needs in Iran.

Nourani (1998) stated that the topic of adaptive behavior has not been investigated in a major way by professionals in non-western countries. He used modified forms of the SSRS and the VABS to explore adaptive behaviors and the social skills of Iranian preschoolers. Both the scales were translated and adapted according to Iranian culture. Many items from the VABS changed as per Iranian culture and some items were excluded as they didn't fit in to Iranian cultural context. Both teachers' and parents' ratings on the SSRS and the VABS were obtained from 207 children aged 3 to 5 years differing in gender and SES. Results showed that parents and teachers of Iranian preschoolers each value different social skills. Comparison of means for the importance ratings revealed that across all subscales a larger number of the SSRS items were judged either "Important" or "Critical" by parents than by teachers. Frequency ratings about children's use of adaptive and social skills also indicated that Iranian parents and teachers of preschoolers have Different perceptions of children's social functioning. This was evidenced by low to moderately low correlations between their ratings on the SSRS subscales and the VABS sub domains. Correlations of parent's ratings of adaptive behaviors and social skills of children were lower than the ratings of teachers across all subscales. In many domains significant effects of demographic factors were evident on the SSRS: (a) Iranian junior preschoolers were found to be less cooperative and less internalized than senior preschoolers, (b) females were more cooperative and less externalized than males, and (c) children of less educated families were rated significantly lower on Assertion, Cooperation and Responsibility and higher on Internalizing than children of families with more education. On the VABS: (a) junior preschoolers demonstrated lower adaptive skills on all domains as rated by parents and on the Daily Living and Motor Skills as rated by teachers. (b) gender differences were not significant, and (c) children of less educated families scored lower than children of families with more education on all adaptive behavior domains. Overall, the findings were consistent with past studies supporting situational specificity of the social competence than those supporting the stability of behaviors across situations. Social skills are more situationally specific than adaptive behaviors.

The researches reviewed in this section reveal important information about adaptive behaviors with reference to cultural and social dimensions. Most of the researchers concluded that cultural and social background and practices influence both development of adaptive behaviors and scores on different adaptive behavior dimensions.

Most of the studies in this section were carried out in developing countries that share significant religious, cultural, social or economic features with Pakistan. Researches from Iran, India, Zambia and China concluded that adaptive functioning was closely related with cultural standards and practices. These studies also pointed that many items adaptive behavior measures developed in western and/or developed countries were not relevant for children living in developing countries because of significant sociocultural variations. This not only supports the need to develop/adapt adaptive measures to address the indigenous needs of children, but also to assess the pattern of adaptive behaviors in different cultures.

Research on Adaptive Skills in Pakistan

The area of adaptive skills was found to be understudied in Pakistan regardless of this area playing a significant role in clinical assessment. This section included the very few studies on adaptive skills conducted in Pakistan.

Yunus, Mushtaq and Qaiser (2012) conducted a research to study the influences of peer pressure on adaptive skills and learning in the adolescents. They developed two scales for their research including an Adaptive Behavior Scale (ABS) and Peer Pressure Scale (PPS) in order to study their main variables. The study participants comprised of 120 adolescents including 60 males and 60 females from Gujrat city selected through purposive in nature. Cronbach alpha was calculated and found to be significant for Peer Pressure Scale (PPS) and its subscales i.e. belongingness subscale, influential learning subscale and for influential consequences subscale while Cronbach alpha was also found significant for Adaptive Behavior Scale (ABS) and its subscales i.e. interpersonal skills scale, self discipline scale. They reported significant correlation between ABS total and its subscale scores, with PPS total scores and its subscales scores. Inter correlation between PPS and its subscales revealed that Peer Pressure scale scores were highly significantly correlated with its four subscales. Inter correlation of ABS and its sub scales showed that total ABS scale scores were highly correlated with its all subscale scores. The results showed that Peer Pressure had a positive influence as those who received high amount of Peer Pressure, had better adaptive abilities. The adaptive behavior scale developed in this study was more of a measure only meant to assess adaptive behaviors specific to learning environments compared to general adaptive behaviors.

Durkin, Hasan and Hasan (1998) reported prevalence and related demographic factors of intellectual disability among children between 2 and 9 years of age in Karachi. They carried out a two phase population survey between 1988 and 1989. In phase I they assessed 617 children living in rural areas and 5748 children living in urban areas. They used the Ten Questions measure based on parental ratings to screen out disabilities among 6365 children from their cluster sample. In phase II, structured psychological and medical examination was conducted for 10 percent of children from initial sample who received negative disability results and all children who had positive results in disability screening. Psychological assessment was based on SBIT to assess intellectual level and adaptive skills tool developed by the authors. The researchers did not mention psychometric details of these two instruments. Structured observation of participants, developmental history, ability to comprehend instructions, and observation of motor skills was carried out during physicians for evaluation of mental retardation. Psychologists classified level of mental retardation according to IQ. Researchers reported to had also used comprehensive medical, psychological, neurological evaluations in areas of hearing, seizures, motor and vision to investigate the intensity of disability. They used serious category of disability by combining severe and moderate disability groups. The researchers reported that the prevalence estimates of 65.3 per 1000 individuals for mental retardation with mild severity and 19.0 per 1000 as prevalence estimates for serious mental retardation. When compared to prevalence in other countries the data from industrialized countries and selected less developed countries reveal considerably lower prevalence rates. Finally, researchers concluded that perinatal difficulties, traumatic brain injuries, neonatal infections, malnourishment and post natal brain infections were found to be significant correlates of intellectual disability in their sample. The maternal educated had strong correlation with prevalence of disability in both groups. The researchers failed to provide any significant details related to the scale development procedures employed to develop adaptive skills instrument and its psychometric properties. The reported information showed that they developed a short checklist only enlisting some common adaptive skills. No information was provided regarding the validity or reliability indices established for the measure.

Rauf, Haq, Aslam and Anjum (2014) employed cross-sectional observational study to studied the chore symptoms and adaptive skills of children diagnosed with autism. They studied 39 boys and girls aged between 3 and 16 years attending special education schools in Rawalpindi and Islamabad from September 2011 to January 2012. The mean age of the participants was 10.6 ± 2.97 years. The participants were selected meeting the criteria of autism. ABS-S: 2, was administered on children (n=21) to assess the adaptive skills and childhood autism rating scale-2 (CARS-2) was used to study the characteristics and severity of symptoms of autism. According to results, participants reported to have marked impairment in verbal communication (mean=3.17 ± 0.90) followed by relating to people (mean=2.75 ± 0.83) and general impression (mean=2.73 ± 0.7). Most of the participants showed average to below average adaptive skills on number and time (n=19, 90.5%), independent functioning (n=17, 81.0%), self direction (n=17, 81.0%), physical development (n=13, 61.9%), responsibility (n=12, 57.1%) and socialization (n=13, 61.9%) as well as poor to very poor adaptive skills on prevocational skill (n=15, 71.4%), language development (n=13, 61.9%) and economic development (n=13, 61.9%). Researchers further reported that the boys with autism was more towards moderate to severely impaired spectrum, without gender differences in any symptom associated with autism. They concluded that the comprehension of the presentation of characteristic symptoms of children with autism will be helpful in devising the indigenous intervention plans that are congruent with the level of adaptive functioning. The research did not consider nor discuss the cultural relevance of the content of adaptive behavior scale used in this research.

Afzal et al., (2017) assessed the Adaptive functioning and sociodemographic characteristics related to it in children with intellectual disability. The study was conducted from January 2011 till December 2013 in the Outpatient Clinic of Psychiatry and Behavioral Sciences District Headquarter (D.H.Q.) Hospital affiliated with Punjab Medical College in Faisalabad, Pakistan. In total the study employed 170 children with ID from 1 to 10 years of age and 62 percent of participants were boys. Demographic information from the participants was recorded and the Portage Guide to Early Education (PGEE) was administered. According to the researchers most parents (62.4%) had consanguineous marriages. Almost 14 percent participants reported to have comorbid epilepsy and 11 percent reported comorbidity of movement disorder. Eighty-one percent of children showed behavioral issues and communication disorders. The researchers reported that the developmental ages of most of the participants in areas of cognition was 1 year of age and language development was around 2 years of age while motor skills, socialization and self-help development was around 4 years of age. They concluded that adaptive functioning deficits were highest in children with cognitive and language delays. There was a high association between these deficits and children who were the product of consanguineous marriages, and children with pre and postnatal complications. An association between adaptive functioning and psychiatric co morbidity was also reported. Early individualized educational programs are recommended to enhance the functioning and help with the continued development of these children. The review of this research points to many technical errors, for instance the scale that was used to adaptive functioning was not considered true adaptive functioning instrument. PGEE was developed and used to measure general developmental functioning not specifically adaptive functioning, but researchers employed it to assess adaptive functioning because some of the items were similar to items in adaptive functioning measures but it could not be considered equivalent to adaptive skills instrument.

The studies mentioned in this section revealed many limitations from using a developmental measure in place of adaptive skills measure, no information on reliability and validity of the measures developed etc. All researches discussed in this section either used the measures that were technically not sound or used instruments developed in western countries ignoring the obvious cultural content biases. All these problems strongly highlighted the need to study the area of adaptive functioning.

Summary

In summary, the researches reviewed in this chapter presented adaptive construct as a multidimensional in nature having various dimensions. Adaptive skills were described as greatly influenced by cultural practices and researchers described that adaptive skills were shaped in light of culture generated role assumptions that vary depending on age and gender. Studies identified presence of many adaptive skills instruments but cross cultural researches raised serious concerns on free use of these tools across cultures. Rather, researchers point to evaluate cultural adequacy of these instruments before using them for clinical and educational decision making. The review of literature failed to reveal any standardized instrument that could be used to assess adaptive skills of children in Pakistan.

Researchers also pointed to the impact of culture on symptoms presentation of many developmental disabilities. Cultural beliefs and practices were also identified as strong predictors of early identification, professional help seeking and source utilization. Cultural beliefs were also noted as influencing the disability attribution, perception of disability and attitude of care givers toward people living with developmental disabilities.

As far as the factors that were associated with adaptive skills were concerned, researches gave a broad range of variables shown to have strong relationship with adaptive skills. Different researches highlighted the role of different intra personal, social and familial factors influencing the acquisition and quality of adaptive skills. Most researches identify IQ as one of the strongest correlate and predictor of adaptive skills. Since the conception of adaptive skills construct, the nature of relationship between IQ and adaptive skills has interested the majority of researchers. Many believed it to be two dimensions of the same construct, however, most of the contemporary studies described these two as significantly distinct yet related constructs influencing each other.

Lastly, most of the researches reviewed in this section concluded that adaptive skills measures had become common place in psychological assessment and can be very helpful for professionals working with children with developmental psychopathologies. The studies indicated that the presentation of adaptive skills was somewhat different and the score on different dimensions change from one problem to another. As children with mild developmental delay score highest on almost all dimensions of adaptive skills as compared to other children and children with autism score less on communication and socialization etc. Age, level of intelligence and severity and type of developmental problems emerged as important factors that could mediate the score on adaptive skills measures.

Purpose of the Present Research

The current research was an attempt to explore the adaptive skills of children. As literature revealed significantly different pattern of adaptive skills in children with Intellectual disability (ID), Autism Spectrum disorders (ASD) and those following typical development (TD), therefore, these three groups are chosen to assess the pattern of adaptive skills across these developmental groups. It also aimed to assess the relationship of adaptive skills with different personal and family demographic factors. The personal variables selected to study include chronological age, gender, diagnostic status/ severity of disability, behavioral problems, intellectual functioning and temperament. The familial factors chosen included number of siblings, parental education, parental age, marital status of parents, family system and family income. The literature revealed dearth of standardized measure of adaptive skills and temperament in Pakistan. It also revealed that the instruments used to assess both adaptive skills and personality were developed and standardized in western countries and had significant linguistic and cultural differences from Pakistan. Experts consider cultural and linguistic differences seriously and treat them as significant biases that can plague both the process and outcome of assessment, these biases are taken seriously whether they exist within or across cultures (Mylonas, & Furnham, 2013). Therefore, the present research planned to develop an indigenous adaptive behavior scale and to translate Children's Behavior Questionnaire (CBQ-T) and Temperament in Middle Childhood Questionnaire (TMCQ). Furthermore, it was intended to establish primary psychometric properties for all three instruments. These three measures would hopefully offer useful assistance in assessing adaptive skills and temperament of children in Pakistan. As literature review could not identify any significant research in Pakistan exploring adaptive functioning and its related correlates and predictors across three developmental groups, therefore, the primary conceptualization of present research was based on the literature representing researches conducted in western countries.

The review of literature raised the following questions, and the present research was conceptualized to provide answers to these questions.

1. Do children with intellectual deficiency, autism and typical development diverge in their performance on adaptive skills measures?

2. Does symptom severity relate with adaptive skills?

3. What is the role of different demographic factors in adaptive skills across three developmental groups?

4. Do children following different developmental pattern also differ significantly on temperamental dimensions?

5. Are temperamental dimensions related significantly with adaptive functioning?

6. Are there any specific differences in adaptive behaviors that can discriminate the three groups?

7. Does the association of different demographic variables differ significantly across developmental groups?

8. Which demographic factors can significantly predict adaptive skills across three developmental groups?

Since adaptive skills impairment is considered an integral part of intellectual disability definition, initially most researches on this topic only involved children with intellectual disabilities. This trend had changed slightly as past four decades had witnessed a dramatic increase in the prevalence of autism spectrum disorders due to increased awareness of ASD and related conditions, consequently the focus shifted and most studies were conducted to examine the adaptive functioning of children with ASD as distinct from that observed in children with ID.

Despite all the popularity gained by adaptive functioning, there were very few researches that compared the adaptive skills of children with different developmental problems. Instead, large majority of researchers restricted their interest to study adaptive skills in isolated developmental problems or compared adaptive skills of children with A-typical development with those having typical development. Inferences drawn from the data of individuals with one specific developmental problem were difficult to generalize on other developmental problems, particularly when most of the literature highlights the differences related to taxonomy and characteristics symptomatology of ASD, ID and other developmental problems regardless of some shared symptoms (APA, 2013; Jacobson, Maulik & Rojahn, 2007). Based on the clinical differences it was decided to include three groups of children following different developmental pattern, while sharing some common traits like chronological age. There were very limited researchers found that assessed adaptive skills of children in Pakistan and even those limited researches employed small samples and non-standardized assessment tools. Another limitation noted was that no study attempted to include a broader range of factors potentially associated with adaptive skills nor did they compare functioning of different developmental groups. Rather most researches restricted their data to small number of children with single developmental problem. Keeping in view the limitations noted in studies conducted in Pakistan and other countries, present research was planned to include children with ID, ASD and a group of children following typical development.

The present project was hoped to make unique contribution to the existing body of research by exploring the significant input of demographic factors in adaptive skills among children following varied pattern of development.

Assessment of adaptive skills was considered an integral part of assessment of children and adolescents in contemporary clinical, counseling, school, educational, forensic and many other fields of psychology. The findings of this research also expected to have some significant implications in educational and clinical fields by providing valid assessment useful in making decisions regarding diagnosis, placement and program planning. Present research would assist clinicians to carry out a comprehensive assessment of children with typical development and those having developmental problems.

The current research would be helpful to assess whether adaptive skills correlates identified in western literature are valid for Pakistan. It is aspired that the present project would benefit professionals by providing indigenous tools to adequately assess adaptive skills and temperament of children in Pakistan by taking into account their socio cultural practices. Having an in depth understanding of adaptive skills and its correlates would particularly help professionals in the process of differential diagnosing.

The findings may also aid the practitioners to plan management programs relevant to children's needs and to monitor children's progress through these management programs. By comparing the pattern of adaptive skills and temperament in children with typical and A typical development this research would make a unique contribution to existing research. The result would help professionals better understand their clients with differing needs and were hoped to help to assist them in making differential diagnosis, designing management programs and program evaluation.

CHAPTER - III

Research Design

The main aim of the present project was to study the adaptive skills of children and their significant correlates and predictors in Pakistani children. A thorough review of literature pointed to an absence of a measure that could provide a comprehensive assessment of adaptive skills in children.

Due to the absence of relevant measures, it was decided to construct the measure of adaptive skills. There was a series of steps designed to construct a measure of adaptive skills and to assess its psychometric features, as a measure without known psychometric features was not considered meaningful (Kline, 2013).

In order to achieve the study aims, present research was carried out in two main phases. Phase - I specifically aimed at developing an indigenous and culturally relevant adaptive skills scale for children in Pakistan and establishing its psychometric characteristics. On the other hand, the aim of Phase - II was to translate the measures of temperament, explore the adaptive skills in children and to identify the main correlates and predictors of adaptive skills in children.

Figure.1.

Flow chart of Present Research Project

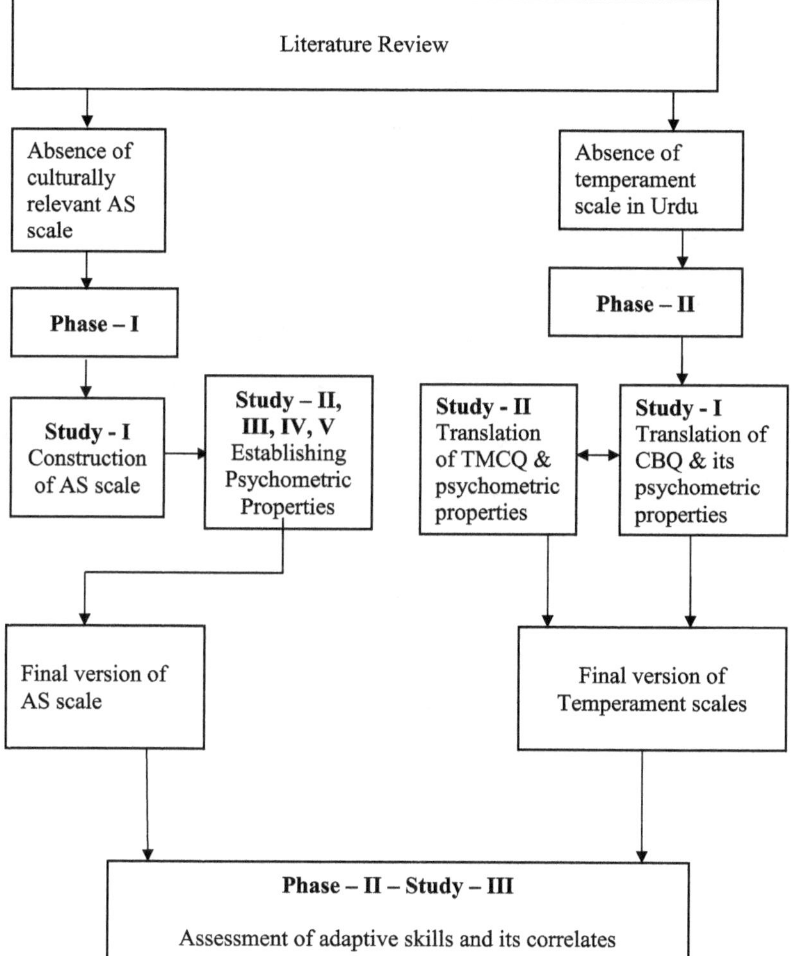

Phase – I

The review of literature indicated the absence of culturally relevant adaptive skills scale for Pakistani children, therefore, it was decided to construct an adaptive skills scale indigenous to Pakistani cultural context in phase-I. Phase- I of present research was planned on Lovinger's model of scale construction and comprised three related studies. Study-I involved development of an indigenous adaptive skills scale for Pakistani children. Study- II assessed the structural validity of adaptive skills scale. Study-III aimed to investigate the external validity and other psychometric properties of the scale. The details of all three studies of phase-I were given below.

Study – I: Substantive Validity Phase

As the literature pointed absence of any well standardized instrument to assess adaptive skills in Pakistan and highlighted the limitations of using measures developed and standardized in western countries, the first phase of this study aimed at developing item pool for an indigenous adaptive skills scale. For this purpose, a combination of rational-theoretical approach and factor analytical approach of item development was suggested to be employed; as experts advocate to use combination of three main strategies of scale development namely rational-theoretical, factor analytical and empirical criterion keying approach instead of relying only on one approach (Simms, 2008).

Objectives of Study – I. The following objectives were focused in first step of this study

1. To select main domains of adaptive skills.

2. To generate a pool of culturally appropriate items to assess adaptive skills.

3. To establish the face validity of the selected items.

4. To conduct an initial pilot testing of selected items.

This study was helpful in identifying culturally relevant domains of adaptive skills and establishing an initial item pool for the indigenous adaptive skills scale. The outcome was an initial draft of adaptive scale with established face validity ready for further evaluation of psychometric functions and practical adequacy.

Study – II: Structural Validity Phase.

After the initial selection of items, the next step was to ascertain content and construct validity of selected items based on the guidelines of Clark and Watson (1995) and Kazdin (2003). In order to achieve this goal following objective were set for this study

Objectives of Study – II. The study – II was designed around the following objectives

1. To establish the content validity of selected items.

2. To determine construct validity of the selected items.

Structural validity is generally referred as one of the core concerns of experts related to psychometric properties (Brown, 1996). It was measured in terms of content and construct validity. Construct validity is considered pertinent as it is believed to overarch the other forms of validity and can directly influence the overall strength of an instrument (Kane, 2006; Polit & Beck, 2012). The study – II assessed construct validity by assessing the factorial structure, convergence and divergence ability of the selected items.

Study – III: Establishing Reliability Phase.

After ascertaining the initial psychometric features, the third study covered the reliability of the items selected in study – I. This study was designed to achieve the following objectives

Objectives. The main objectives of Study – III were

1. To evaluate the test-retest reliability of adaptive skills scale.

2. To determine the cutoff score for adaptive skills scale.

The rationale of study – III was to assess the reliability of the indigenous scale of adaptive skills and establishing the suitable cutoff scores for the new scale. The outcome of this study was expected to have a final scale of adaptive skills with acceptable psychometric properties.

Phase – II

Phase – II of the current research consisted of three studies. Study I was designed to translate "*Childhood Behavior Questionnaire – Teacher Form*" (CBQ-T) and establish psychometric characteristics of both these scales. Study II was planned to translate "*Temperament in Middle Childhood Questionnaire*" (TMCQ) in Urdu language and to determine its essential psychometric features. Study – III was to assess the adaptive skills and to explore the association of several personal and familial demographic factors with adaptive skills of children following variant developmental pattern. The details mentioned below

Study I and II – Translation and adaptation of Temperament Scales

The literature relevant to psychological assessment underscores the importance of translating and adapting assessment instruments not only to make them culturally relevant but to improve the efficacy of those assessment instruments across cultures. Study – I and II of phase – II had specifically been designed to prepare a culturally relevant tool to measure temperament of children.

Objectives. The first two studies were planned around following objectives

1. To translate CBQ-T short form and TMCQ – Short form into Urdu Language.

2. To establish validity of CBQ-T and TMCQ Urdu.

3. To evaluate reliability of CBQ-T and TMCQ Urdu.

The outcome of study – I would be CBQ-T Urdu with well-established psychometric features suitable for assessing temperament in children. The outcome of study – II of phase – II was expected to be providing TMCQ Urdu as a reliable and validity instrument to measure temperament in children.

Study III – Assessment of adaptive skills in three groups of children and identifying associated psychosocial factors.

Adaptive functioning is an integral part of human life influencing the quality of life in many different ways and over the years adaptive skills assessment has become a commonplace practice in clinical assessments of individuals. Consequently, it had attracted lots of professional attention across countries justified due to significance of this construct in one's functioning as well as clinical and educational decision making. Study – III was the main study of the present research project and was conceptualized to assess the adaptive skills of Pakistani children and to explore a range of variables related and could potentially influence the acquisition and quality of adaptive functioning. Literature provided adequate assistance in identifying the personal and social variables that could be associated with adaptive skills.

Objectives. Following were the objectives of study – III

1. To assess and compare the adaptive skills scores of children with intellectual deficiency, ASD and typical development.

2. To explore the association between cognitive level and adaptive skills scores.

3. To identify the age-wise differences in adaptive skills scores of children with ID, ASD and typical development.

4. To analyze the gender differences in adaptive skills scores of the sample.

5. To explore the temperament dimensions of children with intellectual deficiency, ASD and typical development.

6. To explore the gender wise differences in temperament profiles of children with ID, ASD and typical development.

7. To identify the association between adaptive skills and temperament among children with ID, ASD and those having typical development.

8. To study the association of different demographic factors with adaptive skills scores.

The outcomes of this study were expected to provide a good insight into personal and social variables that could better explain the adaptive functioning of children in Pakistani context. The results of this study were also expected to gain better understanding into variables that could potentially predict the adaptive skills outcomes in children.

CHAPTER – IV

Phase – I

The culturally relevant instruments had gained much attention over past decades, engaging experts in developing and critically reviewing the efficacy of assessment measures. The present phase was divided in three main studies. Study – I was based on Loevinger's (1957) classic model of scale development aimed to develop culturally relevant measure to assess adaptive behaviors. Study – II was designed to establish substantive and structural validities for the newly developed scale. The third study was planned to determine internal consistency along with external validity including convergent, discriminant and criterion related validities and finalizing the indigenous adaptive behavior scale.

Figure 2. *Conceptual Model of Phase-I based on Loevinger's Model of Scale Development*

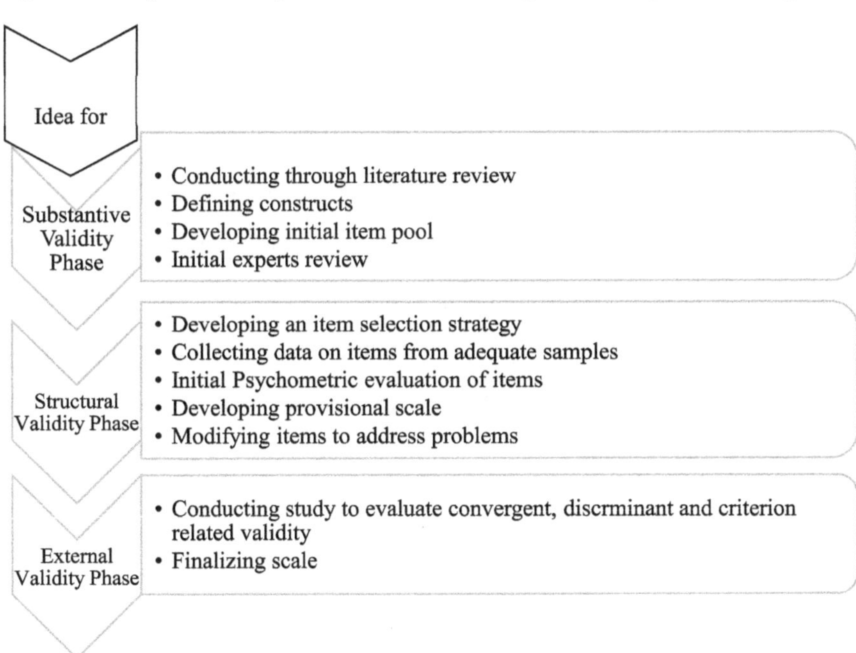

Study – I: Substantive Validity Phase

The first study of this phase aimed at developing item pool for an indigenous adaptive skills scale. For this purpose, a combination of rational-theoretical approach and factor analytical approach of item development was employed; as experts advocate to use combination of three main strategies of scale development, that is, rational-theoretical, factor analytical and empirical criterion keying approach instead of relying only on one approach (Simms, 2008). The study I was broken down into five steps with the following details

Objectives of Study–I.

The first phase of this study was focused on following objectives

1. To select main domains of adaptive skills.

2. To select culturally appropriate items to assess adaptive skills.

3. To establish the face validity of the selected items.

4. To conduct a pilot study.

Many experts (Clark & Watson, 1995; Simms, 2008) in the field of scale construction suggested dividing broadly conceptualized constructs into sub-domains in order to assess all important aspects of the broader construct. Keeping in context the hierarchical nature of the adaptive skills construct, the researcher was sensitive to the fact that the scale may in fact be divisible into sub-domains based on the most frequently mentioned theoretical sub-domains of adaptive skills (Sparrow & Cicchetti, 1984; AAIDD, 2016). The in-depth interviews with experienced clinical psychologists working with children were carried out to discuss the cultural relevance of adaptive functioning construct and domains of adaptive skills relevant to Pakistan. The relevant literature was also thoroughly reviewed to identify primary dimensions of adaptive skills construct. In total, eleven domains of adaptive skills construct were selected to be followed in the indigenous scale namely; communication, socialization, self care, community skills, self direction, health and safety, home living, work, leisure, functional academic skills and motor skills (Mash & Terdal, 1997; Sparrow & Cicchetti, 1985). As almost all of the measures that were developed to assess adaptive skills employed these domains (Thompson et al, 1999; Sparrow, 2008) therefore, it was decided to use these eleven domains to generate items of the initial pool.

In order to fulfill the second objective of present phase, three main steps were carried out to generate a pool of items on selected domains of adaptive skills by following the guiding principles of Loevinger (1957) and other experts that item pool should sample all content potentially relevant to target construct (Clark & Watson, 1995; Anastasi & Urbina, 1997).

Step – I. Generating Initial Item Pool. As a first step, experts were requested to generate items on the domains of adaptive skills selected from comprehensive review of literature.

Sample. The sample for step I comprised 120 participants including clinical psychologists ($n = 25$) trainee clinical psychologists ($n= 40$), special educationists ($n = 15$), teachers ($n = 20$) and mothers ($n = 20$). The mean age of this sample was 29.87 and only those individuals were selected who had an adequate understanding of child development and basic familiarity with adaptive functioning construct.

The inclusion criteria for selecting clinical psychologists was 6 months to 2 years' experience of working with children; for trainee clinical psychologist was completion of clinical training in developmental pediatrics; 2 to 3 years of working experience for special educationists; 5 years working experience and graduation in psychology for teachers and the criteria for mothers was having at least 1 child from 5 to 11 years and graduation in psychology.

The sample was required to not only have a theoretical understanding of adaptive skills concept but was expected to be familiar with the presentation of these skills in Pakistani culture. The relative duration of work was considered with reference to adaptive functioning assessment in their practice. The duration of work experience was used as a criterion to select sample and it was based on a detailed discussion with experts involved in training of both clinical psychologists and special educationists.

Procedure. The purpose and objectives of the present study were explained to all participants through a letter and initial consent was sported from all participants.

- All participants were sent letters requesting to help develop culturally relevant items on 11 domains of adaptive skills (Appendix

- – A). An additional document defining the selected domains of adaptive skills was attached along with the letters (Appendix – B).

- After one month the first reminder was sent to all, followed by the second reminder after a month. Majority of the participants didn't respond to the initial request and/or subsequent reminders made through regular mail, emails and text messages. The total response rate was 22.5 percent. The details of response rate are as follows

Table 3

General Response Rate of Participants

	Before first reminder	After First reminder	After second reminder	Total
Clinical psychologists	1	1	4	6
Trainee clinical psychologists	2	1	7	10
Special educationists	0	0	2	2
Teachers	0	2	1	3
Mothers	2	3	1	6
Total	5	7	15	27

Trainee clinical psychologists had the highest response rate among all participants. The close review of the items revealed that out of 27 participants, 5 failed to develop items on all 11 domains. Though it was clearly requested in the letter to develop items in Urdu (National language of Pakistan), all participants but two sent items in English. A log sheet was made for items sent by participants and all items were pooled into that log sheet. All items were given a code which was a combination of initial letter(s) of the domain and a numeric serial.

Step –II. Review of Literature. Keeping in view the poor response rate of experts, it was decided to review the well-established adaptive skills scales to choose culturally relevant items to be included in the indigenous scale for adaptive skills.

Sample. The sample for step -II comprised 8 measures of adaptive skills including Vineland Adaptive Behavior Scale (2005), AAMD Adaptive Behavior Scale (2000), Ghana Adaptive Behavior Scales (Kniel & Kniel, 2006), Madras developmental programming system (Peshawaria, & Venkatesan, 1992), Curriculum of the Indian National Institute for the Mentally Handicapped (1989), Portage Guide for Early Education, Early Intervention in Mentally Retarded Children Scale (1993), Scales of Independent Behavior (1996) and Childhood Adaptive Behavior Scale . Apart from the adaptive skills scales researcher also reviewed various books and articles of developmental psychology discussing adaptive behaviors related to different age ranges.

Procedure. The first step was to gather the relevant literature, for this purpose electronic data sources, reference sections of libraries and research archives were used to identify and gather the literature relevant to the intended purpose.

- Culturally relevant items were identified after a thorough review of all scales mentioned above.

- Items were selected following two main criteria including (a) the degree to which an item reflected particular dimension of adaptive skills and (b) the degree to which the item was relevant to Pakistani culture.

- The items from step -I and step -II were combined. In total 573 items were pooled together.

- Items were grouped into eleven sub-domains and each item was given a separate code starting from the first letter of subscale followed by a numeric.

- The researcher along with another clinical psychologist and two MS clinical psychology trainees reviewed the selected items and similar items were dropped from the item pool. Consequently, the total number was then dropped to 397 items.

- The selected items were translated into Urdu following the standard translation guidelines of MAPI (2009) and WHO (2013).

- For this purpose, three bilingual psychology graduates were given the items to translate into Urdu. A committee comprising researcher and two bilingual clinical psychologists selected the most adequate Urdu translation on the basis of ICVI values of 1. In total 38 items were sent back for translation due to poor translation.

- The translated items were then sent to four bilingual MS trainees to back translate the items into English. The committee again reviewed all the items and matched the back translation with original items. The items with back translation closest to the original items were selected. Finally, the items were reviewed by a Professor in Urdu to evaluate and refine items the quality of language.

- Many of the items required some material to assess the task given in a particular item. A set of picture cards were designed to provide ease of administration. A committee of two clinical psychologists and two teachers approved the format and content of the supportive material proposed to be used to assess specific items (Appendix- C).

Step – III. Pilot Study. A pilot study was conducted to gain the initial insight into adequacy of the selected items (Lancaster, Dodd & Williamson, 2004). The main objectives of pilot study were to review the adequacy and comprehensibility of items by testing them on representative of intended population, estimation of actual administration time and the appropriateness of the picture cards developed for this project (Croft, Brown, Thorsteinsson & Noble, 2013; Kazdin, 2003).

Sample. In general, a sample of 30 or more participants is considered good for pilot study (Lancaster et al., 2004). Therefore, a non-probability purposive sampling technique was employed to select a sample of 50 children attending mainstream schools including equal number of male and female children. Children 5 to 11 years of age were included and the mean age of this group was 8.91 years.

Procedure. The participants were approached at their homes and an institute offering painting classes in evening after sorting consent from parents and administration of the institute (Appendix – D).

- The purpose of the study and ethical rights were explained to all participants.
- Some items were directly administered on children and many of the items were rated with assistance of primary caregiver.
- A debriefing session was offered to all parents after the interview during which researcher answered any questions of the parents related to the administration.
- All children were given a small bar of chocolate as a token for their participation and primary caregivers were thanked for their time and cooperation.

Conclusion. The administration took 55 to 65 minutes in general, and 10 to 15 extra minutes were spent with children initially for small chat with children to make them feel comfortable and to develop rapport. The session was broken down into two sittings.

The pilot study was found to be very helpful in identifying reinforcers for girls and boys. Reinforces for girls were shiny stickers of Barbie doll and Elsa, boys showed liking for stickers of a cartoon character Ben-Ten, many girls and boys also told to be interested in cartoon character of Douremon (Appendix – E). In this pilot study only one art scissor was used for cutting tasks but on the feedback and observation of the participants two sizes of scissors were included (a small art scissor for five and six year old children and a little large art scissor for children aged seven and above). Children also showed more interest in colored picture cards compared to black and white. They also showed preference for real money and coins over their pictures. Another finding was that children reported to be more comfortable with the maze with broader lines compared to maze B with fine lines (Appendix – F). Another finding was that children preferred reading sheets printed on white paper instead of reading lists printed on colored papers. The pilot study was very helpful in identifying suitable reinforcers for children and to evaluate the suitability of supplementary material.

Discussion

From past many decades there was a surge of interest in assessment instruments aimed to assess children and adolescents and concerns are generally raised regarding the ability of a scale to adequately measure domains of a particular construct (Kamphaus, Petoskey & Rowe, 2000), adaptive functioning in case of present research. A detailed literature review and interviews with the clinical professionals revealed absence of a comprehensive measure to assess adaptive skills of Pakistani children. The Pakistani clinical experts working with children identified many content biases that raise serious concerns regarding cultural relevance of frequently used adaptive skills measures in Pakistan.

This concern led towards the conception of adaptive skills scale based on the cultural role expectation of Pakistani society. The present study aimed to develop a culturally relevant scale of adaptive behavior for children aged 5 till 11 years. This particular age range was selected as this is considered most important to acquire culturally relevant adaptive skills to ensure an adequate functioning (AAMR,2006).

A combination of theoretical and rational approaches to scale development was followed based on the thorough review of literature (Simms, 2012). Experts working with children were requested to generate items keeping in consideration the main adaptive skills domains. Other items for the initial pool were selected after a thorough review of adaptive skills instruments developed in western countries and neighboring Asian countries. This review was done as the response rate of experts chosen to develop items was very low and even the frequent requests couldn't increase the response rate and as the theoretical approach to item development was also considered to be significant by many experts (Husain, 2012).

The outcome of the first step was a pool of 573 items related to adaptive functioning. The initial cleansing of data was done through a thorough review of selected items by a committee, and the repeated items and items representing the same content were removed from the item pool. This exercise reduced the item pool to 397 items, dropping 173 items in total.

These items were then field tested on a group of children which helped the researcher identify some significant factors. One of which is to identify the reinforcers for the children, due to some ethical constraints and policy of many school children couldn't be offered eatable reinforcers. After a long discussion and considering many points it was decided that children would be rewarded with stickers of their choice. Brief discussions with children during the cognitive interviewing helped the researcher to identify the suitable reinforcers. Most of the children were very open in asserting their preference and almost all children selected popular cartoon characters as their reinforcers. The important observation was that the choice of character by girls and boys was different. It was only 12.34 percent children who selected the same character, otherwise girls opted for a popular female character whereas boys choose a male character. It was also helpful in selecting the appropriate sizes, designs and presentation of supplementary material.

CHAPTER - V

Structural Validity Phase

One of the core concerns in test development is evaluating the validity of the psychological measures (Marnat, 2009). Validity is the actual extent to which a tool measures what it claims to measure (Polit, & Beck, 2012). Structural validity is one of the most pertinent features of psychometric characteristics of any instrument. The structural validity can be assessed through many different procedures but content and construct validity are two most frequently employed procedures (Brown, 1996; Brown, 2000; Smith, 2005). The current study was divided into two main steps focus to assess these two essential psychometric features of indigenously developed adaptive behaviors scale.

Study – II: Establishing Content Validity

Once the initial screening of the items was done, the next step of this study was to establish content validity of selected items based on the guidelines of Clark, Watson (1995) and Kazdin (2003). Content validity is the degree to which elements of a test represent all aspects of a specific construct (Haynes, Richard, & Kubany, 1995) or the general relevance of test items with the theoretical construct it is based on. One of the most popular method of establishing content validity is to use experts to evaluate and or rate test content in terms of its relevance and representation of the core construct (Marnat, 2003).

Sample.

The sample for this step comprised 25 participants including clinical psychologists (n= 7), pediatricians (n = 5), special educationists (n = 3) mothers (n = 5) and teachers (n = 5) for rating the initial items. All participants were selected on the basis of their experience with children with disabilities and following typical development. It was made sure that all participants had a sound experience and understanding of both typical and A-typical developmental processes. The sample included 2 mothers of children with ASD and three mothers of children following typical development. Mothers were used as target population judges and in literature it was recommended that members of the target population might be included in establishing validity along with conventional subject experts to further strengthen the content validity (Boateng, Neilands, Frongillo, Melgar-Quinonez & Young, 2018).

Procedure.

The following procedure was employed to establish the content validity of the indigenous adaptive skills scale

- In order to choose content evaluation experts, the Grant and Davis (1997) criteria was used. These criteria included specifying and defining clinical expertise, identifying experts who have relevant training, firsthand experience relevant to the content area and clear theoretical understanding of the construct.

- The inclusion criteria for mothers was having two children aged till 12 years, for all other participants it was at minimum 5 years of working experience with 4 to 12 years old children.

- After explaining the main research aims to all participants, they were requested to rate each item for fidelity to the construct, cultural relevance, redundancy, clarity and its placement within a particular sub-domain on a four-point Likert scale. Instructions sent to these raters can be seen in Appendix – G.

- Only two participants send the ratings within the given time limit of six weeks. Keeping in mind the experience of last study, researcher sorted personal appointments from all participants and requested the ratings during those meetings except four participants who lived in other cities. The response rate is shown in the table below

Table 4

General Response Rate of Experts for Content Validity Ratings

	Before Deadline	After personal meeting	Total
Clinical psychologists	1	5	6
Pediatricians	0	1	1
Special educationists	1	1	2
Teachers	0	3	3
Mothers	1	3	4
Total	3	13	16

Seven participants sent the incomplete ratings and two neither send the ratings nor did they respond to any request other than their initial consent. The response rate of participants was 64 percent and the highest response rate was from clinical psychologists.

Figure 3.

Flow Chart Showing Details of Response Rate of Participants in this Step.

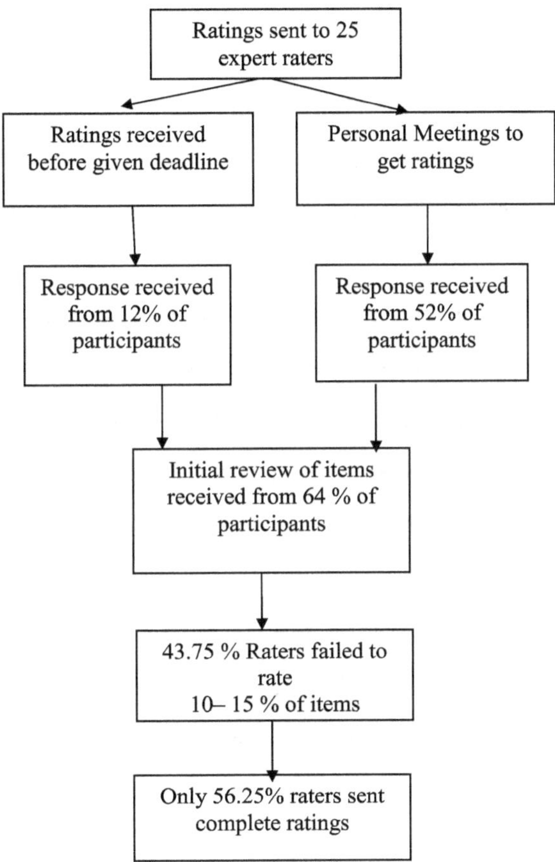

Figure reveals that personal meeting with the raters turned to be an effective strategy to increase response rate. However, even this strategy couldn't not ensure rating for all items.

It was noted that 10 to 15 percent of items were left unrated by nearly half the raters. All those items were towards the end of the list.

Results.

In order to assess whether the selected items were relevant and appropriate to measure adaptive skills construct content validity index ratings were conducted for each item. Content validity index was chosen to calculate the content validity using the ratings of experts. The researcher decided to select 9 experts for ICVI ratings as 7 to 12 experts are generally considered to be a good number for calculating content validity index (Devon et al., 2007; Haynes et al., 1995).

I-CVI was primarily based on content and cultural relevance ratings. All experts were requested to rate each item. Four indices including content and cultural relevance, clarity, simplicity and redundancy were used to assess content validity (Farrokhzad et al., 2014; Yaghmaie, 2003). The details are mentioned in the table given in annexure G.3.

Total 264 items receiving content validity index (I-CVI) of 7.8 and above were finally selected for the scale as this value was mentioned as good cut off value for item selection in I-CVI when more than 7 experts rate items (Haynes et al., 1995).In result of the content validity analysis many items were restated and/or combined with other similar items. Some of the items with repeated content were deleted. The placement of some items in subdomains was also changed in light of the feedback of experts. The breakdown of items into subdomains before and after content validity analysis is mentioned in the following table.

Table 5

Number of Items in Sub-domains Before and After Expert ICV-I Ratings

Domains	No. of Items Before Ratings	No. of Items After Ratings
Communication	57	36
Socialization	58	28
Self care	40	16
Community skills	38	32
Self direction	25	24
Health and safety	15	14
Home living	55	29
Work	13	10
Leisure	16	16
Functional Academic skills	45	32
Motor	35	28

The table above indicates the number of items contained in each domain of adaptive skills and final placement of these items in particular sub-domains. The detail of items is attached in Appendix - H. The number of items in leisure scale remained same, however, the review revealed that some items were shifted to other scales and items from other scales replaced them. Self direction was another scale in which number of items remained almost same, the number of items was also least affected in subscale of health and safety and work subscale.

Figure. 4.

Comparison of Number of Items in Each Scale Before and After ICVI Calculation.

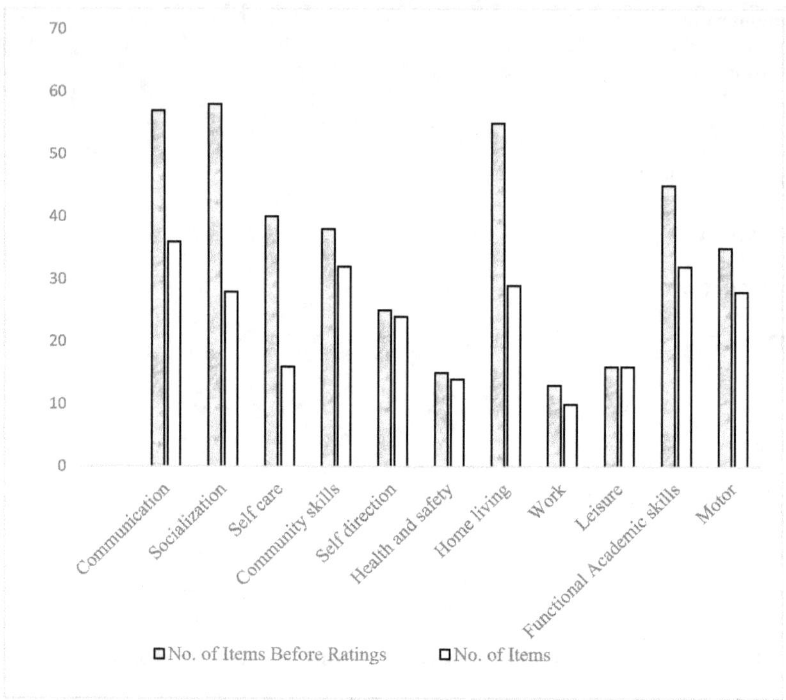

The figure above revealed that all subgroups but leisure went through rigorous change as the number of items differed due to ICVI ratio calculation. The number of items in leisure group remained same, however, some of the items were replaced.

Study – III. Determining Construct Validity

The second step of structural validity phase focused around establishing construct validity of the newly developed adaptive skills scale through three steps. Many experts consider that construct validity can overarch other two primary types of validity procedures (Schotte, Maes, Cluydts, De-Doncker & Cosyns, 1997) and report that a weak construct validity of an instrument also affects the overall strength of the instrument (Messick, 1995). The two main components of construct validity are convergent and divergent validity (Brown, 1996). The most frequently used procedure to establish construct validity is to carry out factor analysis (Kane, 2006; Marnat, 2009), estimating correlation between measures sharing the same theory (Messick, 1995) and evaluating association between the scores on two different instruments measuring two different constructs (Nakamura, Ebesutani, Bernstein & Chorpita, 2009). The present study employed all three procedures to assess the construct validity of the newly developed adaptive skills scale.

Sample

The sample of third study comprised three groups, that is, sample -A for factorial validity, sample -B for divergent and sample –C for convergent validity. Sample A consisted of 800 children including children with developmental psychopathology (n =100) and children with typical development (n =700) attending mainstream schools in Lahore city selected through stratified sampling technique. Whereas, the participants with developmental psychopathologies were selected through purposive sampling technique. The data for this study was collected few months after Army Public school mass shooting incident. The administration of a large majority of the private schools declined the data collection requests due to strict security protocols issued by government at that time. The administration of some public schools also refused to cooperate for security reasons. Consequently, the data collection was restricted to some schools who gave permission to collect data.

Participants were from 5 to 11 years of age. The mean age was 8.46 ($sd = 2.18$) years and only those children were selected who scored 70 percent or above marks in last two exams or school evaluations. This criterion was used to subjectively ruled out developmental delay as it was hard with restricted resources to assess such a large sample. The details of the sample are given on the table below

Table 6

Demographic Characteristics of the Sample – A (N = 800)

Variables	Frequency	Percentage
Gender		
Girls	407	50.9 %
Boys	393	49.1 %
Age		
5 years	88	11 %
6 years	100	12.5 %
7 years	94	11.75 %
8 years	94	11.75 %
9 years	125	15.62 %
10 years	139	17.37 %
11 years	160	20 %
Family System		
Joint	335	41.87 %
Nuclear	465	58.12 %
School Type		
Public	268	33.5 %
Semi Private/ Private	532	66.5 %

Female children out numbered male children, majority of the children was of 11 years of age. The mean family income was noted to be 31 thousand per month and most of the children were living in nuclear family system. Majority of the fathers were found to be educated till intermediate, whereas, most of the mothers had educational level lower than grade 10.

Sample -B was selected for discriminant validity and consisted of 200 children divided in two groups of children with developmental psychopathology ($n = 90$) and children with typical development ($n = 110$) which dropped down to 84 and 102 (the details are mentioned in figure 5.3) respectively. This sample was extracted from sample A. The table below shows detailed information of sample -B.

Table 7

Demographic Characteristics of the Sample – B (N = 186)

Variables		Children with Dev. Psychopathology	Typical Development Group
	Percentage	*Percentage*	*Percentage*
Gender			
Girls	50 %	44 %	54.9 %
Boys	50 %	56 %	45.1 %
Age			
5 years	9.1 %	11.9 %	6.9 %
6 years	10.8 %	11.9 %	9.8 %
7 years	12.4 %	13.1 %	11.8 %
8 years	11.3 %	9.5 %	12.7 %
9 years	16.7 %	8.3 %	23.5 %
10 years	15.1 %	14.3 %	15.7 %

Variables	Combined	Children with Dev. Psychopathology	Typical Development Group
11 years	24.7 %	31.00 %	19.6 %
Family System			
Joint	41.8 %	46.9 %	36.4 %
Nuclear	58.2 %	53.1 %	63.6 %
School Type			
Public	9.7 %		9.7 %
Semi Private/ Private	45.7 %		45.7 %
Special School	46.6 %	46.6 %	
Father age			
Mean	42.79	39.59	42.16
Sd	9.14	8.38	5.55
Mother age			
Mean	34.99	35.13	38.23
Sd	6.94	7.27	5.43

Sample -B included equal number of girls and boys, with 8.60 (sd = 2.00) years mean age whereas most of the participants in developmental psychopathology group were 11 years old and in typical development group most participants were 9 years old. Majority of the participants were living in a nuclear family setup.

Sample -C was employed for convergent validity, for this a random subsample of 65 children was drawn from 102 typically developed children from sample -B. From 65children, only 44 gave consent for continued participation.

Figure 5.

Flow Chart of Sample

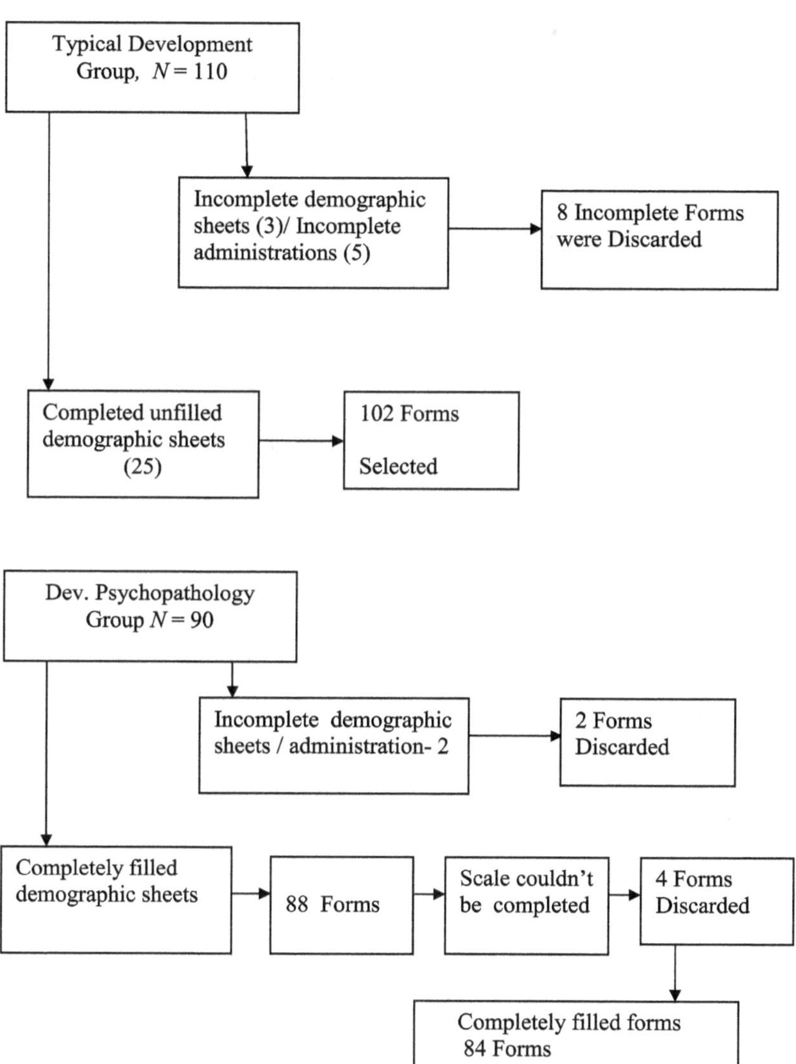

Instruments

Following tools were employed to collect data for this step.

Demographic Form. The demographic form was designed to collect basic information regarding the personal and familial factors of the sample. This included age, gender, some information regarding relationships, grade, marks in last two exams and IQ as personal variables and parental age, education, monthly family income, marital status of parents, family setup etc. (Appendix – I).

Adaptive Behavior Scale. The items selected during the last step were compiled in a scale including all adaptive behavior items (Appendix – H). It included 397 items based on ten domains of adaptive functioning. The indigenous adaptive behavior scale was accompanied by a test booklet including pictures and material needed for some items of the scale and a response sheet (Appendix – J).

Childhood Behavior Checklist. Childhood Behavior Checklist (CBCL) 4- 16 years developed by McConaughy and Achenbach (1988) was used in this study to assess discriminant validity of the adaptive behavior scale. CBCL 4-16 is frequently used to assess the externalized and internalized behavioral problems of children and adolescents. The reliability and validity of CBCL 4-16 is reported to be strong and it has widely been used as reliable tool to assess psychometric characteristics of other tools.

Children's Adaptive Behavior Scale (CABS). To establish convergent validity, Childhood Adaptive Behavior Scale (Richmond & Kicklighter,1980) was used in addition to earlier mentioned scales. The CABS offer composite score and five independent subscale scores. The subscales are namely independent functioning, language development, family role performance, socialization and economic vocational activity. Available data on psychometric properties indicate adequate evidence of validity and reliability (Hearth & Obrzut, 1986; Richmond & Kicklighter, 1980).

Procedure

- A general permission to collect data was taken from Secretary School Education, Punjab. A detailed note explaining the purpose and implementations of the present study was enclosed with the permission letter (Appendix – K). The office of secretary education granted a general permission to collect data from public schools situated in the city of Lahore.

- After sorting the general permission, 50 primary education institutes in Lahore were contacted in person from both public and private sector. The response rate was very poor particularly from private schools, most schools refused to give permission for data collection because of the security or other issues. Only two private and 5 public schools gave permission to collect data. In order to take representation from private schools, tuition centers and summer schools offering swimming and art classes to children were contacted.

- After sorting permission from school administration, a list of students who scored more than 70 percent marks in last two exams was made for each class, all these lists were made with the help of class teachers. Finally, students were randomly selected from that list. The researcher tried to take representation from as many grades as possible.

- A set of tools comprising consent form (signed by concerned teacher) demographic sheet (designed for this study) and adaptive behavior scale developed in study – I was administered on each child in an individual session.

- Initial few minutes were denoted to general discussion with the child regarding their interests and hobbies to put him/her at ease and they were encouraged to ask questions regarding the administration. First of all the demographic sheet was filled which was later corroborated through information mentioned in the school records and parents.

- In cases where teacher and/or children could not provide information about demographic variables, the forms were sent to parents in home work diaries to get them filled.

- As a next step, the scale of adaptive behaviors was administered on each child in individual session. The sequence of administering the items remained same in all administrations and all items were administered on all children.

- The responses on some random items of home living, self care, work and leisure were later checked with one of the parents and items of socialization, community skills and self directions were checked with teachers to control the children's tendency to give false positive responses.

- The session time noted to range from 35 to 45 minutes depending on the working speed of children. Five and six years old children took longest time in responding to questions.

- After administering the scale every child was verbally thanked for participation and given a reinforcer. The reinforcers were in the form of stickers of popular cartoon character of Ben-10 and Douremon for boys and Dora, Barbie and Elsa for the girls.

- All class teachers were offered brief sessions regarding the assessed children or general class room management. Almost 67 percent of teachers availed the debriefing sessions and majority was interested in guidelines regarding class management.

Statistical Analyses

Descriptive analysis, exploratory factor analysis, Pearson product moment correlation and t test were carried out to analyze the data of study – II. All procedures were carried out through Statistical Package for Social Sciences 20 (SPSS).

Step – I. Factor Analysis. Factor analysis (FA) was chosen as it was strongly recommended in literature (Field, 2009; Floyd & Widaman, 1995; Cortina, 1993) to assess the main structure of scale and to establish construct validity of the scale by using the participants from sample A.

Evaluating suitability of data for Factor Analysis. First of all, data was examined to identify potential outliers through basic descriptive procedures and review of bivariate scatter plots as its literature suggested that the factor analysis data be free of outliers (Garson, 2010). All the data was retained but two cases as correlation was not altered substantially when calculated excluding those outliers. Correlation matrices showed that most correlations were above 0.3 suggesting appropriateness for factor analysis (Field, 2009).

Principal component analysis (Hofmann, Kashdan, 2010) of exploratory factor analysis (Preacher & MacCallum, 2003) was selected for the present study. Secondly, Kaiser Myer Olkin (KMO) estimate of sampling adequacy also indicated suitability of the items for adequate factoring, as KMO value (0.97) for the present study was in the range of superb value for factor analysis (Field, 2009). Bartlette test of sphericity was also observed as highly significant (p< .001) supporting the suitability for this particular analysis (Field, 2009).

Initially, both orthogonal (varimax) and oblique (promax) rotation methods were carried out and finally oblique (promax) method (Costello & Osborne, 2005; Hofmann, Kashdan, 2010) was chosen based on the criteria mentioned by Thrichenbeck (2000) as most of the inter factor correlations were above 0.32 which was said to be indication of 10 % or more overlap in variance among factors which suggest adequacy of using oblique rotation over orthogonal (Tabachnick & Fidell, 2007) and also because oblique rotations wre mentioned to be most preferred methods to be used in social sciences than orthogonal rotation methods in FA (Furr, 2010).

Main Factor Analysis. Different factor solutions were tried from 20 factors to three factor solutions. Finally, it was decided to accept four factors solution for the newly developed scale. The decision of choosing the number of factors was based on the frequently mentioned criteria in different texts instead of relying solely on Eigen values above 1. Those criteria include Cattell's Scree plot criteria, supporting the four factor solution (Costello & Osborne, 2005) Item loadings of 0.30 and higher on a particular factor (Kline, 2002), Number of items in a factor and interpretability of factors with reference to main theoretical construct (Floyd & Widaman, 2006). The minimum number of items in any factor was 29 and all items had loading of .3 or above. The other significant criterion was simple solution and interpretability of factor structure, the selected factor solution had both these strengths (Floyd & Widaman, 2006).

Table 8

Item Loadings for Exploratory Factor Analysis With Promax Rotation of Adaptive Behavior Scale

Sr. No.	Item No.	Statements of Items	F1 DLS	F2 SS	F3 SCS	F4 HLS
1	C1	Points to 5 body parts	.58	-.05	-.03	-.09
2	C 4	Identify 5 objects	.78	-.13	.02	-.07

Sr. No.	Item No.	Statements of Items	F1 DLS	F2 SS	F3 SCS	F4 HLS
3	C 5	Follow gestures	.23	-.09	-.04	-.14
4	C 6	Tells age	**.83**	-.09	.01	-.00
5	C 7	Tells name of people	**.77**	-.08	-.01	-.14
6	C 8	Explains pictures	**.71**	-.03	-.08	-.04
7	C 9	Answers questions from story	**.61**	-.17	.10	.05
8	C 10	Write easy words	**.82**	-.12	.02	.01
9	C 12	Name thing you can eat	**.79**	-.03	.04	-.07
10	C 13	Follows 3 instructions	**.83**	-.08	-.02	-.10
11	C 15	Makes phone calls	**.33**	.27	.26	-.00
12	C 16	Name 3 animals with 4 legs	**.74**	.01	-.00	-.05
13	C 17	Words mean	-.03	.16	.24	.01
14	C 18	Tells address	-.08	-.00	**.34**	.29
15	C 19	Tells phone number	.33	.01	-.07	**.40**
16	C 20	Points 10 body parts	**.73**	-.13	.03	.06
17	C 21	Follow 3 instructions (Ver./Writ.)	**.64**	-.10	.08	.27
18	C 22	Responds to head nodding	.27	-.04	-.06	-.05
19	C 23	Names 20 objects from booklet	**.74**	-.12	-.06	.07
20	C 24	Name city	.19	.24	**.39**	.24
21	C 25	Uses past & future tense	.18	.04	.28	.01
22	C 26	Carry on conversation	**.66**	-.07	.06	.11

Continued . . . .

Sr. No.	Item No.	Statements of Items	F1 DLS	F2 SS	F3 SCS	F4 HLS
23	C 27	Describes events in logical order	**.58**	.13	.05	.05
24	C 28	Can write a paragraph	.17	**.41**	.19	.18
25	C 29	Uses swear words for attention	.01	.07	.03	-.08
26	C 30	Enjoys riddles/jokes	.29	.02	.02	.07
27	C 31	Use comparative terms	**.84**	-.06	.01	-.12
28	C 32	Recognizes alphabets	**.73**	.02	.11	-.18
29	C 33	Identify categories	**.73**	.02	.02	-.11
30	C 34	Understands prepositions	**.39**	.10	.19	-.26
31	C 35	Singing national songs in school	**.52**	-.14	.16	.18
32	C 36	Greeting others	.10	**.30**	.26	.02
33	SC 1	Reciting Bismillah	**.67**	-.05	.02	.02
34	SC-2	Washes hand/face	**.48**	-.10	.11	.12
35	SC-3	Uses correct food utensils	**.75**	-.12	.05	-.02
36	SC-4	Bathes self except for back	.01	.07	**.76**	-.02
37	SC-5	Spread soft toppings on Bread	-.11	-.04	**.69**	.24
38	SC-6	Un/buckles belt	-.10	-.05	**.76**	.04
39	SC-7	Dresses self completely	-.03	-.06	**.77**	.05
40	SC-8	Uses brush or miswaq	.25	-.03	**.47**	-.06
41	SC-9	Hangs up cloths on hanger	.02	-.04	**.49**	**.38**
42	SC-10	Why do you take bath/ shower	**.30**	-.03	.37	.03
43	SC-11	Serves self at table	.03	-.11	**.51**	**.40**
44	SC-12	Prepares own sandwich	-.24	.27	.37	**.44**
45	SC-13	Peels and cuts Vegetables	-.12	-.07	**.63**	**.44**

Sr No.	Item No.	Statements of Items	F1 DLS	F2 SS	F3 SCS	F4 HLS
46	SC-14	Toast chapatti	-.22	.26	**.34**	**.47**
47	SC-15	Manners for eating	.29	.25	**.34**	-.17
48	S-2	Afraid being caught	**.73**	-.09	.04	.01
49	S-3	Say if bump into someone	.15	.08	.25	-.17
50	S-4	Permission to use objects	.10	**.45**	**.35**	.04
51	S-5	States feelings about self	.21	**.62**	.13	-.31
52	S-6	Takes care others belongings	**.39**	.02	**.45**	-.01
53	S-7	If best friend asks answer in exam	.01	**.35**	.11	-.05
54	S-9	Happy / proud on achievement	.23	-.08	.04	.01
55	S-10	Makes sure not to lose things	**.52**	.27	-.18	.15
56	S-11	Says please/sorry	.04	**.58**	.10	.04
57	S-12	Helps others	**.36**	**.50**	.02	-.11
58	S-13	Cooperate in group	.19	**.47**	.07	-.01
59	S-14	Returns borrowed objects	.29	.03	**.39**	-.02
60	S-16	Acts properly in public	-.03	**.55**	.25	.07
61	S-17	Follows school rules	.27	**.66**	.08	-.29
62	S-18	Respects given time limits	.29	.19	.26	-.12
63	S-20	Address people by their name	.26	.04	.16	-.19
64	S-22	Not overly dependent	**.42**	**.49**	-.27	.03
65	S-23	Shows interest in others ideas	.23	.00	-.10	.12
66	S-24	Congratulates others	.08	**.48**	.11	.16

Sr No.	Item No.	Statements of Items	F1 DLS	F2 SS	F3 SCS	F4 HLS
65	S-23	Shows interest in others ideas	.23	.00	-.10	.12
66	S-24	Congratulates others	.08	**.48**	.11	.16
67	S-26	Understands could get in trouble	**.36**	.05	**.43**	.04
68	S-27	Understands being put down	.25	-.09	**.35**	-.00
69	SD-1	Follows class rules	**.75**	-.08	.01	-.02
70	SD-2	Completes class tasks in time	**.77**	-.06	-.03	.04
71	SD-3	Control anger when denied	**.55**	.09	-.13	.16
72	SD-4	Keeps working on difficult task	.25	.07	.21	.17
74	SD-6	Tells Her/ His Gender	.22	.04	.06	-.18
75	SD-7	Apologizes for mistakes	**.73**	-.01	.08	.06
76	SD-8	Likes making decisions	**.46**	.07	**.36**	-.17
77	SD-9	Can print name	.28	.14	-.08	.07
78	SD-10	Call rescue services	-.18	.11	**.65**	.16
79	SD-11	Finding reading book	**.47**	.07	.14	.18
80	SD-13	Saying no to activities against will	**.49**	.10	-.01	.17
81	SD-14	Where find doctor	**.56**	-.04	.09	.19
82	SD-15	Method of WUZU	.04	-.04	**.46**	**.41**
83	SD-16	What would you do if lost	.21	-.02	**.46**	.22
84	SD-18	Knows timings of prayers	-.11	**.60**	.18	.19
85	SD-20	Proposes solution in group conflicts	.13	.12	**.48**	.17

Continued . . . .

Sr No.	Item No.	Statements of Items	F1 DLS	F2 SS	F3 SCS	F4 HLS
86	SD-21	Follows advice by elders	**.41**	.14	**.45**	-.21
87	SD-22	Excuses himself for false	.29	.21	.27	-.00
88	SD-23	Accept criticism and suggestions	**.32**	.26	.25	-.03
89	SD-24	Defend himself	.15	.27	**.30**	.11
90	CS-1	Finding way home	.15	-.09	-.11	**.71**
91	CS-2	Waiting in queue	**.46**	**.59**	-.33	-.09
92	CS-3	Leaving seat for elders	.03	**.33**	.26	.174
93	CS-4	Keeps quiet in mosque/library	**.61**	-.06	.04	.12
94	CS-6	Keeping things on place	**.64**	-.07	.04	.18
95	CS-7	Don't misbehave	**.67**	-.04	-.00	-.03
96	CS-8	Seek permission entering class	**.79**	-.05	.07	-.04
97	CS-10	Knowing correct price of 3 things	**.59**	.01	.09	.11
98	CS-11	Collects trash	**.62**	.05	.14	-.09
99	CS-12	Care of baggage	.28	.03	**.43**	.19
100	CS-13	Going to Doctor	**.47**	-.12	.03	.41
101	CS-14	Uses public transport	-.11	**.79**	-.03	-.10
102	CS-16	Knowledge traffic signals	.11	.12	**.57**	-.03
103	CS-17	Identify public bathroom signs	-.24	**.82**	.21	-.09
104	CS-18	Move to new neighborhood	-.08	**.67**	.13	.11
105	CS-19	Why grownups need to work	.16	**.49**	.12	.09

Sr No.	Item No.	Statements of Items	F1 DLS	F2 SS	F3 SCS	F4 HLS
106	CS-20	Car worked on	-.14	**.49**	**.38**	.06
107	CS-21	Need to have police	.21	**.41**	-.00	-.09
108	CS-22	Crossing streets carefully	**.37**	.00	.13	**.31**
109	CS-24	Where does nurse work	.29	.15	.17	.045
110	CS-25	What should you say if get candy	.18	.18	.23	-.21
111	CS-26	Name 3 games played in ground	**.31**	**.36**	.13	-.01
112	CS-27	What should you do if find purse	.11	**.49**	.13	.02
113	CS-28	How old you've to be to vote	-.15	**.53**	.18	.07
114	CS-29	Where should you post letter	-.23	**.65**	.19	.14
115	CS-30	From where can you borrow books	-.26	**.72**	.21	.04
116	CS-31	Takes care of school utensils	.29	.26	**.37**	-.16
117	CS-32	Goes to local store	.10	**.31**	.27	.06
118	HS-3	Asks for school Nurse	**.55**	-.01	-.03	.14
119	HS-4	Conscious of interacting with strangers	**.39**	.15	.01	.14
120	HS-5	Why do you brush your teeth	.24	.11	.22	.01
121	HS-6	Had number for emergency calls	.09	**.65**	.22	-.17
122	HS-7	Follows traffic rules while crossing street	.26	-.29	**.30**	.28

Continued . . .

Sr No.	Item No.	Statements of Items	F1 DLS	F2 SS	F3 SCS	F4 HLS
123	HS-8	Expressing pain/discomfort	.18	**.50**	-.24	-.01
124	HS-9	Avoiding phys contact strangers	**.53**	.12	.02	-.01
125	HS-10	Discriminating family/friends	.27	.06	**.39**	.01
126	HS-11	Where can you buy cough medicine	.00	.17	**.69**	-.10
127	HS-12	Can left to care self/others	-.15	**.68**	**.34**	-.07
128	HS-13	Avoids sharp objects	-.12	-.03	**.67**	.08
129	HS-14	Avoids dangers of electric objects	-.05	-.04	**.68**	-.12
130	W-1	What do you use to nail	**.61**	.02	-.03	-.07
131	W-2	Helps at little household tasks	**.34**	.01	-.03	**.34**
132	W-3	Uses tools/ utensils	-.06	.01	**.71**	.06
133	W-4	Does routine household tasks	**.38**	-.12	.01	**.43**
134	W-5	Regular/punctual in school	**.60**	-.06	.05	-.02
135	W-6	Cooperative	.24	**.52**	-.14	-.07
136	W-7	Does simple creative work	.24	.03	.28	.21
137	W-8	Works patiently	**.38**	.28	-.13	.09
138	W-9	Consistent	**.42**	**.36**	-.23	.03
139	W-10	Identify objects	**.52**	.27	-.08	-.04
140	L-1	Plays with toys/objects	**.64**	-.05	.02	-.15
141	L-2	Takes interest in activities of others	.21	-.11	.02	-.01

Continued . . .

Sr No.	Item No.	Statements of Items	F1 DLS	F2 SS	F3 SCS	F4 HLS
142	L-3	Invites peer to game	**.58**	-.10	.11	.08
143	L-6	Plays competitive games	**.75**	-.10	.01	-.02
144	L-7	Takes interest in magic/tricks	-.16	**.49**	.29	-.03
145	L-8	Making partners n playing	-.08	**.31**	.16	.01
146	L-9	Refuse to play friend	**.42**	-.02	**.39**	-.03
147	L-10	Learns new game	**.62**	-.05	.16	.01
148	L-12	Can keep score	**.57**	-.06	.16	-.02
149	L-13	Reads for entertainment	-.08	-.16	**.39**	**.50**
150	L-14	Attend activities in city	.10	-.10	.21	.27
151	L-15	Enjoys planning	.00	-.18	**.44**	**.46**
152	L-16	Play preadolescent plays	**.41**	.04	.09	.18
153	HL-1	Concentrate for 5 minutes	.22	-.06	.00	.06
154	HL-3	Does small errands in familiar sur	.21	-.05	.07	**.32**
155	HL-4	Takes care of guests	-.31	.23	.28	**.56**
156	HL-5	Helps cleaning house	.00	-.12	-.06	**.72**
157	HL-6	Light candle	.10	-.14	-.04	**.81**
158	HL-7	Makes his bed	-.28	-.10	**.38**	**.63**
159	HL-8	Use Stove without danger	-.27	.17	.24	**.67**
160	HL-9	Washes/ irons own clothing	-.16	-.01	.18	**.71**
161	HL-10	Exchanges amount of coins	-.05	.12	**.39**	**.43**
162	HL-11	Putting things order at home	.07	.20	.26	.13

Sr No.	Item No.	Statements of Items	F1 DLS	F2 SS	F3 SCS	F4 HLS
163	HL-12	Giving correct change	.01	**.53**	.18	.13
164	HL-13	Ensuring discipline in house	-.00	**.64**	.05	.06
165	HL-14	Cook simple meal	-.35	**.41**	.14	**.49**
166	HL-15	Button the shirt	-.19	-.14	**.35**	**.50**
167	HL-17	Taking care of younger siblings	**.35**	.06	-.03	**.37**
168	HL-18	Buying edibles	.08	**.57**	-.36	**.43**
169	HL-19	Care of household items	.24	.05	-.14	**.52**
170	HL-20	Helping younger siblings study	.13	**.41**	-.16	**.40**
171	HL-21	Checking doors/locks	.24	.12	-.18	**.59**
172	HL-22	Making time table for siblings	.06	.18	-.07	**.55**
173	HL-23	Dishwashing	-.23	.22	.19	**.60**
174	HL-24	Helping mother preparing meal	-.24	**.64**	.13	**.31**
175	HL-25	What use to make bread	-.02	-.28	**.90**	-.23
176	HL-26	House is caught on fire	-.16	.01	.09	**.79**
177	HL-27	Clean daal/ rice	-.10	**.42**	-.24	**.59**
178	HL-28	Meets responsibilities	.19	.09	.11	**.32**
179	FAS-1	Indicate right no of objects	**.58**	**.36**	-.21	-.00
180	FAS-2	Distinguish round/rectangular	**.67**	-.08	.04	.07
181	FAS-3	Differentiate yesterday/today	**.70**	-.09	.09	.15
182	FAS-4	Name days of week	**.68**	-.06	.03	.25
183	FAS-5	Reads3 simple words	**.77**	-.09	-.02	.18
184	FAS-6	Counts from 1/ 20	**.88**	-.02	-.06	-.12

Sr No.	Item No.	Statements of Items	F1 DLS	F2 SS	F3 SCS	F4 HLS
185	FAS-7	Reads own name	**.79**	-.04	.02	-.02
186	FAS-8	Copy word of four letters	**.67**	.04	-.03	.10
187	FAS-9	Order objects to color	**.67**	-.01	.10	-.11
188	FAS-10	Adds up to 10	.23	.06	.13	.01
189	FAS-11	Names daytime / related activities	**.56**	.01	.27	.12
190	FAS-12	Names the daytime	**.47**	-.05	.19	.13
191	FAS-13	Name date/day	**.49**	.03	**.34**	.05
192	FAS-14	Writes simple sentences	**.69**	-.04	.03	.24
193	FAS-15	Names coins 1, 2 /5	**.40**	**.46**	.21	**-.35**
194	FAS-16	Locates dates on calendar	.34	**.41**	-.17	.28
195	FAS-17	Reads 10 words	.16	-.02	.27	**.35**
196	FAS-18	Copy simple designs/shapes	**.76**	-.01	-.02	-.00
197	FAS-19	Knows basic colors	.32	**.54**	.20	-.23
198	FAS-20	Capable of remembering address	.38	**.50**	-.28	.26
199	FAS-21	Draws pictures	**.60**	**.44**	-.24	-.03
200	FAS-22	Arranges from smallest to largest	**.51**	.10	**.35**	-.19
201	FAS-23	Urdu books read from right	**.45**	.08	**.36**	.09
202	FAS-24	Reading signs/directions	.11	**.40**	.20	.15
203	FAS-25	Writes imp messages	-.22	**.90**	.14	.03
204	FAS26	Difference between left/right	**.69**	.03	.01	.06
205	FAS27	Understands more/less/same	**.72**	-.01	.07	-.14

Sr No.	Item No.	Statements of Items	F1 DLS	F2 SS	F3 SCS	F4 HLS
206	FAS28	Lists things needed at home	-.20	**.43**	.01	**.38**
207	FAS29	Expense list after shopping	-.29	**.39**	.07	**.35**
208	FAS30	Tells correct time	.05	**.38**	.21	.14
209	FAS31	Correctly Identify money amount	**.42**	**.53**	.02	-.15
210	FAS32	Reading warning on edibles	-.22	**.63**	.05	**.32**
211	M-1	Summersault	.11	.07	.25	.20
212	M-2	Folds paper	.16	**.72**	.03	-.24
213	M-3	Unscrews the lid	**.63**	-.09	.05	.06
214	M-4	Can jump rope	**.52**	-.11	-.12	.57
215	M-5	Cuts piece of paper	.27	.02	-.08	-.04
216	M-6	Hits ball with bat	**.79**	-.04	-.00	.04
217	M-7	Picks objects from ground	**.48**	**.52**	**-.36**	.04
218	M-8	Rides bicycle	**.73**	-.01	-.05	.09
219	M-9	Uses crayon for drawing	.29	.02	-.02	.01
220	M-10	Stands eyes open	**.69**	.02	-.02	-.04
221	M-11	Stands on tiptoes	**.36**	.17	**.33**	.04
222	M-12	Cuts Star by scissor	**.32**	-.04	.21	.24
223	M-13	Bears weight on 1 knee	.20	.29	.14	-.04
224	M-14	Puts small objects in jar	**.53**	.07	.20	-.11
225	M-15	jump in air	**.31**	.23	-.24	-.11
226	M-16	Walk for15 minutes	**.72**	.02	-.14	.09

Sr No.	Item No.	Statements of Items	F1 DLS	F2 SS	F3 SCS	F4 HLS
227	M-17	Can hop on1 foot	**.40**	.15	**.31**	.01
228	M-18	Can draw straight line with ruler	**.69**	-.05	.01	.02
229	M-19	Can open lock	**.50**	-.03	.04	**.30**
230	M-20	Can fold paper put to envelope	**.87**	-.03	-.09	-.06
231	M-21	Can thread needle	.09	-.10	-.07	**.76**
232	M-22	Walks backward on line	.25	.18	-.17	.11
233	M-23	Walks and bounces ball	.23	-.00	-.09	.29
234	M-24	Can jump on step	.11	.20	-.04	.17
235	M-26	Trace path in maze	**.39**	-.10	.06	.28
236	M-27	Manages kite	.10	**.44**	.14	.27
237	M-28	Catches a small ball from 3 meter	**.31**	.03	-.16	.23

Note. Factor loadings > .30 are in boldface. C= communication; SC= self care; S= socialization; SD= self direction; CS= community skills; HS= health and safety; W= work; L= Leisure; HL= Home living; FAS= Functional academic skills; M= Motor. DLS= Daily living skills; SS= Social skills; SCS= Self care skills; HLS= Home living skills.

The table 8 showed details of item loadings across different factors. Initially 264 items were used in factor analysis, and the table above shows the final factor structure which employed 237 items. All the loadings above the selected cutoff point, that is, 0.30 are presented as bold. Some items loaded on more than one factor, loadings on both factors are highlighted. Loadings of 0.30 and above were chosen as cutoff value as experts had explained that in a sample of more than 100 participants, loadings of 0.30 and higher could be considered significant (Kline, 2002). A large majority of the items showed systematically higher intra subscale correlations compared to inter subscale correlations, hence, justifying the establishment of distinct subscales as supported by the literature (Clark & Watson, 1995). The final selection of number of factors was based on a number of frequently used criteria including scree – plot, cut off values and achieving simple structure (Kline, 2000). There were some items that had cross loadings on more than one factor, the placement of those items in a particular factor was decided on item factor correlation and theoretical relatedness of the item with other items within that factor.

Table 9

Eigen Values and Variance Explained by Factors of Adaptive Skills Scale

Factors	Eigen Values	% of Variance	Cumulative Percentage
Daily Living skills	87.08	46.29	46.29
Social skills	14.79	9.17	55.45
Self care skills	7.81	6.25	61.70
Home living skills	6.08	2.53	64.23

The table 9 indicated that together the four factors explain almost 64 percent of total variance which was above the minimum acceptable level of variance which was 50 percent for good factor structure.

The detail of the factors and items is as follows

Factor 1 – Daily Living Skills. Most of the items that loaded on first factor had a common theme depicting the practical aspect of adaptive functioning. Factor had a mix of items from all domains of adaptive skills like communication, functional academic skills, work, motor skills etc. All these items pointed towards the practical application of theoretical knowledge to solve routine problems, therefore, it was decided to name this factor as " *Daily Living Skills*".

Factor 2 – Social Skills. The items that loaded on second factor were those that involved adaptive skills which facilitate the social dimension of growth by helping one understand different social rules, norms, practices and agents and mechanism of socialization. Some of the items loaded on this factor were "Helps others if necessary", "Making partners and carry leisure activity with them", "Leaving seat for elders, greeting familiar people" and "Where should you go to post a letter or a parcel" etc. The second factor included items all of which were the adaptive skills used in one or the other social situation, reveals understanding of different social mechanisms and influences the primary social functioning therefore, this factor was assigned the "*Social Skills*" title.

Factor 3 – Self Care Skills. Items included in factor three depict adaptive skills based on self direction and self help dimensions. The items loaded on this factor reflected the skills that were primarily employed to take care of the personal needs, ensure one's safety and regulate one's self in society like "prepares own sandwich", "Knows the method of WUDU", "Discriminating between family, friends and strangers" and "Why do we need to have police" etc. the personal care demands of our routine life, thus, qualifying for "*Self Care Skills*" title.

Factor 4 – Home Living Skills. The last factor consisted of items revealing skills needed to meet the domestic demands, like taking part in domestic activities, taking care of the small domestic chores and taking care of domestic resources etc. The "*Home Living*

Skills" was selected as the title for this particular factor. The detail of items included in the four factors is given in Appendix – L.

Table 10

Inter Scale Correlation of Adaptive Behavior Subscale

	DLS	SS	SCS	HLS
Daily Living skills				
Social skills	.74**			
Self care skills	.77**	.75**		
Home living skills	.60**	.61**	.73**	
Full Scale	.94**	.88**	.89**	.79**

Note. DLS = Daily Living skills; SS = Social skills; SCS = Self care skills; HLS = Home living skills.
 **Correlation is significant at the 0.01 level (2-tailed).

All the subscale scores shared moderate to high correlation with each other and with full scale scores. All factors found to had strong association with the full scale scores supporting the underline latent trait.

Table 11

Item to Total Correlation of Adaptive Behavior Scale

Sr No.	Item No.	Correlation Coefficient	Sr No.	Item No.	Correlation Coefficient
1	C1	.38	19	C 27	.67
2	C 4	.54	20	C 28	.70
3	C6	.65	21	C 31	.60
4	C 7	.51	22	C 32	.61
5	C 8	.50	23	C 33	.59
6	C 9	.51	24	C 34	.72
7	C 10	.63	25	C 35	.57
8	C 12	.64	26	C 36	.55
9	C 13	.57	27	SC-1	.57
10	C 15	.69	28	SC-2	.50
11	C 16	.61	29	SC-3	.57
12	C 18	.38	30	SC-4	.63
13	C 19	.50	31	SC-5	.55
14	C 20	.58	32	SC-6	.47
15	C 21	.69	33	SC-7	.55
16	C 23	.55	34	SC-8	.64
17	C 24	.60	35	SC-9	.60
18	C 26	.63	36	SC-10	.54

Continued . . . .

Sr No.	Item No.	Correlation Coefficient	Sr No.	Item No.	Correlation Coefficient
37	SC-11	.58	56	S-26	.70
38	SC-12	.59	57	S-27	.39
39	SC-13	.60	58	SD-1	.57
40	SC-14	.58	59	SD-2	.61
41	SC-15	.60	60	SD-3	.55
42	S-2	.59	61	SD-5	.63
43	S-4	.74	62	SD-7	.65
44	S-5	.59	63	SD-8	.62
45	S-6	.68	64	SD-10	.57
46	S-7	.35	65	SD-11	.68
47	S-10	.64	66	SD-13	.61
48	S-11	.63	67	SD-14	.63
49	S-12	.66	68	SD-15	.62
50	S-13	.61	69	SD-16	.65
51	S-14	.55	70	SD-18	.65
52	S-16	.68	71	SD-20	.67
53	S-17	.64	72	SD-21	.67
54	S-22	.57	73	SD-23	.66
55	S-24	.65	74	SD-24	.64

Continued . . . .

Sr No.	Item No.	Correlation Coefficient	Sr No.	Item No.	Correlation Coefficient
75	CS-1	.44	95	CS-27	.60
76	CS-2	.58	96	CS-28	.49
77	CS-3	.69	97	CS-29	.57
78	CS-4	.66	98	CS-30	.54
79	CS-6	.64	99	CS-31	.63
80	CS-7	.53	100	CS-32	.57
81	CS-8	.68	101	HS-3	.54
82	CS-10	.66	102	HS-4	.55
83	CS-11	.62	103	HS-6	.67
84	CS-12	.71	104	HS-7	.57
85	CS-13	.60	105	HS-8	.39
86	CS-14	.47	106	HS-9	.57
87	CS-16	.60	107	HS-10	.51
88	CS-17	.55	108	HS-11	.60
89	CS-18	.66	109	HS-12	.63
90	CS-19	.66	110	HS-13	.48
91	CS-20	.61	111	HS-14	.41
92	CS-21	.43	112	W-1	.48
93	CS-22	.61	113	W-2	.50
94	CS-26	.69	114	W-3	.53

Sr No.	Item No.	Correlation Coefficient	Sr No.	Item No.	Correlation Coefficient
115	W-4	.52	136	HL-7	.38
116	W-5	.49	137	HL-8	.53
117	W-6	.51	138	HL-9	.45
118	W-8	.52	139	HL-10	.63
119	W-9	.50	140	HL-12	.66
120	W-10	.58	141	HL-13	.56
121	L-1	.44	142	HL-14	.45
122	L-3	.55	143	HL-15	.31
123	L-6	.55	144	HL-17	.56
124	L-7	.46	145	HL-18	.54
125	L-8	.57	146	HL-19	.56
126	L-9	.62	147	HL-20	.59
127	L-10	.62	148	HL-21	.54
128	L-12	.55	149	HL-22	.51
129	L-13	.47	150	HL-23	.59
130	L-15	.49	151	HL-24	.62
131	L-16	.56	152	HL-25	.38
132	HL-3	.46	153	HL-26	.57
133	HL-4	.50	154	HL-27	.46
134	HL-5	.33	155	HL-28	.52
135	HL-6	.46	156	FAS1	.64

Sr No.	Item No.	Correlation Coefficient	Sr No.	Item No.	Correlation Coefficient
157	FAS2	.58	178	FAS25	.68
158	FAS3	.69	179	FAS26	.66
159	FAS4	.72	180	FAS27	.58
160	FAS5	.69	181	FAS28	.59
161	FAS6	.62	182	FAS29	.60
162	FAS7	.64	183	FAS30	.62
163	FAS8	.65	184	FAS31	.72
164	FAS9	.58	185	FAS32	.57
165	FAS11	.77	186	M2	.59
166	FAS12	.60	187	M3	.54
167	FAS13	.74	188	M4	.63
168	FAS14	.74	189	M5	.59
169	FAS15	.66	190	M6	.68
170	FAS16	.68	191	M7	.60
171	FAS18	.63	192	M8	.64
172	FAS19	.73	193	M10	.57
173	FAS20	.69	194	M11	.73
174	FAS21	.68	195	M12	.47
175	FAS22	.67	196	M14	.60
176	FAS23	.78	197	M15	.25
177	FAS24	.68	198	M16	.59

Sr No.	Item No.	Correlation Coefficient	Sr No.	Item No.	Correlation Coefficient
199	M17	.71	203	M21	.43
200	M18	.58	204	M26	.49
201	M19	.63	205	M27	.37
202	M20	.62	206	M28	.30

The table revealed that item M 15 "Can jump with both feet in the air" have a corrected item total correlation which was below 0.30 indicating the weakness of this items. As these items also had low factor loadings, therefore, it was decided to drop these items from the scale. However, item M 28 "Catches a small ball from three feet" also had correlation value less than .30 but it was retained as the values was 0.29 which was very close to 0.30 and also had adequate factor loadings. The item was retained because it had a factor loading above 0.30 in factor analysis, had strong theoretical relevance with the motor skills domain and it also had high content validity value, i.e., 0.89.

Table 12

Mean , Standard deviation and Mean Difference Values for Subscales of AB Scale

	Mean	(SD)	Girls Mean	(SD)	Boys Mean	(SD)	t
DLS	226.87	(34.16)	231.88	(30.08)	222.02	(36.91)	3.67
SS	63.92	(15.81)	67.01	(13.99)	60.79	(16.92)	5.01
SCS	55.54	(12.05)	57.62	(10.60)	53.45	(13.03)	4.39
HLS	38.19	(12.47)	40.31	(12.97)	36.03	(11.55)	4.36
Full Scale	384.52	(66.70)	396.83	(61.32)	372.29	(69.28)	4.70

Note. DLS = Daily living skills; SS= Social skills; SCS= Self care skills; HLS= Home living skills

t- values are significant at .000 level of significance.

The table presented mean scores of sample on all subscales and for composite score of indigenous adaptive behavior scale. The mean scores were also calculated for girls and boys which revealed significant mean differences between scores of girls and boys on all subscales of adaptive behavior.

Figure 6.

Selection of Items at Different Stages of Scale Development

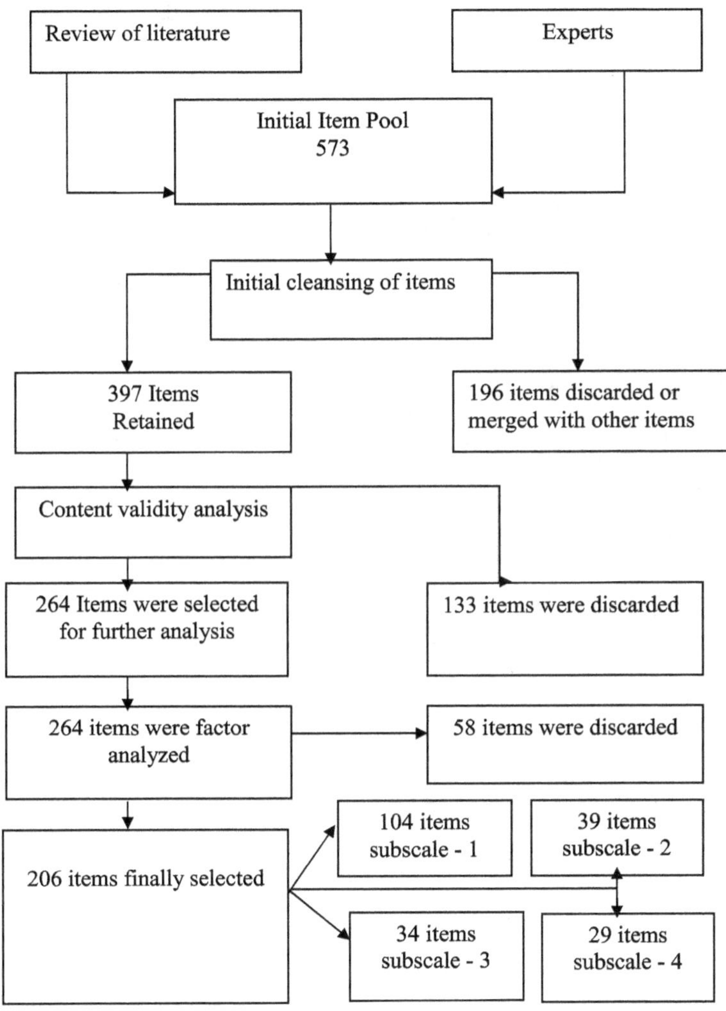

Figure 6 indicated how 573 items went through different stages of scale item

selection and dropped to 206 items comprising a final scale and the number of items were retained at different stages of scale development.

Step – II. Convergent Validity.

The next step was to assess the convergent validity of the scale. For this purpose, scores of children on newly developed adaptive behavior scale were correlated with scores on CABS. The results are presented in the table below

Table 13

Correlation between Scores of AB Scale and CABS

CABS Subscales	Domains of Adaptive Behavior Scale				
	DLS	SS	SC	HLS	Composite
Language development	.87**	.50**	.53**	.48**	.79**
Independent functioning	.84**	.89**	.86**	.78**	.89**
Economic vocational activity	.68**	.54**	.45**	.49**	.60**
Family Role performance	.51**	.49**	. 50**	.84**	.81**
Socialization	.67**	.39**	.48**	.50**	.78**
Composite	.79**	.67**	.68**	.75**	.80**

Note. DLS = Daily living skills, SS = Social skills, SC = Self Care, HLS = Home living skills
**Correlation is significant at the 0.01 level (2-tailed).

The table 13 showed moderate to high values of correlation between scores of adaptive behavior scale and child adaptive behavior scale (1980). These findings suggested that both scales assess the similar domain. This convergence of scores supported the newly developed scale as a valid tool.

Step – III. Divergent Validity

Divergent validity is a procedure covering an essential aspect of construct validity. The procedure generally involves evaluating the degree of association between scores of some independent measures representing two dissimilar theoretical constructs (Hofman & Kashdan, 2010). CBCL and matched groups design were used to evaluate the discriminant validity of the scale. For Matched group design, scores of children with developmental disabilities were compared with those of without any developmental problem.

Table 14

Mean Scores of Clinical and Non- Clinical Groups on AB Scale

	Clinical Group ($n = 84$)		Non-Clinical Group ($n = 102$)				*Cohen's*	*Effect size*
	M	*(SD)*	*M*	*(SD)*	*t*	*p*	*d*	*r*
Subscale 1	157.37	23.16	229.75	12.70	25.64	.00	3.88	.89
Subscale 2	46.36	7.10	64.93	15.84	10.62	.00	1.51	.60
Subscale 3	38.96	7.15	53.64	9.73	11.84	.00	1.72	.65
Subscale 4	27.50	8.03	37.38	12.03	6.68	.00	0.97	.44
Full Scale	270.19	39.89	385.69	43.19	18.78	.00	2.78	.81

Note. t- values are significant at .000 level of significance.
df= 184

The table 14 showed differences in scores of both groups on all subscales. The group of children with typical development scored much higher compared to participants having developmental disability. The lowest difference in scores was on subscale 4.

To further strengthen the discriminant validity ABS scores were correlated with scores on CBCL of 30 participants from non clinical group.

Table 15

Correlation between Scores of Adaptive Behavior Scale and CBCL

CBCL Scales	Domains of Adaptive Behavior Scale			
	DLS	SS	SC	HLS
Anxious Depressed	.25*	-.11	.06	.21*
Withdrawn/ Depressed	.17	-.21**	-.11	.16
Somatic complaints	.11	.15	-.12	.13
Social Problems	.27	-.39*	.18	.30*
Thought Problems	.19	.15	.16	.19
Attentional Problems	.09	.22	-.21*	.06
Rule Breaking	-.21	-.21*	.23	-.31*
Aggressive behavior	.14	-.19	-.20*	.09

Note. DLS = Daily living skills, SS = Social skills, SC = Self Care, HLS = Home living skills. *Correlation is significant at the 0.01 level (2-tailed).

The table 15 indicated low to slightly moderate correlation values between scores on subscales of adaptive behavior and child behavior checklist. This low association between scores indicates the distinct nature of both constructs.

Step IV – Establishing Reliability and Cut off Scores. The second step of the present study was planned to achieve yet another significant milestone in scale development by assessing reliability (Aertssen, Ferguson, & Smits-Engelsman, 2016) and determining cutoff scores for newly developed adaptive behavior scale.

Objectives. The study was focused around following objectives

- To establish test retest reliability over the period of 5 to 12 weeks by using intra-class correlation

- To assess inter rater reliability by correlating ratings of two independent raters.

- To establish cutoff scores for subscales and composite score of adaptive behaviors scale

Sample. The sample for this step was divided into two groups, that is, group A and B. Sample A was selected to evaluate the test retest reliability and composed of 50 children randomly selected from the sample A of step – I , study – III including both boys (66 percent) and girls (34 percent) attending mainstream school. The mean age of was 7.72 years (sd = 1.09) while the age was from 6 to 10 years. Sample B was employed for inter-rater reliability and comprised 30 children randomly chosen from the sample A of step – I study – III including children of both genders with mean age of 8.34 years and having typical development. Sample C consisted of 30 children drawn randomly from sample A of step – I, study – III. All three sample groups were not employed in any other study than step – I of study – III and for reliability analysis of current study.

Ethical Considerations. All the procedures used in this phase were approved by board of studies after a detailed review. The participants were given information about the research objectives, importance of their participation, confidentiality and their right to withdraw at any point in time. Confidentiality and integrity of all participants were respected through all steps. All participants were offered debriefing session and their participation was appreciated through verbal thanks and reinforcers. Participation was based on free will after sorting institutional and personal consent.

Procedure. The instruments and procedure were same as was in the last steps. Demographic form and adaptive behavior scale were main instruments to collect data. After sorting permission from concerned authorities, the indigenously developed adaptive behavior scale was administered on the sample. At the end of the session all participants were appreciated for their time and participation.

Results. The results were computed by using SPSS (20.0) by mainly using descriptive statistics, intra-class correlation and receiver operative characteristics curve. The detailed findings mentioned below

Internal consistency. One of the most salient features of the scale is internal consistency which is traditionally established through alpha coefficient. The results for internal consistency assessed through Cronbach's alpha for the indigenous adaptive behavior scale is given below in table 16.

Table 16

Internal Consistency of Adaptive Behavior Scale

Factors	Number of Items	α
Daily living Skills	106	.98
Social Skills	39	.95
Self Care Skills	34	.96
Home living Skills	29	.93
Full Scale	206	.96

The results revealed that the alpha coefficient values for full scale and subscales fall in the acceptable range recommended for clinical screening tools. The alpha coefficient for the scale was observed to be .95 taken as an excellent indication of internal consistency (Fieldman, 2005).

Test Retest Reliability. Test re test was another significant criterion of evaluating the strength of any assessment instrument. The same set of individuals was assessed using same measures for specific phenomena after a certain gap in time, the magnitude of correlation between two scores was used to determine the reliability (Marnat, 2003). In order to investigate test re test reliability of adaptive behavior scale intra class correlation (ICC) method was used to investigate test re-test reliability of ABS. The same interviewer re-administered ABS to 50 children randomly selected from phase I after 8 to12 weeks of first administration. The table below shows the ICC values between the scores of two administrations.

Table 17

Intra Class Correlation Coefficient for Scores of First and Second Administration of

Adaptive Behavior Scale

Variables	r
Daily Living Skills	.98*
Social Skills	.96*
Self Care Skills	.95*
Home Living Skills	.94*
Composite	.96*

* Correlation is significant at 0.01 level

The table 17 showed correlation between the scores of first and second administration of adaptive behavior scale over the period of time. All values were significant at .001 level of significance and revealed excellent test re-test reliability. All the subscales found to had consistency in scores over the specified period of time.

Step – V. Establishing Cut Off Scores. The next step was to establish cut off scores of the newly developed scale. To achieve this objective, receivers operating characteristic curve was used to determine the cut off scores.

Receivers Operating Characteristic Curve (ROC). Selecting the appropriate cutoff scores for adaptive behavior scale was the next task of this study. Most frequently used methods for selecting cutoff points include discriminant function analysis, ROC curve and mean and standard deviation values (Singh, 2006). ROC curve was applied to establish the cut off score for adaptive behavior scale. ROC curve assesses a test's ability to identify true positive and false positive cases and thus establishes how successfully a test can differentiate between people with a particular problem from those who are not having that problem by determining a valid cutoff (Pintea & Moldovan, 2009).

Table 18

Summary of ROC Analysis for the Sub scales and Composite Score of Adaptive Behaviors Scale.

	Area under Curve	Std. Error[a]	Sig.[b]	95 % Confidence Interval	
				Lower Bound	Upper Bound
Composite Score	.96	.01	.00	.94	.97
DLS	.99	.00	.00	.98	.99
SS	.87	.01	.00	.85	.89
SCS	.87	.02	.00	.84	.89
HLS	.76	.02	.00	.72	.79

Note. DLS= Daily living skills, SS = Social Skills, SCS = Self Care skills, HLS= Home living Skills.
a. Under the non parametric assumption
b. Null hypothesis: true area = 0.5

Significance for all subscales was less than 0.05, indicating that using the indigenously developed adaptive behavior scale was better than guessing. The area under the curve falls in the category of moderate to excellent ability to differentiate between conditions suggesting the screening accuracy of the current scale (Pintea & Moldovan, 2009). The sensitivity and specificity for different cut off scores was also calculated and finally the cut off score of 330.50 was selected. This led to sensitivity of 0.91, therefore, approximately 90.6

% of all children with deficiency in adaptive behaviors would be correctly identified. The detail of different cut off scores and their corresponding sensitivity values were given in appendix – N. AUC values, corresponding significance level and 95% confidence interval values for all factors found to have good to excellent screening accuracy except subscale 4 which showed satisfactory clinical accuracy.

Discussion

After the initial screening of items, the next step was to get the items reviewed by subject matter experts (Netemeyer, Bearden, & Sharma, 2003). Experts were chosen keeping in view the standard criteria for selecting subject matter experts (Grant & Davis, 1997) who were then requested to rate each item for their relevance with the construct, clarity and redundancy (Jew, Green, & Kroger,1999). Literature on scale development strongly suggested to carefully choose the subject matter experts to review the specific content. There are different criteria proposed by various professionals to define the subject matter experts. Generally, it is believed that subject matter experts are those individuals who have sufficient knowledge of the subject, understands the content and it different dimensions well and can practically generalize the knowledge of specific content area to various practical situations (Grant & Davis, 1997; Husian, 2012).

The selected items were then tested on a developmental sample to assess the face validity of the items as it was strongly suggested by experts to first test the adequacy of selected items before formally testing the items (Netemeyer, Bearden, & Sharma, 2003). The preliminary placement of items into subscales was done using clinical judgment of experts. After initial refinement and review of items, content validity was determined through calculating ICVI for each item.

The content validity was assessed by item ratings for degree of relevance with the AB construct and cultural role expectations of Pakistani society. The items with 0.78 and higher I-CVI values were chosen as literature (Haynes et al., 1995) suggested that when more than eight experts were involved in item ratings, the 0.75 was considered satisfactory I-CVI value and I-CVI values of 0.78 and above are considered good. Content validity index was calculated for dimensions of construct and cultural relevance. Equal importance was given to both dimensions, therefore, any item having ICVI values lower than 0.78 on either of the two dimensions was reviewed and/or deleted. This process paved the way for establishing further psychometric properties of the selected items.

Socialization, home living and communication were the subscales that received the most changes in terms of item shifting. In total, 133 items making 33.50 percent of all items were removed from the scale. Some 66. 50 percent items were retained as they received the acceptable level of ICVI value which was 0.78, these 264 items were then rearranged according to their respective sub-scales for further analyses.

As the main aim of this study, FA was carried out to assess the construct validity of scale (Eristi & Akdeniz, 2012). Different factor solutions were conducted from 36 factors to three factor solutions. The four factor solution was finally chosen on the basis of total variances explained by factors, scree plot (Costello & Osborne, 2005; Yong & Pearce, 2013), simple structure (Beavers et al., 2013) and factor interpretability (Floyd & Widaman, 2000). Factor analysis revealed some interesting findings as it showed a factor structure which was slightly different from the factor structure of adaptive skills reported in western cultures. The factor structure was found to be somewhat different from the factor structure given in VABS and AAMR scales as many items loaded on factors other than the expected factor. This finding was somewhat similar to findings of a previous research where researcher reported having a slightly different factor model in Vietnam than one mentioned in VABS manual (Goldberg et al., 2009). This was also consistent with another research which reported that 32 percent of the statements had elevated correlations with domains other than their assigned domains (Bildt, et al., 2005; Bean, Roszkowski, 1982). One possible reason of this was that the domains of adaptive skills were considered to be highly inter related and share overlapping of items.

The items that primarily comprised on factor 1 were those that point to the practical application of concepts like "making phone calls", "Locates important dates on calendar" etc. This factor also included items referring to general understanding of concepts and mechanics of various procedures things "Follows classroom rules", "Can respond correctly to the question like "What day and date do we have today?", "Understands that Urdu books are read from right to left, English books are read from left to" etc. Understanding daily life problems and knowing how to solve them "Acts properly at public place without drawing negative attention", "What should you do if you lose your reading book" etc. as all these practical skills were pertinent to maintain daily life functioning, the factor was named "Daily Living Skills".

Factor 2 was primarily comprised items of sub-domains of socialization, community skill and health and safety. Other than that, some items from self direction sub-domains also loaded on this factor. But regardless of the subscales the underline theme of almost all these items was related to different aspects of social processes. The possible explanation of loading of socialization item 7 (what do you do if your best friend asks an answer of a question during exam) and 17 (follow school rules and discipline) was that these items were about understanding and respecting rules and norms operating within school which was an important agent of society. The possible reason of loading of item 12 (helps others when needed) might be that helping others was not only highly valued by society but was strongly encouraged by religion as well. Therefore, it was considered to be a responsibility of all community members to help those in need. Self direction item 10 (which number do you dial to call rescue services) and home-living item 26 (what would you do if your house is on fire) reflected knowledge of effective use of social resources that could be used to ensure safety. The items 7 of leisure (Takes interest in magic and tricks) and 12 of home-living (I bought a bread of Rs 50 from 100 how much is left with me) but related to understanding of a social system. Magic shows and tricks are staged as regular part of social community functions and buying and selling is also an operation taking place as community activity. A close review of social skills domain revealed an overlap of activities which possibly had resulted in loadings of community and home living items on this factor. The factor was labeled as "Social Skills".

Factor 3 was mainly consisted of items of self care domain. From leisure domain items 13 and 15 loaded on this factor, both are about activities related to pleasure. Pleasure seeking is an important aspect of well being and satisfies secondary human needs which are positively associated with well being and can be considered related to self care. The item from work (3 – uses utensils) domain that loaded on factor 3 was basic task that ensures independent functioning. Item 10 (discriminate friends from strangers) and 11 (from where can you buy cough syrup) from HS domain assessed the knowledge of safety behaviors that were also related to self care. Items 12 (cares for baggage while travelling), 16 (knowledge of traffic signals), 19 (why do grownups work) and 21 (why we need to have police) of community domain also loaded on this factor. These items reflected the ability to take care of one's self, ensured safety and the knowledge of the ways to meet one's needs, all these could be explained as different elements that directly influence independent functioning (all these could be explained as different aspects of independent functioning). Other items were also related to self regulation dimension of self care. Keeping in view this common theme the factor was named "Self Care Skill".

Majority of home living items constituted Factor 4. Apart from home living, items 2 and 4 (helps in simple domestic chores; does routine domestic chores) from work also loaded here. These items were primarily based on tasks carried out at home due to which they might have high loading on factor 4 than factor 1. Item 1 (can find a way home from school) from community skills also had high loadings on factor 4, initially this item was placed in home living but on feedback of reviewers it was shifted to community skills domain. However, the factor loadings supported the initial placement. Item 28 (can make a list of items needed at home) and 29 (making a list after shopping) of FAS domain and item 21 of motor scale (can thread a needle) were also loaded on this factor. The first two items assessed the practical use of numeral skills whereas the item from motor scale was about fine motor skills, but all these skills were closely related to domestic activities/chores. The detailed review of all the items loaded on factor 4 other than the home living domain showed that they were related to activities that take place or were closely related to home. "Home Living Skills" was deemed appropriate for this factor.

Other than the factorial validity the other two types of construct validity that is, convergent and divergent validities were examined. Discriminant validity was established by using two methods that is, correlating the AB construct with theoretically different construct and by using matched group design that had also been used in other researches for the same purpose (Jamil & Khalid, 2012; Hussain, 2012). For the first purpose scores on CBCL (1986) were correlated with scores of AB, CBCL not only a widely used clinical scale but was also frequently used for research purposes (Achenbach, & Ruffle, 2000). CBCL assessed behavioral problems that belong to a construct theoretically very different from the construct of AB and was also used in previous researches to establish discriminant validity of different adaptive functioning instruments (Bildt et al., 2005; Alonso et al., 2010). The findings of the current study revealed low correlation between all the scales and composite score of CBCL and ABS supporting the discriminatory power of the present scale. The literature (Husain, 2012) usually considered low, negative and no correlation between two unrelated scales as a strong indicator of discriminant power of scales. Therefore, this finding supported the present scale as a valid tool which could successfully identify problems related to adaptive behaviors. The matched group method was also used to assess current scales' ability to discriminate the children with adequately developed adaptive skills from children with delayed adaptive skills. The mean scores of both groups showed a statistically significant mean difference on all subscales. The difference in scores on daily living skills was highest among all factors and the lowest difference in scores of both groups was observed to be on home living skills. The significant differences between the scores of children with developmental delay from those following typical development suggested strength of the newly developed scale to discriminate the children with normal development with those having developmental delays specifically with reference to adaptive behaviors. Factor covariance carried out in last phase offered another indication of discriminant validity, all values of which were statistically significant though small. This indicated relatively poor factor distinctiveness which in fact supports discriminant validity of the test (Hall, Hughes, 2007).

The next step was to assess the convergent validity of the scale, this purpose was achieved by using CABS (1980). Significant positive correlation was observed between sub scales of CABS and present scale and all correlations were found to have moderate to high values of correlation. The significant positive correlations suggested that both constructs assessed the same behavioral domain, that is, adaptive behaviors. This positive correlation clearly supported this new tool as a valid measure of adaptive functioning (Osa, Ezpeleta, Domenech, Navarro, & Losilla,1997). However, there was also observed to be moderate correlation indicating that many items of CABS were not culturally relevant and must had resulted in low scores. This finding was also supported by the item to subscale correlation assessed in factorial validity step. The items showed significantly high positive correlation with subscales in which the items were retained and low correlation with other subscales (Appendix – M), this convergence of scores could also be taken as a good evidence of validity (Clark & Watson, 1995). The study not only shed light on the factor structure of newly complied adaptive behavior scale but also supported the multidimensional nature of the AB construct as was noted in many key researches in both western and non western cultures (Klein & Klein, 2012; Sparrow et al., 2005; AAMR , 2006).

Apart from validity another important psychometric concern with reference to newly developed scales was reliability (Eisen, Normand, Belanger, Spiro, & Esch, 2004). The first attempt was to establish internal consistency of the newly developed scale. All four subscales extracted from factor analysis found to have Alpha coefficient that falls in the excellent range of reliability. The correlation of items with total subscale scores also supported the item's placement in a particular factor as most of the items had moderate to high correlations with the total score of the factor in which they were retained and weak correlation with the total scores of other factors. There were few exceptions where items showed moderate to high correlations with another factor's total score. The close review revealed that these items loaded on more than one factor in factor analysis and their placement in a particular factor was based on their theoretical relevance.

The reliability of the total scale and subscales was observed to be ranging from 0.91 to 0.98 which was adequately required for clinical screening tools (Nunnally & Bernstein, 1994). The alpha coefficients, item total and subscale correlations all suggested strong internal consistency. The alpha coefficients of subscales and item to subscale correlations supported the internal consistency and factor structure of the scale. Items placement on different factors remained more or less same across different factor solutions particularly when the number of factors was restricted to 3, 4 and 5 factors.

The test retest reliability showed significant high correlations suggesting the tool's strength to provide consistent scores over the period of almost two to three months. The significant change was observed on items related to socialization (for instance, "permission to use objects", "says please/sorry" etc.) self care ("spread soft toppings on bread", "why do you take bath", "uses correct food utensils" etc.) , home living ("what is used to make bread....", "lighting candle", "taking care of household items" etc.) and motor skills (like jumping, forwards summersault and working with scissors). Most of the items were easy to learn and the items related to health and safety, self care and home living were those that children were never get the chance to perform for example, hanging clothes on hanger, lighting candle etc. The correlation value of 0.80 was mentioned as a minimum value for good test retest reliability in literature (Kline, 2000). The results of this study revealed that all correlation values were above 0.80 supporting the newly developed tool.

Analysis of the essential psychometric characteristics of the scale paved the way to next step of determining the cut off score for the scale. ROC curve was employed to establish the cut off scores for subscales and composite score (Hanley, & McNeil, 1982). The goodness of a test is revealed by an ROC curve which is very much above the diagonal ROC line and peak towards the upper left corner of the graph (Pinteaa & Moldovan, 2009). The ROC curves of the indigenous adaptive behavior scale fulfilled both these characteristics. Although researchers used different summary indices associated with ROC to determine cut off points, area under curve (AUC) was one of the most popular index from all (Park, Goo & Jo, 2004). Therefore, AUC was used as the primary index to evaluate the clinical utility of the present tool developed in phase I. AUC is a combined estimate of specificity and sensitivity and is explained as an average value of sensitivity for all likely values of specificity (Obuchowski, 2003). In light of different ranges of AUC values mentioned in literature (Flonkowski, 2008; Park, Goo & Jo, 2004) the results showed that the present scale in general indicated good accuracy to differentiate children with under developed adaptive behaviors from those with typical development. This finding was in line with most of the findings observed in previous steps of this research and further supports the validity of indigenously developed scale. According to experts, the optimal cut off point in a scale is the one which minimizes the probability of false positive and false negative and maximizes the probability of true positive and true negative (Pintea & Moldovan, 2009). This criterion was clearly fulfilled by the AUC value for the present scale which was significant and most of the cutoff points for subscales also revealed that they support the correct identification of true positive with reduced probability of incorrectly identifying children with typical development as having developmental problems.

The next significant question was to decide the other criteria and evaluating the tradeoff between cut off scores based on sensitivity or specificity. The sensitivity values point out the strength of the tool to correctly identify children with under developed adaptive functioning (true positives). Experts (Park, Goo & Jo, 2004; Baughman et al., 2004) suggested that sensitivity values should be given preference over specificity while determining cut off point for tools for which subsequent confirmatory measurement was available. An important consideration in this regard is that adaptive behaviors assessment is generally carried out in combination with intellectual assessment and the results of both these domains usually support each other (Nahira, 1999). An individual suffering from developmental psychopathology mostly scores lower on tools assessing intellectual and adaptive functioning compared to an individual following typical development pattern. The availability of subsequent assessment tools like intellectual assessment and developmental profiling through in-depth clinical interviews suggested that the cut scores should be chosen on the basis of sensitivity values. After closely assessing different cut off scores and valuing the tradeoff between sensitivity and specificity the score of 330.50 was chosen as a cut off for total scale score. Accuracy of identifying true positives of selected cut off scores for subscale one was 97 % and 96% , 89.6 % and 85.8% for subscales two, three and subscale four respectively. This also indirectly supported the discriminant and content validity of the scale. AUC and sensitivity were used in combination to determine the cutoff point of a scale (Fawcett, 2006), and both these criteria supported that the score of 330.50 could be adequately used as a cutoff point for this scale as was mentioned in literature (Flonkowski, 2008; Park, Goo & Jo, 2004).

In sum, the findings of this phase provided an adequate support with reference to clinical utility of indigenously developed adaptive behaviors scale.

Conclusion.

The validity and reliability analyses carried out in this study supported the adequacy of items of current AB scale to be used in Pakistani cultural context. Despite some of the limitations, the adequate to good psychometric findings suggested that the present tool could be used as a useful screening tool for adaptive skills assessment.

CHAPTER –VI

Phase - II

The present chapter covers the details of studies carried out in phase-II. Phase-II of this project was focused on assessing the adaptive skills of children and to explore their relationship with multiple psychosocial factors. Temperament was identified as an important variable related to adaptive skills. However, literature pointed to very limited number of standard scales in Urdu to measure temperament in middle childhood. Therefore, it was decided to translate and standardize two temperament questionnaires to be used in this study. Consequently, Phase- II was subdivided into three main studies aimed to translate and standardize two temperament measures and to assess adaptive skills along with their psychosocial correlates and predictors in children. The following section provides a detailed account of these three studies.

Study – I. Translation of Children Behavior Questionnaire – Teacher Short Form

Cross cultural psychology experts (Van de Vijver & Leung, 2000) stressed the need to develop both structural and measurement equivalence of assessment instruments used across cultures (Hilton & Skrutkowski, 2002; Van de Vijver, 1997). The current study was an attempt to achieve this goal by developing a culturally valid translation of both CBQ-T and TMCQ and determining the psychometric characteristics of translated versions with Pakistani children. The present study was divided into different steps with the following details.

Objectives.

The present step was planned around following objectives.

1. To translate CBQ-T short form into Urdu Language.

2. To evaluate the substantive, structural and external validity of CBQ-T Urdu version.

Figure. 7.

Flow Chart of Studies of Phase – II

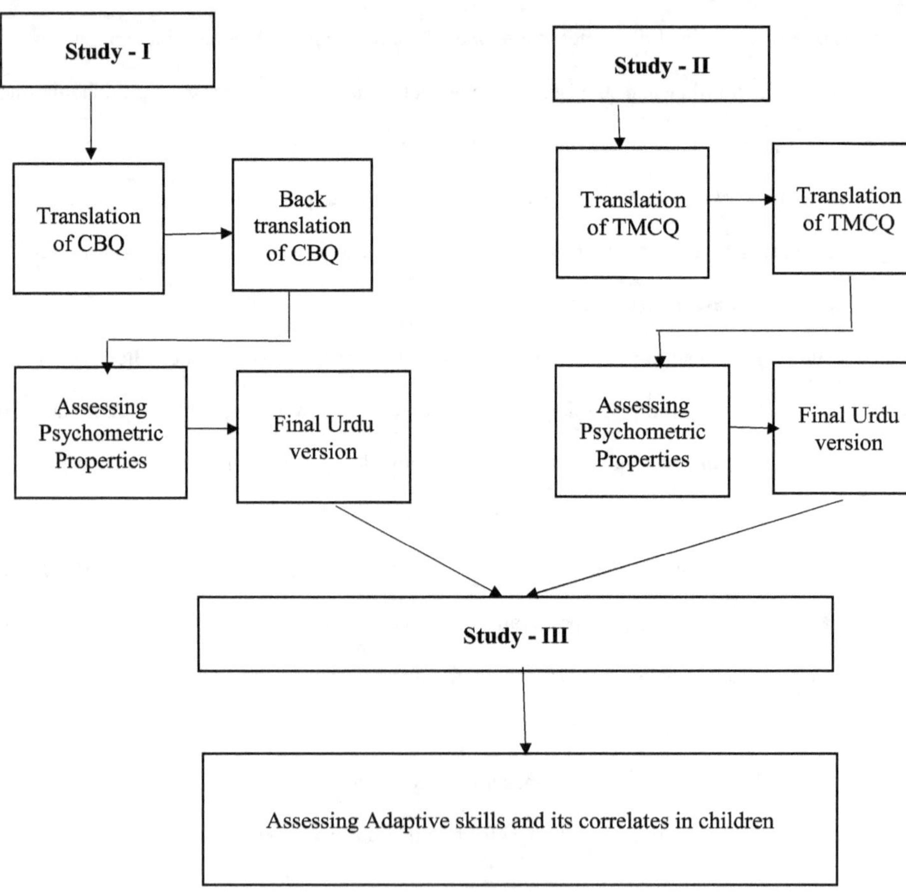

Sample.

The sample for this phase was divided into three groups. Sample A included 25 (for 2 steps of this study) bilingual graduates selected from Psychology, English and Education departments of Beaconhouse National University, University of The Punjab, Forman Christian College University and Government College University Lahore. Sample B consisted of two language experts, two PhD scholars, two clinical psychologists and a school teacher, all having 8 to 10 years of professional experience along with good command over Urdu and English language. The third sample (C) comprised 463 children including both girls (38 %) and boys (62 %) selected through random sampling technique at grade level with mean age of 6.18 years. In total 29 school teachers, teaching 5 to 7 years old children in Lahore district filled forms for 463 students. Only those teachers were included who were well familiar with children for whom they had filled the scale. The gender ratio of teachers was 24 percent male and 76 percent female teachers. The mean age of teachers was 36.52 years and the mean teaching experience was noted to be 8.14 years. Only those teachers who gave consent were included in the study. Teachers were approached at 4 public and 5 private sector schools and 6 private coaching centers of Lahore. Majority of the schools declined data collection requests and only few schools agreed. Therefore, the data could not be collected from many schools.

Instruments.

A consent form along with a basic demographic form covering socio-demographic information of participants from previous studies were used along with the following instruments

Children's Behavior Questionnaire – Teacher Short Form. CBQ-T short form consists of 94 items and developed by Teglasi (2003), assessing 15 temperamental dimensions mentioned earlier. Teachers are requested to rate children on different statements using 7 point Likert scale from extremely untrue (1) to extremely true (7) by keeping in mind the child's behavior in past six months. If a particular behavior is not observed in a given situation then 0 is given (Teglasi, 2003; Putnam, Rothbart, 2006). Like other temperamental scales of Rothbart, CBQ-T reported to have good evidence of adequate reliability and validity. The alpha ranges from .67 to .89 (Teglasi, 2003), .65 to.93 and interrater reliability ranging from .45 to .80 with good stability over time (Putnam & Rothbart, 2006) (Appendix – O).

Children's Adaptive Behavior Scale (CABS). CABS developed by Richmond and Kicklighter (1980) was used in addition to earlier mentioned scales to establish the discriminant validity of the translated scale. The CABS computes a total adaptive behavior score and separate scores for five subscales. The subscales are namely independent functioning, language development, economic vocational activity, family role performance and socialization. The standardization data available on psychometric features point out reasonable validities and reliabilities values for total and subscale scores (Hearth & Obrzut, 1986; Richmond & Kicklighter, 1980).

Procedure.

The author of CBQ – T and TMCQ were approached and a formal request was launched to translate and adapt both these scales (Appendix – P). In order to develop a culturally relevant translation of CBQT a series of steps was carried out by following the translation guidelines of MAPI and integrated model of cultural adaptation and translation proposed by Sidani, Guruge, Miranda, Ford-Gilboe and Varcoe (2010) and was consisted of the following steps.

Step 1: Translation of CBQ in Urdu. After receiving permission from the authors, items of CBQ- T form were translated into Urdu. For this purpose, CBQ- T was sent to 15 graduates of Sample A (Appendix – Q). A detailed instructional letter was enclosed with the forms requesting participants to avoid too literal translation, be mindful of content equivalence and not to leave any item (Appendix – R.1). Although translated forms were only sent to consented participants, 6 participants failed to return the translation of CBQ-T within the given time period of three weeks and 4 participants sent incomplete translations. All the translated items were thoroughly scrutinized by a committee of experts mentioned as sample C including PhD scholars, clinical psychologists and a school teacher. The experts were requested to evaluate the translation of each statement on a rating scale for grammar, content equivalence and comprehensibility; the Urdu translation selected by these experts was then sent to an Urdu language expert for final review. On the feedback of experts, 5 items were sent back for translation and 7 items faced minor modifications made by the language expert. A final list of all items translated into Urdu was prepared for next step.

Step 2: Back Translation of Translated Items. In this step, items of CBQ-T translated into Urdu language were sent to 10 participants of sample A. Again, a detailed instructional letter mentioned in step one was enclosed with the forms requesting participants to translate the Urdu items into English language. In total 8 participants sent the translations within given time and 4 participants sent incomplete translations. All the items were carefully scrutinized by the experts committee from step one with the exception of an English language expert in place of Urdu language expert. The experts used the same evaluative criteria as was in last step to select the back translation and critically compared the back translation with the original version of CBQ-T. The finally selected items were sent to an English Language expert, who suggested minor modifications related to syntax of few items.

Step 3: Content Review of Translated Items. Once the procedure of translation was completed, a committee of experts constituted in step 1 evaluated the content of all CBQ-T items for cultural relevance. The exception was that language experts were excluded from this content review committee. After a thorough review and calculation of scale content validity index (S-CVI) and item content validity index (I-CVI) for all items using indices suggested by Farrokhzad et al., (2014) and Yaghmaie (2003), and guidelines proposed by Polit and Beck (2006). Five items of CBQ-T were identified as not having culturally relevant expression and/or content.

Step 4: Review of Back Translation by Original Author. The final back translation of both scales was sent to the original authors of CBQ-T for their review. A separate list that included the items having different cultural expression and/or content with an explanation was enclosed with that. After a discussion with the author those items were modified, in order to make them culturally more relevant for Pakistani children (Appendix – R.2). A final version of CBQ – T Urdu version was prepared after the authors of original questionnaire approved that substantive meaning of all original statements had been maintained.

Step 5: Pilot Study. In order to verify the applicability of CBQ – T, a pilot study was conducted (Lancaster et al., 2004). The final Urdu version of CBQ-T was administered on 20 teachers (teaching 5 to 7 years old children) who filled the scales for their students. All administrations were carried out individually and participants were requested to give their feedback. In light of participant's feedback few changes were made in the presentation of items, including increasing the font size and adding rating scale on top of every page of the forms.

Step 6: Establishing Psychometric Characteristics of CBQ – Teacher (Urdu). The last step of this phase was marked with establishing the psychometric properties of translated versions of CBQ – T short form. The task was to evaluate internal consistency, inter rater and test re test reliability along with establishing construct, convergent and discriminant validities for CBQ-T Urdu. Like the newly developed tools, the tools translated and adapted in other language are also assessed for their psychometric properties (Anastasi, 1997).

Convergent validity. The item to subscale total correlation and degree of agreement on parental and teacher ratings of the Urdu CBQ-T items was examined to establish the convergent validity. For this purpose, 75 students were randomly selected from sample C and their mothers were requested to fill the CBQ-T scales, from which 50 filled forms were returned.

Discriminant validity. The scores on CBQ-T and CABS were used to evaluate the discriminant validity of the scale. For this purpose, a group of 45 students was randomly extracted from the sample and CABS was administered on them in individual in addition to CBQ-T.

Test re test reliability. CBQ-T was administered on a small group of 29 children from sample C to evaluate the test re test reliability. The time gap between two administrations was almost 9 weeks. It was made sure to re-administer the questionnaire on same set of children by the same rater.

Results.

Descriptive statistics, Cronbach's alpha coefficient, Pearson product moment, intraclass correlation and independent sample t-test were employed to analyze the data of study – I of phase - II. The results and trend of scores of CBQ-T was also compared with the scores trend of original CBQ-T. The descriptive analysis of the Urdu CBQ – T was carried out to see the general trend in scores and the details are mentioned below.

The initial psychometric review of scores on Urdu CBT- T is mentioned in this section. The following table (19) shows a general trend of CBT- T scores among girls, boys and in total sample.

Table 19

Mean and Standard Deviation of Scale Scores For CBQ–T Scale Urdu

Scales	Girls (*n* = 173)		Boys (*n* = 290)		Total Sample (*N* = 463)		*d*
	Mean	*(SD)*	*Mean*	*(SD)*	*Mean*	*(SD)*	
Activity Level	4.10	(2.46)	4.48	(2.29)	4.34	(2.35)	-.15
Approach/ Positive Anticipation	3.53	(2.01)	4.00	(1.99)	3.82	(1.99)	-.23
Anger/ Frustration	3.24	(2.00)	3.73	(1.98)	3.54	(1.99)	-.26
Discomfort	3.30	(1.97)	3.54	(1.82)	3.45	(1.87)	-.12
Falling Reactivity/Soothability	3.54	(2.07)	3.71	(1.98)	3.65	(2.00)	-.08
Attentional Focusing	3.56	(2.04)	3.82	(1.93)	3.72	(1.96)	-.13
High Intensity Pleasure	3.46	(2.03)	3.58	(1.86)	3.54	(1.91)	.06
Fear	3.30	(1.96)	3.47	(1.96)	3.41	(1.95)	.08
Impulsivity	3.33	(1.93)	3.46	(1.86)	3.41	(1.88)	.06
Sadness	3.42	(2.03)	3.61	(1.88)	3.54	(1.93)	.09
Shyness	3.46	(2.09)	3.79	(1.95)	3.66	(1.99)	.16
Inhibitory Control	3.56	(2.10)	3.82	(1.99)	3.72	(2.02)	.12
Low Intensity Pleasure	4.31	(2.44)	4.32	(2.21)	4.32	(2.29)	.00
Perceptual Sensitivity	3.66	(2.12)	3.57	(1.96)	3.60	(2.01)	.04
Smiling and Laughter	3.72	(2.13)	3.73	(1.88)	3.72	(1.97)	.00

The mean scores of Urdu version of CBQ-T revealed that the mean scores of girls were slightly lower than those for boys on most of the scales. The mean total scores of this group were observed to be relatively similar to scores of original CBQ-T.

Reliability. In order to assess the reliability of CBQ-T internal consistency, inter scale correlation and correlation of test retest scores were established. The details are given below

The internal consistency of CBQ-T questionnaire Urdu version was evaluated through Cronbach's alpha coefficient. The details of this analysis are provided below

Table 20

Internal Consistency of CBQ – T Urdu and CBQ - T

Scales	Number of Items	CBQ – T Urdu α	CBQ – T (Original) α
Attentional Focusing	6	.92	.79
Anger/ Frustration	6	.91	.86
Activity Level	7	.93	.88
Approach/ Positive Anticipation	6	.92	.81
Falling Reactivity/ Soothability	6	.91	.80
Fear	6	.90	.70
Discomfort	6	.88	.83
High Intensity Pleasure	6	.89	.89
Sadness	7	.92	.68
Impulsivity	6	.88	.83

Scales	Number of Items	CBQ – T Urdu α	CBQ – T (Original) α
Shyness	6	.89	.88
Inhibitory Control	6	.89	.82
Perceptual Sensitivity	6	.89	.71
Low Intensity Pleasure	8	.90	.67
Smiling and Laughter	6	.91	.87

Table showed that all scales of Urdu CBQ-T exhibit good internal consistency as revealed through Cronbach alpha values. The alpha values of Urdu CBQ-T were comparatively higher compared to alpha values of CBQ-T original and ranged from .88 to .93.

Table 21

Test Re Test Reliability of CBQ – T Urdu

Scales	r
Activity Level	.66
Approach/ Positive Anticipation	.54
Anger/ Frustration	.79
Attentional Focusing	.63
Falling Reactivity/ Soothability	.89
Discomfort	.47
High Intensity Pleasure	.53
Fear	.69

Scales	r
Inhibitory Control	.43
Impulsivity	.68
Perceptual Sensitivity	.73
Low Intensity Pleasure	.87
Shyness	.91
Sadness	.49
Smiling and Laughter	.49

**All correlation values are significant at the 0.05 level

Table 21 showed that the intra class coefficients of correlation for all scales of Urdu CBQ-T were in the medium to high range, thus, suggesting excellent stability in scores over a period of time.

Construct Validity of CBQ-T Urdu was established by calculating inter scale and item to subscale total correlation.

Table 22

Correlation Coefficients of Scale Scores of CBQ – Teacher Form Urdu

Scales	1	2	3	4	5	6	7	8	9	10	11	12	13	14	15
1. Activity Level															
2. Anger/ Frustration	.90														
3. Approach/ Positive Anticipation	.92	.88													
4. Attentional Focusing	.94	.92	.93												
5. Discomfort	-.53	.92	.91	.93											
6. Falling Reactivity/ Soothability	.89	.86	.92	.89	.86										
7. Fear	.59	.87	.85	.91	.86	.85									
8. High Intensity Pleasure	.89	.87	.89	.90	.87	.87	.84								
9. Impulsivity	.92	.86	.59	.49	.92	.89	.86	.87							
10. Inhibitory Control	.91	.85	.91	.90	.85	.92	.89	.86	.88						
11. Low Intensity Pleasure	.93	86	.92	.91	.89	.90	.83	.87	.90	.92					
12. Perceptual Sensitivity	.87	.85	.87	.85	.84	.87	.84	.84	.84	.87	.90				
13. Sadness	.49	.89	.90	.91	.90	.89	.85	.88	.86	.88	.83	.79			
14. Shyness	.65	.84	.49	.88	.83	.91	.84	.86	.85	.91	.85	.86	.86		
15. Smiling and Laughter	.91	.53	.91	.91	.88	.90	.85	.88	.90	.89	.90	.86	.49	.89	

**All values are significant at the 0.01 level (2-tailed).

Inter subscale correlation coefficients reveal moderate to strong association among

different subscales of CBQ-T Urdu. Activity level and discomfort shows inverse

relationship.

Table 23

Correlation of Items to Subscale Total of CBQ – T Urdu

Scales	r
Activity Level	.90*
Impulsivity	.81*
High Intensity Pleasure	.84*
Approach/ Positive Anticipation	.90*
Smiling and Laughter	.88*
Shyness	.89*
Anger/ Frustration	.93*
Discomfort	.78*
Falling Reactivity/ Soothability	.89*
Fear	.85*
Sadness	.72*
Inhibitory Control	.60*
Low Intensity Pleasure	.68*
Attentional Focusing	.93*
Perceptual Sensitivity	.79*

* Correlation significant at 0.01 level

The table 23 showed that all items shared very high correlation with the total of their relevant subscales. All correlations between scale scores and total factor score were observed to be positive and significant at p<.01. The detailed analysis revealed that apart from showing a strong correlation with their respective factor subscales showed very low and even inverse

correlation in some cases with scores of others factors

Convergent Validity. Convergent validity was established by examining the degree

of agreement on parental and teacher ratings of the Urdu CBQ-T through correlation.

Table 24

Intra Class Correlations between Parent and Teacher Scores

Scales	r
Activity Level	.73*
Approach/ Positive Anticipation	.61*
Anger/ Frustration	.54*
Attentional Focusing	.89*
Discomfort	.53*
Fear	.76*
Falling Reactivity/ Soothability	.56*
High Intensity Pleasure	.71*
Inhibitory Control	-.55*
Impulsivity	.79*
Perceptual Sensitivity	.88*
Low Intensity Pleasure	.43*
Smiling and Laughter	.60*
Shyness	.69*
Sadness	.70*

p* < 0.05.

All the correlation values were found to be significant and revealed to have moderate to high strength. Parents and teachers significantly agreed while rating attentional focusing and perceptual sensitivity. Teachers and parents tend to disagree the most on inhibitory control scale.

Discriminant Validity. Discriminant validity was evaluated by calculating correlation between scores of CABS and CBQ-T. The results are mentioned in the table below.

Table 25

Correlation between Scores of CABS and Urdu CBQ-T.

Variables	LD	IF	EVA	FRP	Soc
Activity Level	.27**	.40**	.23**	.38**	.69**
Anger/ Frustration	.34**	.19	.11	-.57**	.21
Approach/ Positive Anticipation	.24	.31	.29	.35**	.30
Attentional Focusing	.16	.12	. 26	.10	.23
Falling Reactivity/ Soothability	-.80	-.80	.16	.06	-.16
Discomfort	-.20	.05	.19	.10	.07
High Intensity Pleasure	.09	.17	.09	.26**	.27**
Fear	.15	.11	.03	.17	.13
Inhibitory Control	.02	.01	.07	.05	.01
Impulsivity	.30**	.17	.16	.09	-.18**
Low Intensity Pleasure	.19	.10	.13	-.01	.11
Sadness	.09	.07	.12	.07	.01
Per. Sensitivity	.14	.10	.08	.11	.20
Shyness	-.36	.04	.09	-.49**	-.54**

Note. LD = Language Development; IF= Independent Functioning; EVA= Economic Vocational Activity; FRP= Family Role Performance; Soc = Socialization. **Correlation is significant at the 0.01 level (2-tailed).

Table 25 showed low to moderate values of correlation between scores of CABS and Urdu CBQ-T. This low association between scores indicated the distinct nature of both constructs. The Shyness was negatively associated with language development, family role performance and socialization scales of CABS. Falling reactivity/soothability had negative correlation with language development, independent functioning and socialization scales of CABS. Anger/frustration, discomfort, impulsivity and low intensity were observed to have negative correlation with family role performance, language development, socialization and family role performance respectively. The highest positive correlation was between activity level and socialization while highest negative correlation was between falling reactivity/soothability and language development and independent functioning.

The results in general provided evidence of adequate substantive and external validity for Urdu CBQ-T scale.

Discussion

In past few decades linguistic diversity emerged as an important cultural factor that influences the process of psychological assessment (Hambleton, 2006). The relevant literature in this area underscores the importance of translating and adapting assessment instruments not only to make them culturally relevant but to improve the efficacy of those assessment instruments across cultures. Present research is a related attempt to translate and adapt CBQ-T short scale in Urdu to make it culturally relevant.

The first part of the current study was focused around preparing a culturally relevant tool that can be used to assess temperament of children. Standard guidelines and procedures were used to translate and adapt CBQ –T questionnaire in Urdu. The translation procedures employed in the present study were those suggested in literature (Hambleton, 2006) and supported by the theorists working particularly in temperament and personality research (Rothbart et al., 2001). During the course of translation process, seven items of CBQ-T scale were modified in order to make them culturally more relevant and to increase their comprehension. For instance, the word "boogie man" in item 17 ("Is afraid when hearing about ideas such as *boogie man*" or when hearing about *burglars*" or others who pose a threat") was replaced with "ghosts/monsters" as boogie man is not frequently used in Pakistan. The CBQ-T item 90 ("Remains pretty calm about upcoming desserts like ice cream") was slightly changed and words like custard, kheer and halwa were added into it, as experts believed that a large majority can relate more easily with the names of local desserts. Qualitative review of each item and content validity index were used to finalize the Urdu version of CBQ-T.

The qualitative expert review and CVI ratings assisted in establishing the content validity as part of substantive validity of the translated CBQ-T version (Allana et al., 2013). The items were assessed for degree of relevance with the temperament construct, cultural relevance and comprehensibility with reference to Pakistan. Each translated item was evaluated through item content validity index (I-CVI) followed by calculation of scale content validity index (S-CVI) to assess the quality of translation. Items with I-CVI value of 1 was chosen as literature suggested that when less than eight experts are involved in item rating, I-CVI value of 1 is considered good (Haynes et al., 1995). Equal importance was given to all three dimensions mentioned above, therefore, any item having ICVI value lower than 1 on either of the two dimensions was reviewed and sent either for revised translation or modified after discussion with original author of the scale. All of the items but seven found to have adequate CVI values and therefore, suggested adequate evidence of content validity of the Urdu version as mentioned in literature (Devon et al., 2007; Yaghmaie, 2003). The items that received ICVI values lower than 1 were modified as mentioned earlier (Allana et al., 2013). This process paved the way for establishing further psychometric properties of the selected items.

All fifteen subscales of Urdu CBQ-T achieved alpha coefficients greater than .80 and falls in the good range of reliability (DeVellis, 1991). Although, the alpha value of 0.7 is considered a good benchmark for internal consistency, measures developed for clinical purposes typically expected to have higher alpha values (Nunnally & Bernstein, 1994). The reliability of Urdu CBQ-T scales was observed to be ranging from 0.86 to 0.94 which is adequately required for clinical screening tools (Parsian & Dunning, 2009) and therefore, suggest strong internal consistency. The inter scale correlation was also observed to be significantly high supporting the alpha values and therefore, the internal consistency of the scale (Nunnally & Bernstein, 1994).

The association between mother and teacher's rating was carried out to ascertain convergent validity for Urdu CBQ-T questionnaire. In general, correlation coefficients were significant but of varied strength. The scales that assessed dimensions of temperament that usually remain stable across school and home environment received higher degree of agreement like attentional focusing scale. However, on the other hand, the negative association on inhibitory control scale may indicate the influences on that dimension of behavior. Usually, children are observed to be more compliant and concerned about maintaining discipline in school compared to home; this might have resulted in negative association on scores of this particular scale. The moderate to high correlation coefficients on most of the scales provided a good evidence of external validity and supported the Urdu CBQ – T as a valid tool. Results about the discriminant validity of the scale presented an interesting picture. Although, most of the correlation values were observed to be low or negative supporting the distinct constructs of the two scales, still some values revealed significant positive associations. For instance, the correlation coefficient between (CBQ-T subscale)"activity level" and (CABS's subscales) "socialization" and "independent functioning" noted to have significant positive correlation. These three scales are theoretically related and share some common underline characteristics which might have resulted in significant positive correlation among these dimensions. In general, low and negative correlation values are interpreted as indicator of discriminant power of scales (Husain, 2012) which supports the present scale as a valid tool which can used to assess temperament of children.

Overall, the mean scale scores for boys were slightly higher than the scores of girls across most of the Urdu CBQ-T scales. This finding revealed a trend of scores in line with the trend shown in CBQ-T and CBQ – T short scales, where the mean scale scores of male children were somewhat higher compared to female children of the same age. This could also be taken as an indication of adequate validity as the Urdu CBQ-T shared similar features with original CBQ – T and short form of CBQ – T.

The current study was the first systematic investigation to translate and establish psychometric properties of CBQ-T. In general, the present study revealed acceptable levels of internal consistency as well as substantive and external validity and it appeared that Urdu

CBQ-T (Appendix – R) might provide accurate assessment information about children's temperament.

Study – II. Translation and Adaptation of Temperament in Middle Childhood Questionnaire.

The importance of culturally relevant measures cannot be undermined, they also stress that to achieve this goal the process of instrument translation and adaptation should focus on establishing conceptual, idiomatic, experiential and semantic equivalence (Borsa, Damasio & Bandeira, 2012). TMCQ is often used to assess different dimensions of temperament among 8 to 11 years old children. However, the content and language biases and absence of local norms limit the utility of TMCQ in Pakistan. Keeping in view these limitations, this phase of the study was planned around following objectives.

Objectives.

1. Translating TMCQ – Short form into Urdu.

2. To establish the psychometric properties of TMCQ Urdu version.

Sample

The sample for this phase was divided into three groups, sample A and B was primarily used to translate and back translate the scale. Whereas, sample C comprised participants on whom the translated version of TMCQ was administered to test the psychometric characteristics of the scale. Sample A comprised a group of 20 (for the 2 steps of this study) bilingual graduates of Beaconhouse National University, University of Punjab, Kinnaird College and Government College University, Lahore with good understanding of both Urdu and English language. Sample B consisted of two language experts, two PhD scholars, two clinical psychologists and a school teacher, all having 8 to 10 years of professional experience along with good command over Urdu and English language. In sample C a group of 248 children including both boys (52%) and girls (48%) was selected through random sampling technique at grade level. The mean age of this sample was 9.91 ($SD = 1.15$ years), the details are mentioned in appendix – S. Total 9 teachers out of 10 gave consent to fill the forms for their students, the mean age of teachers was 30.1 years and mean teaching experience was 3.2 years. This group was approached at 2 public, 3 private schools and 2 private academic coaching centers of Lahore. Only those teachers were selected who were well familiar with children for whom they had filled the scale.

Procedure

The procedure of translation employed in last phase was used to translate TMCQ teacher scale through following steps.

Step 1: Translation of CBQ in Urdu. After receiving permission from the authors, TMCQ form was sent to 10 participants of Sample A along with a detailed instructional letter used in study-I of this phase. Only 2 participants failed to return the translation within the given time period of three weeks, whereas, 3 participants sent incomplete translations with 23 percent items missing. All the translated items were thoroughly scrutinized by a committee of experts mentioned as sample B following the same procedure used in last phase.

Step 2: Back Translation of Translated Items into English. Then the Urdu translation of TMCQ was sent to another 10 graduates from sample A requesting them to translate the Urdu items back in English language. Only four participants send complete back translation within given time period. After back translation all the items were carefully reviewed by the experts committee.

Step 3: Content Review of Translated Items. The committee of experts then evaluated the cultural relevance for content of all items of TMCQ scale. Five items in TMCQ were identified as not having culturally relevant expression and/or content on the basis of ICVI and SCVI values.

Step 4: Review of Back Translation by Original Author. The final back translation of TMCQ was sent to the authors of instrument for their review by following the procedure followed in last study. Once the original authors approved that conceptual meaning of original statements had been maintained; a final version of TMCQ-T short form Urdu version was finalized.

Step 5: Pilot Study. A group of 10 teachers of sample D rated 10 selected children on TMCQ. The procedure of pilot study mentioned in last phase was employed. The result did not suggest making any pertinent changes.

Step 6: Establishing Psychometric Characteristics of TMCQ – Teacher Scale (Urdu). This step aimed at developing psychometric characteristics of translated version of TMCQ-T short scale. Construct, convergent and discriminant validities were established along with internal consistency, inter rater and test re test reliabilities.

***Convergent validity*.** Convergent validity was established by examining the degree of agreement on parental and teacher ratings of the Urdu TMCQ scale. For this purpose, 50 students were randomly selected from sample C and their mothers were requested to fill the scale along with teachers.

***Discriminant validity*.** Intellectual functioning measured in terms of IQ was used to evaluate the discriminant validity of the scale. For this purpose, a group of 30 children was randomly extracted from the sample and SIT was administered on them in individual sessions.

Test re test reliability. To calculate the test re test reliability TMCQ Urdu was administered on a small group of 33 children from sample C. The time gap between two administrations was almost 8 to 11 weeks. Same rater was used to perform the two ratings.

Results.

This section consists of main analyses done to evaluate the initial psychometric properties of the Urdu TMCQ. The main aim was to assess the general trend of scores, evaluate basic indices of validity, including content validity, convergent and divergent validity. Other than that this study also attempted to assess the consistency of the measure and its outcome scores, to do so internal consistency and the stability of scores over a period of time was assessed. To achieve all these objectives the descriptive statistics, Pearson product moment, independent sample t-test, intraclass correlation and Cronbach's alpha coefficient were calculated to analyze data of present study. All procedures were carried out through SPSS (20.0). The first section presents the descriptive analysis of the Urdu TMCQ to see the general trend in scores and compared it with the scores of original TMCQ. The second section represents the psychometric evaluation of the Urdu version. The details of all these procedures are covered in table 26 through table 33.

Table 26

Mean and Standard Deviation of Scale Scores For TMCQ *Scale Urdu*

Scales	Girls (n = 119)		Boys (n = 129)		Total Sample (N = 248)		Variance	d
	Mean	*(Sd)*	*Mean*	*(SD)*	*Mean*	*(SD)*		
Active Control	2.94	(.71)	2.76	(.65)	2.85	(.68)	.91	.26
Affiliation	3.41	(.86)	3.25	(.97)	3.35	(.91)	.84	.17
Activity Level	3.26	(.88)	3.49	(1.03)	3.38	(.95)	.91	-.24
Anger	3.31	(1.21)	3.21	(1.25)	3.25	(1.22)	1.49	.08
Assertiveness/ Dominance	3.22	(1.03)	2.98	(1.07)	3.10	(1.05)	1.10	.22
Attentional Focusing	2.82	(.94)	2.47	(.92)	2.64	(.93)	.87	.37
Discomfort	3.26	(.95)	3.06	(.81)	3.17	(.89)	.79	.22
Soothability	2.87	(.75)	2.94	(.61)	2.88	(.68)	.46	-.10
Fantasy	3.42	(.80)	3.16	(.90)	3.29	(.85)	.73	.30
Fear	3.65	(.87)	3.25	(1.00)	3.45	(.99)	.99	.42
High Intensity Pleasure	3.42	(.89)	3.39	(.92)	3.40	(.90)	.81	.03
Impulsivity	3.22	(.78)	3.29	(.94)	3.25	(.86)	.74	-.08
Inhibitory Control	2.97	(.85)	2.79	(.77)	2.90	(.83)	.69	.22
Low Intensity Pleasure	3.32	(.85)	2.93	(.86)	3.12	(.88)	.77	.45
Perceptual Sensitivity	3.21	(.77)	3.01	(.93)	3.12	(.86)	.75	.23
Sadness	3.12	(.82)	2.96	(.74)	3.05	(.78)	.62	.20
Shyness	2.99	(.92)	2.96	(.84)	2.98	(.87)	.75	.03

The table 26 presented the mean score of girls and boys on all subscales of temperament. The mean scores of both boys and girls were relatively similar.

Table 27

Mean and Standard Deviation of TMCQ Original and TMCQ Urdu

Scales	TMCQ Original		TMCQ Urdu		Variance	*d*
	Mean	*(SD)*	*Mean*	*(SD)*		
Active Control	3.42	(.49)	2.85	(.68)	.91	.72
Affiliation	4.20	(.45)	3.35	(.91)	.84	1.18
Activity Level	3.86	(.67)	3.38	(.95)	.91	.58
Anger	2.79	(.63)	3.25	(1.22)	1.49	-.47
Assertiveness/ Dominance	3.53	(.48)	3.10	(1.05)	1.10	.52
Attentional Focusing	3.41	(.83)	2.64	(.93)	.87	1.00
Discomfort	2.30	(.60)	3.17	(.89)	.79	-1.14
Soothability	3.66	(.59)	2.88	(.68)	.46	1.22
Fantasy	4.07	(.53)	3.29	(.85)	.73	1.10
Fear	2.32	(.67)	3.45	(.99)	.99	-1.33
High Intensity Pleasure	3.41	(.60)	3.40	(.90)	.81	.01
Impulsivity	2.67	(.67)	3.25	(.86)	.74	-.75
Inhibitory Control	3.44	(.56)	2.90	(.83)	.69	.76
Low Intensity Pleasure	3.66	(.50)	3.12	(.88)	.77	.75
Perceptual Sensitivity	3.31	(.61)	3.12	(.86)	.75	.25
Sadness	2.50	(.53)	3.05	(.78)	.62	-.84
Shyness	2.57	(.77)	2.98	(.87)	.75	-.49

The table 27 presented mean score of TMCQ Urdu and TMCQ original providing a relatively similar trend and comparable mean scores.

Reliability Estimation. In order to assess the reliability of TMCQ internal consistency, inter scale correlation and correlation of test retest scores were established. The details are given below

Internal Consistency. The internal consistency of TMCQ Urdu version was assessed though Cronbach's alpha coefficient.

Table 28

Internal Consistency of TMCQ Urdu and TMCQ Original

Scales	Number of Items	TMCQ Urdu α	TMCQ (Original) α
Attentional Focusing	7	.79	.92
Activity Level	9	.83	.89
Assertiveness	8	.84	.74
Activity Control	15	.76	.80
Affiliation	10	.69	.77
Anger/ Frustration	7	.89	.79
Fantasy	9	.77	.80
Soothability	5	.78	.76
Discomfort	10	.84	.76
Fear	9	.86	.75
Impulsivity	13	.87	.90

High Intensity Pleasure	11	.82	.82
Inhibitory Control	8	.72	.73
Perceptual Sensitivity	10	.78	.82
Low Intensity Pleasure	8	.76	.67
Sadness	10	.84	.77
Shyness	5	.65	.83

Table 28 showed that all scales of Urdu TMCQ exhibited acceptable to good internal consistency as revealed through Cronbach alpha values. The alpha values of Urdu TMCQ were from .65 to .89 compared to alpha values of TMCQ original that ranged from .67 to .92.

Table 29

Test Re Test Reliability of TMCQ Urdu

Scales	r
Activity Level	.56*
Attentional Focusing	.43*
Anger/ Frustration	.39*
Activity Control	.46*
Affiliation	.67*
Assertiveness	.48*
Discomfort	.50*
Fantasy	.49*

	r
Fear	.60*
High Intensity Pleasure	.47*
Inhibitory Control	.81*
Soothability	.39*
Impulsivity	.66*
Low Intensity Pleasure	.50*
Shyness	.60*
Sadness	.53*
Perceptual Sensitivity	.62*

All values are significant at p<.05

Table 29 showed that the intra class coefficients of correlation for all scales of Urdu TMCQ were significant and in the medium to high range, thus, suggesting good consistency in scores over a period of time.

Validity Estimates. The following section contains details about validity analyses of TMCQ Urdu. First in this regard subscale to total factor and interscale correlations are established. The details are given below

Table 30

Subscales to total Scores Correlation Coefficients for TMCQ - Urdu

Scales	r
Activity Level	.90**
Activity Control	.79**
Affiliation	.81**

Anger/ Frustration	.88**
Attentional Focusing	.92**
Assertiveness	.88**
Fear	.91**
Discomfort	.85**
Fantasy	.90**
Soothability	.83**
High Intensity Pleasure	.91**
Inhibitory Control	.80**
Impulsivity	.93**
Low Intensity Pleasure	.86**
Sadness	.89**
Perceptual Sensitivity	.79**
Shyness	.84**

**p<.01

In table 30 all items revealed to have strong positive correlation with the total score of subscales in which they were placed.

Table 31

Correlation Coefficients for Subscales of TMCQ Urdu

Variables	1	2	3	4	5	6	7	8	9	10	11	12	13	14	15
1. Alev															
2. HIP	.76**														
3. Imp	.71**	.82**													
4. Shyn	.39**	.47**	.49**												
5. Aff	.18*	.06	.01	-.04											
6. Assert	.45**	.43**	.37**	-.13	.18*										
7. ACon	.42**	.34**	.27**	.22**	.34**	.14									
8. Afoc	.38**	.32**	.26**	.48**	.05	-.01	.48**								
9. ICon	.37**	.31**	.29**	.54**	.05	-.12	.49**	.76**							
10. LIP	.44**	.47**	.41**	.56**	.09	.04	.42**	.59**	.67**						
11. Per	.45**	.49**	.43**	.57**	.20*	.07	.46**	.58**	.58**	.74**					
12. AFru	-.47**	-.39**	-.40**	-.43**	-.22*	-.06	-.33**	-.35**	-.41**	-.44**	-.28**				
13. Disc	-.63**	-.56**	-.62**	-.44**	-.03	-.24**	-.27**	-.37**	-.39**	-.43**	-.35**	.74**			
14. FO	.17*	.19*	.09	-.07	.35**	.42**	.13	-.01	-.05	.14	.17*	-.01	-.01		
15. Fear	-.59**	-.55**	-.57**	-.37**	-.03	-.28**	-.22**	-.29**	-.31**	-.36**	-.29**	.69**	.94**	-.07	
16. Sad	-.57**	-.49**	-.53**	-.43**	-.11	-.21*	-.28**	-.35**	-.39**	-.46**	-.33**	.83**	.91**	-.09	.91**
17. So	-.45**	-.47**	-.55**	-.43**	-.04	-.18*	-.13	-.24**	-.28**	-.40**	-.31**	.69**	.79**	-.01	.76**

Note. Activity level, High intensity pleasure; Impulsivity; Shyness; Affiliation;
Assertiveness; Activity control; Attentional focusing; Inhibitory control; Low intensity
pleasure; Perceptual sensitivity; anger frustration; Discomfort; Fantasy openness; Fear;
Sadness; Soothability.
**p < . 01, *p < . 05

The table 31 presented correlation between subscales of TMCQ Urdu and revealed

non significant negative to significant positive correlation among different subscales.

Convergent Validity. Convergent validity was established by examining the degree of agreement on parental and teacher ratings of the Urdu *TMCQ* scales through correlation.

Table 32

Intra Class Correlations between Parent and Teacher Scores

Scales	*r*
Activity Level	.82*
Affiliation	.55*
Impulsivity	.45*
Shyness	.40*
High Intensity Pleasure	.47*
Anger/ Frustration	.62*
Activity Control	.79*
Soothability	.69*
Discomfort	.78*
Fear	.50*
Attentional Focusing	.73*
Low Intensity Pleasure	.77*
Inhibitory Control	.60*
Perceptual Sensitivity	.59*
Sadness	.42*

p * < 0.05.

All the correlations were observed to be significant and of moderate to high strength. The ratings of mothers and teachers suggest adequate consistency and agreement over all scales of TMCQ Urdu.

Divergent Validity. Divergent validity was evaluated by calculating correlation between scores of SIT and *TMCQ*. The results are mentioned in the table below.

Table 33

Correlation between Scores of IQ and TMCQ Urdu.

TMCQ Scales	*r*
Activity Level	.30**
Affiliation	.03
Impulsivity	.28**
Shyness	.25**
High Intensity Pleasure	.32**
Assertiveness	.17*
Anger/ Frustration	-.28**
Activity Control	.21**
Fantasy	.07
Soothability	-.21*
Discomfort	-.31**
Fear	-.29**
Attentional Focusing	.39**
Low Intensity Pleasure	.34**
Inhibitory Control	.37**

Perceptual Sensitivity	.31**
Sadness	-.30**

**p<.01 , *p<.05 (2 tailed).

The correlation coefficients presented in table 33 revealed significant negative correlation to low significant positive correlation of IQ with various scales of TMCQ Urdu. IQ assessed through Slosson Intelligence Test and compared with the scores of TMCQ Urdu. The table suggested a weak association between these two constructs as IQ revealed inverse association with indices that were generally believed to adversely affect the score on intelligence measures like fear, anger, sadness and low association even with the positive temperamental traits (Matrnat, 2009) supporting the underline distinct nature of both intelligence and temperament constructs.

Overall the results of this study provided good evidence of adequate substantive and external validity for TMCQ Urdu.

Discussion

For clinical experts using psychological measures that can give accurate and reliable reflections of an individual's functioning has always been a significant concern (Mushquash & Bova, 2007). Cultural and linguistic relevance emerged as two significant dimensions in literature that can affect the accuracy of assessment outcome (Paniagua, 1994; Flanagan, McGrew & Oritz, 2000; Sattler, 2001). The present study was designed to translate and adapt TMCQ in Urdu language and to evaluate the psychometric features of the newly adapted questionnaire. A standard procedure was followed for translation and adaptation covering significant technical aspects. Both forward and back translation procedures and final review and approval of original authors were used to ensure the translation and content adequacy and as these procedures were used by other researches translating Rothbart's temperament instruments (Klein, Putnam, & Linhares, 2009).

This study used two significant types of reliability namely internal consistency and test re test to evaluate translated version of TMCQ (Mehmood, 2010; Peneva et al., 2013). Alpha values for all subscales of TMCQ Urdu were generated as most experts consider it a good practice to evaluate alpha for all subscales rather than only relying on single alpha for total scale (Tavakol, Dennick, 2011). The findings of internal consistency analysis revealed a somewhat similar trend observed in original scale reported recently (Kotelnikova, 2016). Two subscales of TMCQ have alpha coefficient values between .65 and .69, Putnam and Rothbart (2006) also observed alpha coefficients in .60 to .69 range for some subscales of CBQ short form and very short forms. The two subscales revealed relatively weak alpha values that experts usually denote to fewer number of items, in lowest alpha value is present case was observed for shyness subscale that only contained 5 items (Tavakol, Dennick, 2011). Inter rater and test re test reliability analyses though reveal relatively low intra class correlation values compared to values observed for CBQ-T Urdu, still managed to provide satisfactory evidences to support the reliability of TMCQ Urdu. As these three methods are often employed as good measures of consistency to investigate the reliability of assessment instruments it can be concluded that the adapted TMCQ Urdu is a reliable instrument to measure temperament in children (Hossein et al.,2013).

For validity, the first step was to calculate the ICV-I based on the expert's ratings for all items and only those items were selected that received that ICVI value of 1. ICVI method is valued for providing a good indication of cross cultural relevance and accuracy of item translation (Squires et al., 2012). The construct validity of TMCQ Urdu was established by evaluating the trend in scale mean scores, inter subscale correlation and item to subscale correlations. The mean scores follow the general trend reported in original TMCQ. The item to subscales and inter scale correlations also support the evidence of construct validity by presenting relatively similar trends. The correlation between intellectual functioning and TMCQ scales also show an interesting trend that indirectly supports the construct validity as it revealed negative correlation of IQ with subscales like fear, Anger frustration, discomfort and sadness. These states are often considered to adversely affect or suppress the performance on measures of intellectual functioning (Marnat, 2009).

Negative and weak correlation between intellectual functioning measured in terms of IQ and TMCQ Urdu scores provided evidence of acceptable levels of discriminant validity. The moderate to high correlations between item and total subscale scores, consistency of reporting across teachers and mothers ratings and markers of internal consistency all supported an acceptable level of good convergent validity for TMCQ Urdu.

The strong efforts were made to employ the set of procedures frequently mentioned in literature to establish psychometric characteristics of measurement instruments (Carter, Briggs-Gowan, Jones & Little, 2003). Strong preliminary validity of TMCQ Urdu was evidently supported by almost all the analyses used in the present study.

Study – III. Assessment of Adaptive Skills: Psychosocial Correlates and Predictors in Children with ID, ASD and Typical Development.

Development of children is a complex process that continues over a period of significant time of human life. During the course of development, children get exposed to a broad number of factors that directly or indirectly influence the quality and pace of developmental dimensions in varied ways. The present study of this research was designed as an attempt to assess adaptive skills and to explore the contribution of personal and familial demographic variables in development and prediction of adaptive skills among children following different developmental patterns. Children's age, gender, cognitive functioning, behavioral problems, presence of disability and temperament are believed to influence their development in multiple ways, therefore, these variables were selected as main personal demographic variables to study. Apart from the personal variables, family variables like family system, number of siblings, parental age, education, marital status and family income were amongst the main variables of interest in the present study. Following objectives were made in order to assess the influence of these variables on the development of adaptive skills.

Objective.

The objectives of this study mentioned as follows

1. To assess and compare the pattern of adaptive skill scores of children with intellectual disability, autism spectrum disorder and typical development.

2. To explore the association between cognitive level and adaptive skills scores.

3. To identify age wise differences in adaptive skill scores of children with typical development, ID and ASD.

4. To evaluate gender differences in adaptive skill scores of the participants.

5. To explore and compare the temperamental traits of children with ID, ASD and those having typical development.

6. To explore the gender differences in temperament profiles of children across three groups.

7. To identify the association between adaptive skills and temperament among children of three developmental groups.

8. To assess the association of demographic variables with adaptive skill scores.

Hypotheses.

Following hypotheses were made to meet the mentioned objectives

1. There is significant mean difference in adaptive skill scores of children with typical development, ID and ASD.

2. Cognitive functioning is positively associated with adaptive skill scores.

3. The adaptive skill scores of children with intellectual disability are significantly higher than children with Autism spectrum disorder.

4. Younger children have significantly lower score on all domains of adaptive skills than older children across groups.

5. The adaptive skill scores of boys and girls are significantly different.

6. Behavioral problems among ID and ASD children are negatively associated with adaptive skills scores.

7. Parental education has significant positive relationship with adaptive skills scores.

8. Parental marital status (intact marriage) is significantly associated with adaptive skills scores.

9. Family income is positively correlated with adaptive skill scores.

10. Number of siblings is positively associated with adaptive skill scores.

11. Joint family system is positively related to adaptive skill scores.

12. Domains of temperament differ significantly across developmental groups.

13. Adaptive skill scores are inversely associated with negative affectivity.

14. Intellectual quotient is a significant predictor of adaptive skill scores.

15. Gender is a significant predictor of scores on different adaptive skill sub domains.

16. Family income is a strong predictor of adaptive skill scores.

17. Disability status is a strong predictor of adaptive skill scores.

Sample. Non probability purposive sampling method was employed to select a sample of 436 children for this study. The g-power analysis holding significance level of 0.05 with medium effect size was used to calculate the sample for main statistical procedures. The sample was divided into three subgroups, A, B and C. Sample comprised children with intellectual disability ($n = 105$), sample B included children with ASD ($n = 92$) and sample C consisted of typically developing children ($n = 239$). The age range for all participants was from 5 to 11 years and included both boys and girls. The sample A and B were approached in developmental pediatric department, child psychiatry departments and special education institutes of Lahore city. Case files of all children seeking services were reviewed and only those children were selected who fulfilled the inclusion criteria. Children with typical development were recruited from mainstream public and private schools, academic coaching centers and institutes that offer swimming, martial arts, music and arts courses during summer vacations. The selection of schools was based on convenient sampling.

Inclusion Criteria. From mainstream schools only those children were selected who got more than 70 percent scores in their last two examinations and who gave assent for the procedure. For clinical group children with a single diagnosis of ID and ASD were selected. Only those children were selected in clinical group who were assessed on standardized tools and whose reliable informant was available.

Exclusion Criteria. Children below 5 or above 11 years of age were excluded from the sample. Comorbid developmental psychopathologies, incomplete or no standardized assessment and absence of a reliable informant were the other exclusion criteria for children in the clinical group.

Instruments. The measures used to collect information in this study included consent form, demographic questionnaire, Adaptive Behavior Scale, Childhood Behavior Questionnaire and Temperament of Middle Childhood Behavior Questionnaire. The details are mentioned below

Consent Form. Consent form designed and used in previous studies of this research project was used in this study (Appendix – D).

Demographic Questionnaire. The demographic questionnaire used in previous studies was completed for each child along with the other measures. It requested basic questions related to personal information of the children and their family. For children with developmental disabilities, few changes were made in the demographic form like instead of marks in last two exams, IQ was included. Some new information regarding clinical diagnosis was also added such as clinical diagnosis, history of psychiatric illness in the family, details of structured assessment, behavioral management plans, type of professional services seek and total duration of professional help seeking (Appendix – I).

Indigenous Adaptive Behavior Scale. The indigenous adaptive behavior scale developed in study I was completed for each child to assess the adaptive skills of children studied in this phase. The scale was individually administered and consisted of a composite adaptive functioning score and four subscales score. The four subscales are daily living skills, social skills, self-care skills and home living skills. In total 29 items are scored on a scale ranging from 0 to 4, whereas, all other items are scored as 0 or 1. This scale demonstrated satisfactory psychometric characteristics along with adequate sensitivity and specificity analyses (Appendix – L).

Children's Behavior Questionnaire – Teacher Short Form (CBQ-T). In order to assess the temperament of children CBQ-T, Urdu version was used. It consists of 94 items and developed by Teglasi (2003), assesses three broader big five domains and 17 temperamental dimensions. The scale is usually used to assess the temperamental traits of children ages 5 to 7 years. Teachers rate children on 7 point Likert scale from extremely untrue (1) of this child to extremely true (7) of this child keeping in mind the child's behavior in past six months. If the child is not observed in a given situation then 0 is given (Teglasi, 2003; Putnam, Rothbart, 2006). Like other temperamental scales of Rothbart, CBQ-T reported to have good evidence of adequate reliability and validity. The alpha ranges from .67 to .89 (Teglasi, 2003), .65 to.93 and interrater reliability ranging from .45 to .80 with good stability over time (Putnam & Rothbart, 2006). The questionnaire was translated and adapted to be used in the present study. The translated questionnaire revealed strong psychometric characteristics (details are mentioned in last study).

Temperament in Middle Childhood Questionnaire (TMCQ). TMCQ comprised 157 statements and developed by Rothbart in 1989, assesses 15 sub temperamental dimensions grouped into three broader big five domains namely surgency, effortful control and negative affectivity. Parents and or teachers rate children on 5 point Likert scale from extremely (1) untrue of this child to extremely true (5) of this child keeping in mind the child's behavior in past six months. If the child is not observed in a given situation then 0 is given (Rothbart, 1989). TMCQ noted to have a good evidence of adequate psychometric characteristics. The alpha ranges from .79 to .90 (Putnam & Rothbart, 2001), the reliability ranges from .59 to.96 and validity ranges from .36 to .81 (Putnam, 2005). TMCQ is a frequently used scale to assess the temperament of children from 8 to 11 years of age.

Procedure. For typically developing children, after sorting a general permission from Secretary School Education, Punjab and school administration, consent was also taken from teachers. A list of students was prepared for each class, and students were randomly selected from that list. Each teacher was given the list of randomly selected students and was requested to fill the temperament scales for all identified children from their classes. The researcher assisted teachers in filling out the first few forms and gave behavioral examples as needed. Only two teachers seek this assistance for first few scales and filled later scales independently. The demographic sheets were sent home to be filled by the parents or any other family member and the adaptive behavior scale was administered by the researcher. In the end all participants were verbally thanked for participation and offered a free session to discuss principles of effective class room management or provided information on any other topic of their interest related to effective teaching. In total 89 percent participants were availed the free session.

For clinical group, after sorting permission from concerned authorities and consent from parents, researcher first reviewed the personal files of the children seeking professional services for developmental psychopathologies. Only those files were chosen that included a formal clinical diagnosis along with complete developmental and syndrome specific assessment on standardized tools by a professionally trained clinical psychologist. Files that lack the assessment details and or clinical diagnosis were not considered for selection. Then the relevant details of assessment like clinical diagnosis, IQ, duration of professional service utilization and nature of individualized educational plan were noted. An interview was conducted with the caregivers for completing the above mentioned measures. At the end caregivers were offered a free debriefing session which was availed by almost 91 percent participants.

The research design and procedures were reviewed and approved by both the research supervisor and committee of experts that analyzed both technical and ethical considerations. The researcher took care of all relevant ethical considerations. Consent to collect data was sorted from administration of concerned institutes, teachers and parents. Assent was also taken from children before starting the administration. The scales were not administered on any child who didn't give any assent.

Results. The data was analyzed with the assistance of SPSS (20.0) and findings are reported in the following section. The first section discusses the personal and familial characteristics of the participants, whereas, the later section presents the findings related to the hypotheses formulated for this study. Descriptive statistics, correlation, multiple linear regression analysis, t test, analysis of variance and multivariate analysis of variance are carried out to analyze the data of this study.

Sample Characteristics. The first section of results presents details of the personal demographic characteristics of participants along with their family demographic variables, all these characteristics are explored for combined sample as well as for each sub sample separately. The details are mentioned in the tables below.

Table 34

Personal Demographic Characteristics of the Sample

	ID	ASD	TD	Full Sample
	(n = 105)	*(n = 92)*	*(n = 239)*	*(N = 436)*
Gender				
% Girls	43.8 %	33.7 %	43.1 %	41.3 %
% Boys	56.2 %	66.3 %	56.9 %	58.7 %
Age				
Mean	9.02	8.62	7.94	8.34
SD	2.02	1.87	1.99	2.02
IQ				
Mean	41.67	37.37	91.41[a]	91.41[b]
SD	14.52	8.09	7.28	7.28

Note. ID = Intellectual Disability; TD = Typical Development; ASD = Autism Spectrum Disorder.

a. Only 54 children in typically developing group were assessed for cognitive functioning. b. N = 250.

The sample was distributed in three groups, 24 percent of the total sample comprised intellectual disability group, 20.5 percent represented in autism spectrum group and 55.5 percent consisted of children with typical development. Overall, the percentage of girls in this sample is lower compared to the boys, this difference is highest in ASD group. Majority of the children in total sample were first born (mode = 1; percentage = 34.9), whereas most of the children in typically developed group were second born (31.7 percent), first born in both ID (39 percent) and ASD (42.2 percent) groups. Only 54 children in typically developing group were assessed for intelligence. The mean IQ of children in typically developing group was highest, whereas, of children in ID group was slightly higher compared to children in ASD group. In total, 45.9 percent children in ID group reported to have behavioral problems and this percentage is 46.5 % in ASD sample.

Other than the personal characteristics of children, significant demographic characteristics of family were also assessed. The information is mentioned in the following table.

Table 35

Family Demographic Characteristics of Sample (N = 436)

Variables	ID	ASD	TD	Full Sample
Family System				
% Joint	53.3 %	53.3 %	59.8 %	57.0 %
% Nuclear	46.7 %	46.7 %	40.2 %	43.2 %
Mother's Age				
Mean	35.73	36.32	37.70	36.95
SD	7.52	5.47	4.65	5.68
Father's Age				
Mean	40.35	41.56	42.22	41.62
SD	7.14	6.71	4.67	5.85
Marital Status of Parents				
% Married	82.9%	71.7 %	95 %	87 %
% Divorced	14.3 %	19.6 %	3.7 %	9.8 %
% Widow	2.9 %	8.7 %	1.3 %	3.2 %

Variables	ID	ASD	TD	Full Sample
Family Income				
Mean	51750.00	53164.38	46208.33	43908.49
Mode	30000	30000	60000	15000

Majority of the children in all three groups had 3 siblings with 34.9 percent in total sample, 26.7 percent in TD, 23.8 percent in ID and 27.2 percent in ASD groups. The range of number of sibling is from having no sibling to 10 siblings among typically developing children and ASD groups; however, this range was from no sibling to 8 siblings in ID group. Majority of children was living in joint family setup and this trend was observed to be same across all groups. The mode family income was 15000 and it ranged from 6000 to 500000. For ID group the range of family income was from 6000 to 170000, for ASD and TD groups it was from 10000 to 500000 and from 8000 to 200000 respectively. The occupation of father differed across groups, majority of fathers in TD group were associated with business (41 percent), with job in ID (23.3 percent) and ASD (31.7 percent) groups (Appendix- T, U and Appendix-V). A large majority of mothers in all groups was found to be housewives. In TD group majority of mothers were educated till graduation (29.7 %) whereas most of the mothers in ID (28.7%) and ASD (26.8 %) groups were illiterate. Similarly, majority of the fathers were educated till graduation in TD (32.7 %) and ASD (27.1) groups, however, in ID group most of the father received education till tenth grade (21.7).

Table 36

Education and Occupation of Fathers Across Groups

	ID	ASD	TD
	Percentage	*Percentage*	*Percentage*
Education			
Illiterate	20.55 %	13.7 %	13.6 %
Below Matric	18.1 %	11 %	6.4 %
Matric	21.7 %	13.7 %	9.1 %
Intermediate	15.7 %	15.1 %	14.5 %
Graduation	8.4 %	27.1 %	32.7 %
Masters	15.7 %	20.5 %	21.8 %
Post Masters	-	-	1.8 %
Occupation			
Laborer	11 %	7.9 %	23.6 %
Domestic Helper	-	1.6 %	-
Skilled worker	20.5 %	7.9 %	3.6 %
Farmer	4.1 %	-	.5 %
Banker	4.1 %	9.5 %	3.2 %
Engineer	5.5 %	4.8 %	.9 %
Doctor	2.7 %	6.3 %	1.8 %
Teacher	6.8 %	1.6 %	.9 %
Business	21.9 %	28.6 %	46.8 %
Lawyers	-	-	.5 %
Job	23.3 %	31.7 %	18.2 %

The occupation of fathers differed across groups, majority of fathers in TD group were associated with business (46.8 %), on the other hand, in ID (23.3 %) and ASD group

(31.7 %) most of the fathers were doing office jobs. Most of the fathers were educated till graduation in TD (32.7 %) and ASD (27.1%) group, however, in ID group the educational attainment of most of the fathers was till matric (21.7%).

Table 37

Education and Occupation of Mothers Across Groups

	ID Percentage	ASD Percentage	TD Percentage
Education			
Illiterate	28.7 %	9.4 %	14 %
Below Matric	19.8 %	11.8 %	7.2 %
Matric	23.8 %	22.4 %	13.5 %
Intermediate	12.9 %	29.4 %	20.7 %
Graduation	10.9 %	14.1 %	29.7 %
Masters	4 %	11.8 %	14.4 %
Post Masters			.5 %
PhD		1.2 %	
Occupation			
Domestic Helper	6 %	5.9 %	.4 %
Skilled worker	1.2 %	1.5 %	-
Banker	-	-	1.3 %
Doctor	1.2 %	5.9 %	1.3 %
Teacher	10.8 %	5.9 %	5.8 %
Business		2.9 %	.4 %
Housewives	80.7 %	77.9 %	90.6 %

In TD group majority of mothers were educated till graduation (29.7 %) whereas, most of the mothers in ID (28.7%) and ASD (29.4 %) group were illiterate. A large majority of mothers in all groups were found to be housewives. The detailed group-wise personal and family demographic information is attached in appendices – T, U and V.

Demographic Variables, Adaptive Skills and Temperament. This section of the results represents the relationship between adaptive behaviors and main personal and family demographic variables including age, temperament, family system behavioral problems and intelligence quotient etc. In order to find out the relationship among the above mentioned variables Pearson product moment correlation procedure was carried out. Detailed findings are given below.

Table 38

Correlation between Domains of Adaptive Skills Score and Behavioral Problems[a]

	ID (*n* = 105)	ASD (*n* = 92)
Daily Living Skills	-.14	-.49*
Social Skills	-.46**	-.34*
Self Care	-.30	-.33*
Home Living Skills	-.57**	-.29
Composite Score	-.33*	-.28*

Note. [a] Children in TD group didn't have any behavioral problem.

* Correlation is significant at the 0.05 level (2-tailed).

** Correlation is significant at the 0.01 level (2-tailed).

Table 38 revealed significant inverse association between behavioral problems and adaptive skill domains across two groups. The scores of children with ID showed significant correlation for social skills and home living skills. However, ASD group showed a significant negative correlation between behavioral problems and all domains of adaptive skills except home living skills, the strength of the correlation was from low to moderate.

In general, behavioral problems observed to have a significant negative correlation with adaptive skills scores which supported the hypothesis that "behavioral problems among children with ID and ASD are negatively associated with adaptive skills scores".

Table 39

Correlation between Domains of Adaptive Skill Score and Family System

	ID	ASD	TD
Daily Living Skills	-55*	-.28*	-.47**
Social Skills	-.21	-.16	-.23
Self Care	-.33	-.16	-.29
Home Living Skills	-.19	-.26*	-.19
Composite Score	-.44*	-.24*	-.34*

* Correlation is significant at the 0.05 level (2-tailed).

** Correlation is significant at the 0.01 level (2-tailed).

The table 39 indicated that joint family system was negatively associated with all dimensions of adaptive skills across all groups, the strength of the correlation was from low to moderate. Daily living skills and composite score revealed to have significant correlation in all groups. Joint family system was negatively associated with all dimensions of adaptive skills, the strength of the correlation was from low to moderate among typically developing children.

Hypothesis that "joint family system is positively associated with adaptive skills scores" was not supported by the findings. As joint family system was observed to have negative correlation with adaptive skills scores across all groups, therefore, the hypothesis turned out to be insignificant.

Table 40

Correlation between Adaptive Skills Score and Family Income

	ID	ASD	TD
Daily Living Skills	-.31**	.27**	.46*
Social Skills	-.16	-.13	.31**
Self Care	-.23*	-.08	.14*
Home Living Skills	-.14	-.10	-.08
Composite Score	-.25*	-.31*	.24*

* Correlation is significant at the 0.05 level (2-tailed).

** Correlation is significant at the 0.01 level (2-tailed).

Table 40 revealed that family income was inversely related to all domains of adaptive skills in ID and ASD groups. However, this pattern was reversed in TD group which indicated significant positive correlation between family income and all domains of adaptive skills but non significant negative correlation with home living skills. Family income had a significant positive correlation with daily living skills and significant negative correlation with composite score in ASD group. Whereas, the ID group had significant correlation with daily living skills, self care and composite score.

In general, the above mentioned findings of ID and ASD group did not support the hypothesis that "family income is positively related to the adaptive skills scores". Rather, the findings stood contrary to the hypothesis as the family income was observed to have significant negative correlation with composite adaptive behavior score in ID and ASD groups. However, this hypothesis was supported by the findings of TD group.

Table 41

Correlation between Domains of Adaptive Skills Score and Number of Siblings (N=436)

	ID	ASD	TD
Daily Living Skills	.20*	.19	-.34*
Social Skills	.19	.19	-.27**
Self Care	.25	.24*	-.14*
Home Living Skills	.13	.12	.26*
Composite Score	.16	.26	-.20*

** Correlation is significant at the 0.01 level (2-tailed).

* Correlation is significant at the 0.05 level (2-tailed).

Table 41 indicated that number of siblings shared positive association with all adaptive skills domains across ID and ASD groups, but only daily living skills in ID group and self care in ASD group had significant correlation. In typically developing children, the number of siblings shared significant negative association with most of the adaptive skills domains except home living skills that had significant positive correlation among typically developing children.

Hypothesis that "number of siblings is positively associated with adaptive skill scores" was supported by the findings in ID and ASD groups. However, this hypothesis turned out to be insignificant in TD group.

Table 42

Correlation between Domains of Adaptive Skills and Parental Education and Age

	Father's Education	Mother's Education	Father's Age	Mother's Age
Daily Living Skills	.24	.22*	.08	.14**
Social Skills	.28**	.29**	-.06	-.02
Self Care	.22*	.21*	-.03	.02
Home Living Skills	-.21*	-.18*	.02	.05
Composite Score	.29*	.26*	.04	.07

** Correlation is significant at the 0.01 level (2-tailed).

* Correlation is significant at the 0.05 level (2-tailed).

The table 42 presented a significant positive correlation between father and mother's education and all domains of adaptive skills but HLS. There was an inverse correlation between father's age and self care and social skills, whereas, home living skills, daily living skills and composite score were positively associated with father's age. However, all domains of adaptive skills except social skills were observed to be positively associated with mother's age. All the correlations were observed to be weak in nature.

Table 43

Correlation between Domains of Adaptive Skills Score and Parental Marital Status

	ID	ASD	TD
Daily Living Skills	- .32*	-.39	-.45*
Social Skills	-.19	-.26	.21
Self Care	-.18	-.16	-.19*
Home Living Skills	-.26	-.31*	-.28
Composite Score	.25**	.21	-.39*

** Correlation is significant at the 0.01 level (2-tailed).

* Correlation is significant at the 0.05 level (2-tailed).

Table 43 showed that the scores of children were negatively associated with parental divorce and single parenthood. Consequently, adaptive skills scores of children were positively associated with intact parental marriage. Therefore, the assumption that parental marital status was significantly associated with adaptive skills scores was supported by the findings of this study.

Adaptive Skills and Pattern of Development. The individuals following different patterns of development are considered to present a varying performance on domains of human functioning. Adaptive skills are one such area of functioning which is believed to be different in individuals having dissimilar characteristics. This section of results attempts to assess the domains of adaptive skills across developmental groups.

Table 44

Means, Standard Deviations and F value of Composite Adaptive Skills Score for Three Groups (N =435)

Groups	N	M	(SD)	95% CI		F	p
				LL	UL		
ID	105	207.15	64.70	194.63	219.67	8.46	.00
ASD	91	135.23	71.91	120.25	150.21		
TD	239	308.52	38.99	303.55	313.49		
Total	435	247.80	89.42	239.37	256.23		

Between groups *df* = 6; within groups *df* = 429; groups total *df* = 435

Note. ID = Intellectual disability; ASD = Autism spectrum disorder; TD = Typical development. CI = confidence interval; LL = lower limit; UL = upper limit.

*p < .05

The table 44 presented mean differences in adaptive skills scores of children having differing developmental status. The findings revealed a significant mean difference in scores of children of typical development, ID and ASD groups. Post Hoc analysis revealed that children with ASD scored significantly lower from children in ID and typical development groups. Whereas, typically developing children scored significantly higher than those who were in ID group.

The difference between mean adaptive skills scores of children in ID and ASD groups. Literature at large suggested that although ASD and ID share some common features, they had large variability in terms of symptomatology, course and prognosis of the disorders. On the basis of this claim it was assumed that the children with ID and ASD will differ significantly in their performance on adaptive skill domains.

Table 45

Mean, SD and t values of Adaptive Skill Scores for ID and ASD Groups

	ID ($n = 105$)		ASD ($n = 92$)				95 % CI		Cohen's
	M	*(SD)*	*M*	*(SD)*	*t*	*p*	*LL*	*UL*	*d*
DLS	98.18	27.42	66.98	34.42	6.97	.00	22.37	40.04	1.00
SS	42.33	15.58	20.39	10.89	11.25	.00	18.09	25.78	1.63
SC	44.21	15.63	27.78	16.34	7.21	.00	11.93	20.92	1.03
HLS	22.43	11.22	12.13	10.37	6.64	.00	7.47	13.36	.95
Total Score	207.15	64.70	135.23	71.91	7.37	.00	52.67	91.17	1.05

Note. $df = 194$. CI = Confidence Interval; LL = Lower limit; UL = Upper limit.

DLS = Daily living skills; SS = Social skills; SC = Self care; HLS = Home living skills.

Table 45 presented adaptive skills scores for children with intellectual disability and children with ASD. Children with intellectual disability scored significantly higher on all adaptive skills scales compared to children with ASD. The mean difference in scores of both groups found to be significant which in turn supported the hypothesis that the "AB scores of children with intellectual disability are significantly higher than children with ASD".

As the number of items in each sub scale of indigenously developed adaptive skills scale was different it was decided to calculate the percentage of mean scores for all these subscales to make the comparison more meaningful. When the scores were arranged in terms of the acquired percentage it presented an interested picture presented in the figure below

Figure 8 .

Pattern of Adaptive Skills Scores Across Three Groups

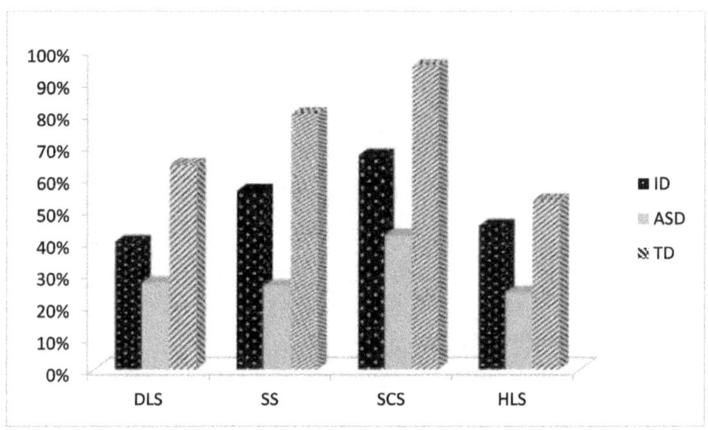

DLS = Daily living skills; SS = Social skills; SC = Self care; HLS = Home living skills.

The figure revealed that the children in ID group had highest score on *Self care skills* domain, followed by *Social skills* and *Home living skills* and they scored lowest on *Daily living skills* domain. On the other hand, children in ASD group scored highest on *Self care* domain, then on *Daily living skills, Social skills* and their lowest score was on *Home living* domain. Whereas, children with typical development had highest score on *Self care skills*, then *Social skills* and *Daily living skills* and scored lowest on *Home living skills*.

Cognitive Levels and Adaptive Skills. An important objective of the present study was to examine the association of cognitive functioning with adaptive skills scores of children across three developmental groups. Cognitive functioning was quantified in terms of IQ. This relationship was explored in total sample and across groups. Pearson product moment method was employed to assess this relationship. The findings are given in the following section.

Table 46

Correlation between Domains of Adaptive Skills Scale, Temperament and IQ (N= 436)

Variables	1	2	3	4	5	6	7	8	9
1. Surg									
2. EC	.43**								
3. NA	-.43**	-.28**							
4. DLS	.46**	.49**	-.47**						
5. SS	.39**	.41**	-.47**	.84**					
6. SC	.37**	.43**	-.49**	.87**	.88**				
7. HLS	.25**	.32**	-.57**	.61**	.67**	.69**			
8. ABS Total	.44**	.47**	-.52**	.96**	.93**	.94**	.74**		
9. IQ	.59**	.53**	-.42**	.80**	.51**	.58**	.48**	.71**	

Note. Surg = Surgency; EC= Effortful control; NA= Negative affectivity; DLS = Daily living skills; SS = Social skills; SC = Self care; HLS = Home living skills. ASB= Adaptive behavior scale.

** Correlation is significant at the 0.01 level (2-tailed).

Table 46 suggested inverse association between negative affectivity domain of temperament with all domains of adaptive skills, temperament and IQ. All other factors share significant positive association with each other, though the strength of correlation varied from weak to very strong. Significant positive association between IQ and adaptive skills supported hypothesis that "there is a significant positive relationship between cognitive functioning and adaptive skills".

Table 47

Correlation between Scores of Adaptive Skills and IQ Across Groups

Variables	ID	ASD	TD
	(n =105)	*(n = 92)*	*(n = 54)*
Daily Living Skills	.50**	.60**	.55**
Social Skills	.37**	.47**	.47**
Self Care	.42**	.53**	.24
Home Living Skills	.15	.34**	.15
Composite Score	.43**	.56**	.45**

Note. ID = Intellectual disability; ASD = Autism spectrum disorder; TD = Typical development.
** Correlation is significant at the 0.01 level (2-tailed).

Table 47 indicated that cognitive functioning shared significant positive association with adaptive skills composite score and sub domains. ASD group shown to have comparatively higher correlation between adaptive skills scores and cognitive functioning compared to children in ID group. This supported the hypothesis that "cognitive functioning is positively associated with adaptive skills scores".

After establishing the association between intellectual and adaptive functioning the next task was to assess the difference in mean scores across different IQ levels. For this reason, MANOVA was calculated for children with ID, ASD and those following typical development.

Table 48

MANOVA Results of Adaptive Skill Domains by Exceptionality

Effects	Value	F	p	Partial Eta Squared
Intellectual Quotient				
Pillais' Trace	.89	11.63	.00	.22

* $p<.05$.

The overall effect in the MANOVA was statistically significant F (4, 246) = 11.63p< .05. This finding indicated the four exceptionality groups differed on their adaptive skills domain performance. Approximately 22% of the variance between groups was explained by their performance on adaptive functioning domains. The results for the dependent variables were also considered individually in Post-Hoc analysis (Tukey HSD), the findings are given in Table 49.

Table 49

Difference Between Adaptive Skill Domain Scores Across Groups

	F	p	Partial Eta Squared	Pattern Revealed in Post Hoc
DLS	69.22	.00	.63	Profound =Severe, Mild< Moderate<above 70
SS	15.59	.00	.28	Profound, Severe < Mild<Moderate< above 70
SCS	19.83	.00	.33	Profound, Severe = Mild<Moderate<above 70
HLS	12.11	.00	.23	Profound, Severe=Mild<Moderate<above 70

The post hoc analysis revealed significant differences in mean scores of adaptive skills across IQ categories. On adaptive domain of daily living skills F (4, 246) =69.22, p=.00, explained almost 63 % variance, profound (M =77.31, SD =23.36), severe (M =69.89, SD =32.85) and mild (M =89.15, SD =29.83) groups did not differ significantly from those in moderate IQ (M =116.09, SD =26.90) and with above 70 IQ range (M= 173.50, SD = 12.09) who scored significantly higher on this domain compared to three other groups.

The social skills domain had F (4, 246) =15.59, p=.00, explained almost 28 % variance, profound (M =32.08, SD =12.47), severe (M =29.98, SD =17.51) and mild (M = 36.63, SD =16.39) groups did not differ significant and children with moderate IQ (M =49.97, SD = 16.03) and above 70 IQ (M =68.50, SD =17.71) scored significantly higher on this domain compared to children in mild, severe and profound groups. The significantly higher score performance was made by children in above 70 IQ group.

The self care domain had F (4, 246) = 19.83, p=.00, explained almost 33 % variance, profound (M =30.23, SD =12.21), severe (M = 31.47, SD =17.41) and mild (M = 37.24, SD = 15.51) groups did not differ significantly and children with moderate IQ (M = 52.53, SD = 16.25) and above 70 IQ (M =59.89, SD =14.92) scored significantly higher on this domain compared to other three groups.

The domain of home living had F (4, 246) = 12.11, p = .00, explained almost 23 % of group variance. Children in profound IQ (M = 11.23, SD = 4.94), severe (M = 15.68, SD = 11.21) , mild (M = 17.44, SD = 11.65) didn't differ significantly from each other but showed significant differences from children with moderate IQ (M = 23.53, SD = 14.58) and with above 70 IQ (M = 32.17, SD = 5.60).

ANOVA was also run to observe the individual mean differences on adaptive behavior across all intellectual levels within the developmental groups. The details of all these analyses are given below

Children in ID group observed to have varying degree of intellectual functioning from profound to mild intellectual delay. The results of mean differences across adaptive scores and IQ presented an interesting picture. The table 50 covers the details of the analysis

Table 50

Means, Standard Deviations and F value of Composite Adaptive Skills Score for IQ Categories in ID Group

Groups	N	M	(SD)	95 % CI		F	p
				LL	UL		
IQ below 25	13	156.85	52.35	125.21	188.47	7.87	.00
IQ 25 – 39	40	198.10	49.61	182.23	213.96		
IQ 40 – 54	23	201.35	61.37	174.81	227.88		
IQ 55 – 70	29	246.79	71.01	219.78	273.80		
Total	105	207.15	64.70	194.63	219.67		

Note. CI = confidence interval; LL = lower limit; UL = upper limit.

Between groups $df = 3$; within groups $df = 101$; groups total $df = 104$

*$p < .05$

The table 50 represented mean scores of children with intellectual disability divided according to IQ categories and showed that the mean composite scores of adaptive functioning significantly differ across IQ groups. The Hochberg Post Hoc test on group differences revealed that children with mild intellectual delay had significantly ($p < .05$)

different mean scores from all other groups as children in this category had significantly

higher mean scores compared to children in other categories. On DLS domain the F (3, 101)

= 10.37, p = .00 and post hoc test also revealed significant mean difference particularly

profound and moderate intellectual disability group. The Self care domain had F (3, 101) =

8.97, p = .00 with mild intellectual group having most significant mean differences than all

other groups. The analysis for Social skills domain revealed F (3,101) = 5.96, p = .001 and

children with mild intellectual delay had significantly different scores from profound and

severe delay cases. The Home living scale revealed no significant difference with an F (3,

101)= 1.35, p = .26 in mean scores across exceptionality groups.

Table 51

Means, Standard Deviations and F Value of Composite Score of Adaptive Skill for IQ

Categories in ASD Group

				95 % CI			
Groups	N	M	*(SD)*	*LL*	*UL*	F	p
IQ below 25							
IQ 25 – 39	52	109.59	66.06	91.20	127.99	9.44	.00
IQ 40 – 54	36	167.11	67.72	144.19	190.02		
IQ 55 – 70	3	197.00	7.93	177.28	216.71		
Total	91	135.23	71.91	120.25	150.20		

Note. CI = confidence interval; LL = lower limit; UL = upper limit. Between groups *df* = 2;
within groups *df* = 88; groups total *df* = 90.

*p < .05

The table 51   represented mean scores of children with intellectual disability divided

according to IQ categories and indicated that the mean scores for self care domain of adaptive functioning significantly differ across IQ groups. The Hochberg Post Hoc test on group differences revealed that children with mild intellectual delay had significantly different mean scores from children in all other IQ categories and the mean difference was significant at .05 level. On DLS the F (2,88) = 12.71, p = .00 revealed significant mean differences on adaptive skills score children with severe intellectual delay had significantly different scores than children with mild and moderate delay. Social skills had F (2,88) = 5.84, p = .004 also suggested significant mean differences on adaptive scores where children with mild intellectual delay had significantly higher scores than children with profound and severe delay. The scores on social skills domain indicated F (2,88) = 7.17, p = .001suggetsing significant mean difference particularly in children with severe delay who significantly scored lower than children with mild delay. The F (2, 88) = 2.61, p = .079 on home living did not support any mean differences in adaptive skill scores across intellectual functioning levels.

Table 52

Means, Standard Deviations and F value of Composite Score of Adaptive Skill for IQ Categories in TD Group

Groups	n	M	(SD)	LL	UL	F	p
				95% CI			
70 – 84	10	270.00	29.48	248.90	291.09	8.38	.00
85 – 99	38	305.15	28.25	295.87	314.44		
Above 100	6	333.00	50.23	280.28	385.71		
Total	54	301.74	35.38	292.08	311.39		

Note. CI = confidence interval; LL = lower limit; UL = upper limit. Between groups df = 2; within groups df = 51; groups total df = 53

The table 52 represented mean scores of children with typical development divided into different IQ categories and revealed significant differences in mean scores of children across groups. The Hochberg post hoc test indicated that the scores of children in group 70 to 84 IQ were significantly lower than scores of other two groups. The F $(2,51)$ = 15.72 , p = .00 on DLS suggested significant mean difference in adaptive performance of children particularly with IQ between 70 to 84 from all other children . The Social skills domain had F $(2,51)$ = 8.66, p = .001 also suggesting significantly different mean adaptive behavior scores. The self care domain has F $(2,51)$ = 1.79, p =.18 indicating non significant difference in mean scores of children with varying levels of intellectual functioning. The home living skills domain also revealed non significant mean differences in adaptive behavior scores of children with different intellectual functioning level as F $(2,51)$ = .71 was non significant at p = .49 advocating no significant difference in means scores across groups.

Age and Adaptive Skills. To explore the relationship between age and adaptive behavior domains Pearson product moment correlation was employed. To assess age wise differences in mean scores of adaptive skills of children from all three samples one way ANOVA was carried out for composite and subscale scores. The findings are mentioned in the table 53.

Table 53

Correlation between Domains of Adaptive Skills and Age among Three Groups

	Age of ID Group	Age of ASD Group	Age of TD Group
Daily Living skills	.27*	-.03	.38**
Social Skills	.15*	-.09	.46**
Self Care	.38**	-.05	.31*
Homeliving Skills	.18	.16	.25*
Composite Score	.34*	-.04	.54*

Note. ID = Intellectual disability; ASD = Autism spectrum disorder; TD = Typical development.

** Correlation is significant at the 0.01 level (2-tailed).

* Correlation is significant at the 0.05 level (2-tailed).

Table 53 represented low inverse association between age and adaptive skills scores except home living domain. Whereas, the relationship between adaptive behaviors and age adaptive behavior was observed to be positive among children with intellectual disability and typical development. Assumption that younger children had a lower score on all domains of adaptive functioning was not supported in the ASD group. However, this hypothesis was supported in children with typical development and children with intellectual disability.

Table 54

Mean and Standard Deviation of Adaptive Skill Scores for Three Groups

Groups	N	M	(SD)	n	M	(SD)	N	M	(SD)
		ID Group			ASDD Group			TD Group	
		(n = 105)			(n = 91)			(n = 239)	
5 year	7	178.14	(42.03)	5	152.20	(115.75)	23	292.87	(34.59)
6 year	8	199.50	(60.68)	5	121.80	(87.47)	44	307.59	(32.23)
7 year	12	212.83	(93.41)	18	142.11	(84.97)	63	319.78	(41.13)
8 year	17	196.00	(48.45)	20	127.85	(56.27)	15	296.33	(41.10)
9 year	6	215.00	(99.45)	11	141.27	(61.26)	18	319.33	(31.56)
10 year	15	195.20	(68.47)	6	147.00	(48.34)	40	300.30	(42.39)
11 year	40	220.10	(58.25)	26	130.19	(75.62)	36	308.75	(39.49)
Total	105	207.15	(64.70)	91	135.23	(71.91)	239	308.52	(38.99)

Note. ID = Intellectual disability; ASD = Autism spectrum disorder; TD = Typical development.

For the ID group the minimum mean score was observed to be 22 and maximum 366. The mean score of children in ASD group was between 0 and 330. The mean score of children in TD group ranged from 292 to 308. The children in typically developing group scored relatively higher on all domains of adaptive skills compared to children of other two groups. The children in ASD group had relatively lowest scores on across all domains of adaptive skills compared to children with other two groups.

Figure 9.

Presenting Mean Scores Across Age Groups.

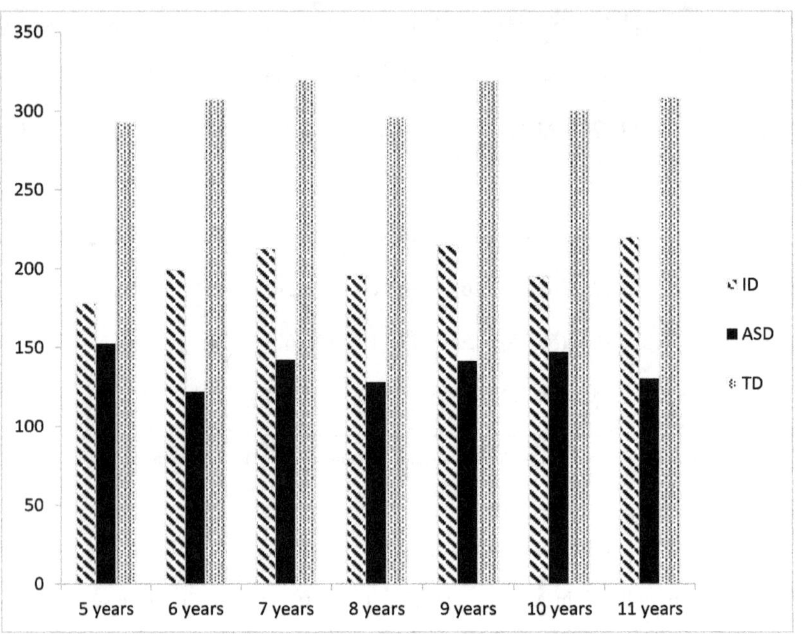

The figure above presented an interesting picture of scores. Almost all groups had a low performance during the 8 year of development. Children in ASD group presents a pattern relatively reversed to one presented by scores of children in ID and TD group. Children in ASD showed better performance in initial years and with age there was a decline in adaptive skills scores.

Table 55

Means, Standard Deviations and F value of Composite Adaptive Behavior Scores

Groups	N	M	(SD)	95% CI		F	p
				LL	UL		
5 years	35	249.83	79.84	222.40	277.26	6.02	.00
6 years	57	276.12	74.48	256.36	295.89		
7 years	93	271.59	94.01	252.23	290.95		
8 years	52	198.73	84.58	175.18	222.28		
9 years	35	245.49	98.09	211.79	279.18		
10 years	61	259.38	76.59	239.76	278.99		
11 years	102	228.47	89.87	210.82	246.12		
Total	435	247.80	89.42	239.37	256.23		

Note. CI = confidence interval; LL = lower limit; UL = upper limit. . Between groups df = 6; within groups df = 248; groups total df = 434

p < .05

The table 55 presented mean score of different age groups and findings revealed that the mean score on ABS differ significantly across age groups. When sample was divided into subgroups to see the age wise differences in adaptive skills scores, the difference turns out to be non significant but only in TD group. The F ratio value for ID group was found to be .708 with *p*.64, in ASD group F ratio was .19 and *p*.97 and finally in typically developing children the F ratio value was 2.34 with significance value of .03. Tukey's (HSD) post hoc comparison was carried out to further explore the differences in mean scores across age groups.

Table 56

Tukey's – HSD Post Hoc Comparison on Adaptive Skills Across Age Groups

I (Age)	J (Age)	MD (I – J)	SE	95% CI LL	95% CI UL	p
8 years	5 years	-51.09	18.91	4.91	-107.10	.10
	6 years	-77.39[*]	16.58	-28.27	-126.52	.00
	7 years	-72.86[*]	14.97	-117.22	-28.50	.00
	9 years	-46.75	18.91	-102.76	9.25	.17
	10 years	-60.65[*]	16.32	-108.99	-12.29	.00
	11 years	-29.74	14.73	-73.39	13.91	.40

Note. SE = Standard error of mean; MD = Mean difference; CI = Confidence interval; LL = Lower limit; UL = Upper limit.

*p < .05

Results in table 56 revealed the mean scores of 8 years old children differ significantly from scores of 6,7 and 10 years old children. The findings presented in the table above supported the assumption that children of differing age would have different scores on adaptive skills.

Table 57

Means, Standard Deviations and F value of Daily Living Skills domain of Adaptive Skill for Age Groups

Groups	N	M	(SD)	95% CI		F	p
				LL	UL		
5 years	35	132.29	(41.13)	118.16	146.41	8.46	.00
6 years	57	143.00	(37.13)	133.15	152.85		
7 years	94	137.99	(47.53)	128.25	147.73		
8 years	52	98.85	(43.61)	86.70	110.99		
9 years	35	121.46	(48.74)	104.71	138.20		
10 years	61	130.92	(36.77)	121.50	140.33		
11 years	102	111.14	(43.44)	102.61	119.67		
Total	436	124.92	(45.19)	120.67	129.17		

Between groups df = 6; within groups df = 429; groups total df = 435

Note. CI = confidence interval; LL = lower limit; UL = upper limit.

*p < .05

The table 57 presented mean differences in adaptive skills scores of children with differing age on daily living skills domain. The findings revealed a significant mean difference in scores of children of different age groups. Post Hoc analysis revealed that 8 years old children scored significantly lower from 5, 6, 7 and 10 years old children. Whereas, 6 and 7 years old children scored significantly higher than those who were 11 years of age.

Table 58

Means, Standard Deviations and F value of Social Skills Domain of Adaptive Skills for Sample

Groups	N	M	(SD)	95% CI		F	p
				LL	UL		
5 years	35	52.09	(19.16)	45.50	58.67	3.95	.00
6 years	57	53.63	(17.75)	48.92	58.34		
7 years	94	53.35	(21.71)	48.91	57.80		
8 years	52	39.67	(20.24)	34.04	45.31		
9 years	35	49.57	(22.07)	41.99	57.15		
10 years	61	51.43	(17.25)	47.01	55.84		
11 years	102	45.76	(19.49)	41.94	49.59		
Total	436	49.31	(20.16)	47.41	51.21		

Between groups df = 6; within groups df = 429; groups total df = 435

Note. CI = confidence interval; LL = lower limit; UL = upper limit.

The table 58 showed mean differences in adaptive skills scores of children with differing age on social skills domain. The findings revealed a significant mean difference in scores of children of different age groups. Post Hoc analysis revealed that 8 years old children scored significantly lower from 6, 7 and 10 years old children.

Table 59

Means, Standard Deviations and F value of Self Care domain of Adaptive Skills for Sample

Groups	N	M	(SD)	95% CI		F	p
				LL	UL		
5 years	35	50.40	(17.22)	44.48	56.32	3.19	.00
6 years	57	56.02	(17.22)	51.45	60.59		
7 years	94	52.96	(22.28)	48.39	57.52		
8 years	52	41.88	(17.46)	37.02	46.75		
9 years	35	50.06	(23.59)	41.95	58.16		
10 years	61	54.44	(17.75)	49.90	58.99		
11 years	102	48.44	(20.35)	44.44	52.44		
Total	436	50.75	(20.09)	48.86	52.64		

Between groups $df = 6$; within groups $df = 429$; groups total $df = 435$

Note. CI = confidence interval; LL = lower limit; UL = upper limit.

The table 59 represented mean differences in adaptive skills scores of children with differing age on self care domain. The results suggested a significant mean difference in scores of children from different age groups. Post Hoc analysis suggested that 8 years old children scored significantly lower from 6, 7 and 10 years old children.

Table 60

Means, Standard Deviations and F value of Home Living Domain of Adaptive Skills

Groups	N	M	(SD)	95% CI		F	p
				LL	UL		
5 years	35	15.06	(9.59)	11.76	18.35	4.74	.00
6 years	57	23.47	(11.77)	20.35	26.60		
7 years	94	24.84	(12.15)	22.35	27.33		
8 years	52	18.33	(9.72)	15.62	21.03		
9 years	35	24.40	(9.67)	21.08	27.72		
10 years	61	22.59	(10.91)	19.80	25.38		
11 years	102	23.13	(11.82)	20.81	25.45		
Total	436	22.35	(11.49)	21.27	23.43		

Between groups df = 6; within groups df = 429; groups total df = 435

Note. CI = confidence interval; LL = lower limit; UL = upper limit.

*p < .05

The table 60 presented mean differences in adaptive skills scores of children with differing age on home living domain. The findings suggested a significant mean difference in scores of children with different age. Post Hoc analysis suggested that 5 years old children had a significantly different (lower) score from children of all other age groups except 8 year old children. The 7 years old children had significantly different score than 5 and 8 years old children.

The assumption that adaptive skills scores differ across age groups was supported by the findings of this section. As the mean of composite and all domain scores revealed significant differences across all age groups.

Gender Differences on sub domains and total score of Adaptive behavior scale.

Independent samples *t* - test and MANOVA were performed to study the gender differences between scores of girls and boys on adaptive behavior scale and its subscales. The tables from 61 to table 64 present findings of gender differences across developmental groups and table 61 also presents the findings of MANOVA to explore the gender differences in combined sample.

Table 61

MANOVA Results of Gender on Adaptive Skills for Combined Sample(N= 436)

			Girls		Boys		Pillai's Trace	*F*	*p*
	M	*(SD)*	*M*	*(SD)*	*M*	*(SD)*			
DLS	124.78	(45.23)	127.06	(45.85)	123.41	(44.74)	.02	1.87	.12
SS	49.27	(20.16)	51.49	(19.89)	47.77	(20.24)			
SC	50.73	(20.08)	52.76	(20.06)	49.34	(20.03)			
HLS	22.35	(11.48)	23.53	(12.10)	21.52	(10.98)			
Total	247.59	(89.43)	242.04	(88.49)	209.41	(65.62)			

*Note.*DLS = Daily living skills; SS = social skills; SC = Self care; HLS = Home living skills.

The table 61 showed that the girls scored higher on daily living skills than boys, whereas, the mean scores on all other factors revealed no gender differences. *Wilk's* Λ= .95, *F* (3, 428) = 6.70, *p* < .001, multivariate $\dot{\eta}^2$= .15. The table indicated approximately 2% of multivariate variance of dependent variables was related with the group element and significant mean differences in scores of the two gender clusters on total score of adaptive skills and its four domains (dependent variables) . The follow-up univariate ANOVAs

pointed out that neither composite score nor subscale scores of adaptive skills were

significantly different for girls and boys. For composite score F (1, 433) = 2.59, p >.001, η^2

= .01, for DLS, SS, SC and HLS F (1, 433) = .92, p >.001, η^2 = .002, and F (1, 433) = 4.15,

p> .001, η^2 = .01, F (1, 433) = 3.65, p >.001, η^2 = .01 and F (1, 433) = 3.62, p >.001, η^2 =

.01respectively.

Figure 10.

Presenting Mean Differences in Adaptive Scores Across Gender.

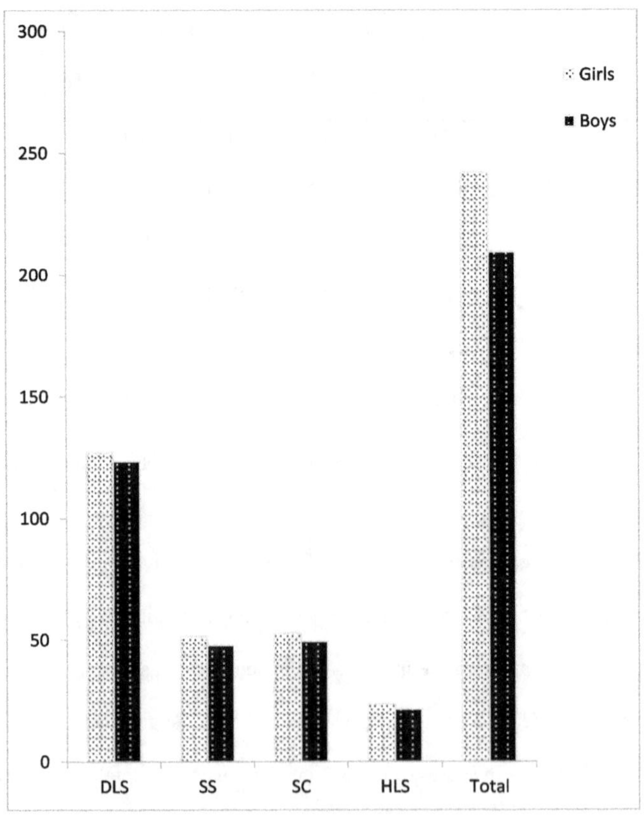

The figure 10 depicted the general trend of adaptive skills scores across gender groups. The girls had slightly higher score on all domains of adaptive skills compared to boys, however this difference was not significant.

Table 62

Gender Differences in Mean Scores of Subscales of Adaptive Skills for ID Group

Subscales	Boys ($n = 59$)		Girls ($n = 46$)		t	p	Cohen's d
	M	(SD)	M	(SD)			
DLS	96.07	(25.88)	101.53	(29.36)	.89	.37	.19
SS	42.68	(16.40)	42.42	(14.32)	-.26	.79	-.02
SC	44.12	(15.71)	44.78	(15.57)	.07	.94	.04
HLS	22.53	(11.05)	22.62	(11.48)	-.10	.92	.01
Composite Score	209.41	(65.62)	205.39	(64.49)	.32	.75	.06

Note. df = 103. DLS = Daily living skills; SS = social skills; SC = Self care; HLS = Home living skills.

The table 62 showed that the girls scored higher on daily living skills than boys, whereas, the mean scores on all other factors revealed no significant gender differences. There was no significant gender difference revealed on any sub domain or composite score.

Table 63

Gender Differences in Mean Scores of Adaptive Skills Subscales for ASD Group

	Girls (*n* = 30)		Boys (*n* = 61)		*t*	*p*	Cohen's *d*
	M	(*SD*)	*M*	(*SD*)			
DLS	61.58	(40.57)	69.76	(30.57)	-1.20	.23	-.23
SS	20.52	(11.99)	20.18	(9.80)	.14	.88	
SC	27.84	(18.79)	27.69	(14.99)	.23	.82	.01
HLS	12.40	(10.88)	11.94	(10.12)	.27	.78	.04
Composite							
Score	132.77	(84.10)	136.44	(65.84)	-.228	.82	-.05

Note. df = 89. DLS = Daily living skills; SS = social skills; SC = Self care; HLS = Home living skills.

Table 63 represented gender differences on scores of adaptive skills subscales. The boys in ASD group scored higher on daily living skills and lower on home living skills compared to girls. Whereas, the mean scores on social skills and self care were almost similar. No mean score revealed significant gender difference on any domain.

Table 64

Gender Differences in Mean Scores of Adaptive Skills Subscales for TD Group

Subscales	Girls ($n = 103$)		Boys ($n = 136$)		t	p	Cohen's d
	M	(SD)	M	(SD)			
DLS	158.65	(13.42)	159.21	(12.99)	-.327	.74	-.04
SS	62.78	(12.17)	59.32	(13.82)	2.02	.04	.27
SC	63.88	(12.42)	61.39	(13.34)	1.47	.14	.19
HLS	27.46	(10.42)	25.38	(8.48)	1.64	.10	.22
Composite Score	312.77	(40.41)	305.30	(37.71)	1.47	.14	.19

Note. df = 237. DLS = Daily living skills; SS = social skills; SC = Self care; HLS = Home living skills.

The table above revealed that the mean score of girls was slightly higher on social skills and lower on daily living skills compared to boys in this groups. Only the mean score on social skills revealed significant gender differences, however, the mean scores of boys and girls did not reveal any mean differences on composite or other sub domains of adaptive skills. In general, the findings do not support the hypothesis that "The adaptive skills scores of boys and girls differ significantly". This hypothesis was only supported by scores on social skills in typically developed children group.

Relationship between Constructs: Adaptive skills and Temperament . In order to investigate the relationship between two main constructs of present study namely, adaptive skills and temperament Pearson product moment correlations were carried out. This section of results presents the findings of association between four domains of adaptive functioning, three broad domains of temperament based on Big Five Model and eighteen sub dimensions of temperament for the combined and sub samples. The section will review the association between these two variables in total sample followed by group wise analysis.

Table 65

Correlation of Three Domains of Temperament and Adaptive Scale for the Sample (N=436)

	Surgency	Effortful Control	Negative Affectivity
Daily Living Skills	.46**	.49**	-.46**
Social Skills	.40**	.41**	-.46**
Self Care	.38**	.43**	-.48**
Homeliving Skills	.26**	.32**	-.56**
Composite Score	.44**	.47**	-.51**

** Correlation is significant at the 0.01 level (2-tailed).

The findings in table 65 revealed significant negative correlation between adaptive skills domains and negative affectivity. However, significant positive correlation was observed between surgency, effortful control and adaptive skill domains.

Table 66

Correlation of Surgency and Domains of Adaptive Scale for the Three Groups (N=436)

	ID	ASD	TD
Daily Living Skills	.42**	.35**	.40**
Social Skills	.41**	.33**	.13*
Self Care	.39**	.33**	.08
Homeliving Skills	.29**	.21*	.04
Total Score	.42**	.40**	.36**

Note. ID= Intellectual disability; ASD= Autism spectrum disorders; TD= Typical developing.

** Correlation is significant at the 0.05 level (2-tailed).

* Correlation is significant at the 0.01 level (2-tailed).

The domains of adaptive functioning observed to have positive correlation with surgency, this trend was consistent across all three groups.

Table 67

Correlation of Effortful Control and Domains of Adaptive Scale for the Three Groups (N=436)

	ID	ASD	TD
Daily Living Skills	.49**	.45**	.14*
Social Skills	.35**	.41**	.04
Self Care	.46**	.44**	-.01
Homeliving Skills	.29**	.30**	.05
Total Score	.45**	.39**	.24**

** Correlation is significant at the 0.01 level (2-tailed).

Table 67 presented that the effortful control dimension of temperament was positively correlated with domains of adaptive skills across ID and ASD groups, whereas, in TD group this dimension was negatively associated with self care. However, the correlation value was weak and non significant.

Table 68

Correlation of Negative Affectivity *and Domains of Adaptive Scale for the Three Groups*
(N=436)

	ID	ASD	TD
Daily Living Skills	-.39**	-.37**	-.27**
Social Skills	-.43**	-.34**	-.21**
Self Care	-.49**	-.32**	-.23**
Homeliving Skills	-.53**	-.52**	-.39**
Total Score	-.48**	-.46**	-.36**

Note. ID= Intellectual disability; ASD= Autism spectrum disorders; TD= Typically developing.

** Correlation is significant at the 0.01 level (2-tailed).

Findings in the table 68 revealed significant negative association between adaptive skills domains and negative affectivity. However, significant positive association was observed between surgency, effortful control and adaptive skills domains.

Table 69

Correlation between Daily Living Skills and Temperament Domains for the Three Groups

	ID	ASD	TD
Activity Level	.29**	.27**	.30**
Activity Control	.23*	.06	.25**
Affiliation	.11	.04	-.21**
Anger/ Frustration	-.47**	-.26*	-.21**
Approach/ Positive Anticipation	.16	.23	.18**
Assertiveness	.06	.10	.33**
Attentional Focusing	.35**	.16	.09
Discomfort	-.43**	-.35**	-.15*
Falling Reactivity/ Soothability	-.41**	-.33**	-.30**
Fear	-.40**	-.41**	-.31**
Fantasy Openness	.03	.09	-.22**
High Intensity Pleasure	.30**	.36**	.36**
Impulsivity	.36**	.33**	.42**
Inhibitory Control	.42**	.20	.09
Low Intensity Pleasure	.36**	.34**	.26**
Perceptual Sensitivity	.41**	.25*	.31**
Sadness	-.49**	-.35**	-.22**
Shyness	.41**	.24*	.09

Note. ID= Intellectual disability; ASD= Autism spectrum disorders; TD= Typical developing. ** Correlation is significant at the 0.01 level (2-tailed).

Most of the subscales of temperament observed to have significant positive association with adaptive skills subscales. Anger frustration, discomfort, soothability, fear and sadness subscales had significant negative correlation with subscales of adaptive skills. Approach positive anticipation, assertiveness and fantasy openness had non significant correlation.

Table 70

Correlation between Social Skills and Temperament Domains for the Three Groups

	ID	ASD	TD
Activity Level	.36**	.14	.13*
Activity Control	.20*	-.09	.03
Affiliation	.11	-.03	.06
Anger/ Frustration	-.51**	-.27**	.07
Approach/ Positive Anticipation	.33	.19	-.21**
Assertiveness	.08	.18	.12
Attentional Focusing	.30**	.23*	.03
Discomfort	-.48**	-.29**	-.09
Falling Reactivity/ Soothability	-.44**	-.34**	-.25**
Fear	-.45**	-.36**	-.24**
Fantasy Openness	.01	-.003	.06
High Intensity Pleasure	.33**	.29**	.23**
Impulsivity	.42**	.30**	.29**
Inhibitory Control	.31**	.24*	.08
Low Intensity Pleasure	.27**	.38**	.01

	ID	ASD	TD
Perceptual Sensitivity	.33**	.34**	.13
Sadness	-.53**	-.33**	-.18**
Shyness	.37**	.23*	.04

Note. ID= Intellectual disability; ASD= Autism spectrum disorders; TD= Typical developing. ** Correlation is significant at the 0.05 level (2-tailed). *Correlation is significant at the 0.01 level (2-tailed).

The social skills domain revealed to have positive dimensions of temperament and had negative association with most of the scales that are included in negative affectivity. Discomfort, fear, sadness, falling reactivity indicated significant inverse association with social skills across all developmental groups. The scores of children in ASD group show significant inverse correlation of most of the scales of temperament with social skills. Whereas, the other two groups suggested a positive association between most temperamental dimensions and social skills domain.

Table 71

Correlation between Self Care and Temperament Domains for the Three Groups

	ID	ASD	TD
Activity Level	.36**	.20	.17*
Activity Control	.29**	.01	.09
Affiliation	.19*	.06	.13
Anger/ Frustration	-.56**	-.29**	.16*
Approach/ Positive Anticipation	.31	.24	-.11
Assertiveness	.12	.01	.29**
Attentional Focusing	.32**	.18	.14*
Discomfort	-.54**	-.31**	-.18**

Falling Reactivity/ Soothability	-.51**	-.27*	-.24**
Fear	-.51**	-.37**	-.23**
Fantasy Openness	.09	.08	.15*
High Intensity Pleasure	.35**	.36**	.30**
Impulsivity	.44**	.29**	.35**
Inhibitory Control	.35**	.21*	.15*
Low Intensity Pleasure	.35**	.38**	.04
Perceptual Sensitivity	.40**	.32**	.22**
Sadness	-.59**	-.31**	-.19**
Shyness	.39**	.23*	-.13*

The self care domain revealed to have significant positive relationship with most of the subscales of temperament. The three groups showed somewhat similar pattern of association between self care and temperamental domains. However, anger frustration dimension of temperament presented a reverse pattern. In ID and ASD groups, this dimension had significant negative association with self care, whereas, typically developing group revealed significant positive correlation though the strength was very low. A similar trend could be observed on shyness, TD groups had significant negative correlation between shyness and self-care, but ID and ASD groups had significant positive correlation between these variables.

Table 72

Correlation between Home Living and Temperament Domains for the Three Groups

	ID	ASD	TD
Activity Level	.29**	.17	.12
Activity Control	.29**	.14	.02
Affiliation	.26**	.19	.07
Anger/ Frustration	-.57**	-.29**	.07
Approach/ Positive Anticipation	.26	.32	-.28**
Assertiveness	.16	.12	.16
Attentional Focusing	.20*	.02	.12
Discomfort	-.56**	-.52**	-.30**
Falling Reactivity/ Soothability	-.57**	-.49**	-.32**
Fear	-.50**	-.52**	-.42**
Fantasy Openness	.14	.25*	.06
High Intensity Pleasure	.26**	.31**	.19**
Impulsivity	.41**	.27**	.22**
Inhibitory Control	.23*	.11	.11
Low Intensity Pleasure	.22*	.22*	.11
Perceptual Sensitivity	.28**	.17	.19**
Sadness	-.58**	-.49**	-.30**
Shyness	.32**	.17	-.18**

** Correlation is significant at the 0.05 level (2-tailed). *Correlation is significant at the 0.01 level (2-tailed).

In general, the findings of this section supported the hypothesis that negative affectivity has inverse association with adaptive skills scores. This hypothesis was supported by findings of correlation in combined sample and across groups. Negative affectivity was found to have significant negative association with composite and domain scores of adaptive skills. Surgency and effortful control were observed to have significant positive association with composite and domain scores of adaptive skills in all three groups.

The Gender Differences on Scores of Temperament Across Three Groups. The following section presents the differences and similarities of temperament across three developmental groups in relation to gender. MANOVA was carried out to find out whether the performance of groups differed on sub domains of adaptive behavior and temperament. Mean scores on temperament are presented in table 73 and table 74 presents the findings of MANOVA.

Table 73

Mean and Standard Deviations of Scores on Three Main Domains of Temperament For Sample

	Full Sample	ID	ASD	TD
		(*n* = 105)	(*n* = 92)	(*n* = 238)
	M (SD)	*M (SD)*	*M (SD)*	*M (SD)*
Surgency	17.95 (6.91)	16.72 (5.24)	15.33 (6.68)	20.66 (6.65)
Effortful Control	13.96 (4.12)	14.97 (4.69)	13.29 (3.81)	16.90 (3.09)
Negative Affectivity	27.76 (15.65)	14.40 (6.73)	19.01 (5.57)	12.64 (5.53)

Note. ID= Intellectual disability; ASD= Autism spectrum disorders; TD= Typical developing.

In total sample the score on surgency ranged from 5.33 to 37, the range in ID, ASD and TD groups was 8.28 – 30.45, 6.68 – 33.76 and 5.33 – 37 respectively. The score on Effortful control was from 6.10 to 29.4 in total sample, in ID group it ranged from 5.66 - 27.00, ASD 6.52 – 26.00 and 7.00 – 32.17 in TD group. The score on negative affectivity ranged from 5.25 – 25.83 in ID, 5.54 – 27.91 ASD and 5.69 – 39.07 in TD group.

Figure . 11.

Mean Scores of Three Groups on Surgency, Effortful Control and Negative Affectivity Dimensions of Temperament.

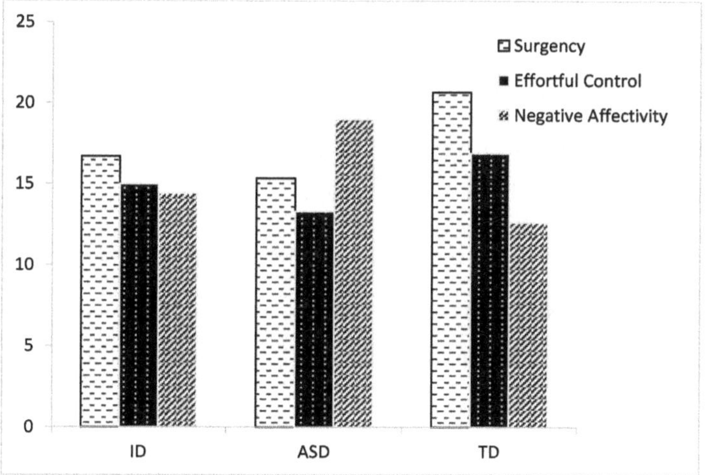

The figure revealed that ASD group scored highest on negative affectivity and lowest on effortful control. Whereas, typically developing group scored highest on surgency and lowest on negative affectivity.

Table 74

Gender Differences in Mean Scores of Temperament Subscales for TD Group

Effects	Value	F	Sig.	Partial Eta Squared
Gender				
Wilke's Lambada	.95	6.70	.00	.15

Wilk's Λ= .95, F (3, 428) = 6.70, p < .001, multivariate $\dot{\eta}^2$= .15.

The table 74 indicated significant variations in mean scores of two gender groups on three dependent variables, that is, dimensions of temperament. Approximately 15% of multivariate variance of the dependent variables was observed to be associated with gender. The follow-up univariate ANOVAs indicated that all three dimensions of temperament were significantly different for girls and boys. For surgency F (1, 430) = 5.27, p < .001, η^2 = .12, effortful control was F (1, 430) = 5.71, p < .001, η^2 = .13, and F (1, 430) = 1.03, p> .001, η^2 = .02 were the observed values for negative affectivity domains. The detailed analysis revealed that girls across all three groups scored relatively high on negative affectivity whereas, boys scored relatively higher on surgency. Girls from all groups also scored comparatively higher on effortful control across all groups.

Predictors of Adaptive Skills. In order to investigate the relationship between adaptive skills and different psychosocial factors, the hierarchical multiple linear regressions were carried out. Family income, family structure, child's age, gender and IQ score were employed as predictors to explore their influence on adaptive functioning score. The details are mentioned below.

Table 75

Multiple Linear Regression Analysis for Family Income, Age and IQ as Predictors of Adaptive Skills Scores

Variables	Model 1		Model 2			
	B	β	B	B		95.0% CI
(Constant)	161.89		37.95			[-22.53, 98.43]
Family Income	.00	-.18		-.17		[-2.11, 8.33]
Age	2.39	.06	3.11	.08		[.00, .00]
IQ			2.90**	.45**		[2.02, 3.79]
R^2	.04				.24	
F	2.97*				16.61**	
ΔR^2	.03				.21	
ΔF					42.34**	

Note. CI = confidence interval

*p < .05. **p< .01.

Table 75 revealed that only the presence of psychopathology significantly predicted the adaptive skills scores. The hypothesis that "family income significantly predicts the adaptive skills" score proved insignificant. However, the hypothesis that "IQ significantly predicts adaptive skills" observed to be significant. Family income and age together accounted for 3.6 percent of variance, whereas, when IQ was added into the model the percentage of variability accounted for increased to 24.2 percent, depicting a significant increase. The value of F ratio was also significant and supported that IQ was a significant predictor of adaptive skills.

Table 76

Multiple Linear Regression Analysis for Diagnosis, Family System and Gender as Predictors of Adaptive Skills Scores

Predictor	Model 1		Model 2		
	B	β	B	β	95.0% CI
(Constant)	138.18**		157.31*		[124.82, 189.79]
Disability	45.21**	.66	45.12*	.66**	[40.26, 49.98]
Family System	-12.46	-.07	-12.77	-.07	[-25.58, .05]
Gender			-11.57	-.06	[-24.44, 1.30]
R^2	.44		.44		
F	166.74**		112.75**		
ΔR^2			.00		
ΔF			3.12		

Note. CI = confidence interval
*p < .05. **p < .01.

Table 76 showed that only the presence of developmental psychopathology (disability status) significantly predicted the adaptive skills scores. When gender was added into the model it failed to increase the percentage of variability accounted for prediction, the value of F ratio also supports the disability status as an important predictor of adaptive skills score instead of gender. Therefore, the hypothesis that "gender significantly predicts the adaptive skills scores" proved insignificant.

Table 77

Multiple Linear Regression Analysis for Surgency, Effortful Control and Negative Affectivity as Predictors of Adaptive Skills Composite Scores

Predictor	Model 1 B	β	Model 2 B	B	95.0% CI
(Constant)	53.90		175.79		[136.36, 215.22]
Surgency	3.89**	.29	2.05	.16	[.88, 3.21]
Eff. Control	7.74**	.34	6.87	.30	[4.99, 8.75]
N. Affectivity			-5.14	-.36	[-6.29, -3.98]
R^2	.29**			.39**	
F	87.26**			93.46**	
ΔR^2					
ΔF	87.26**			75.51**	

Note. CI = confidence interval
*$p < .05$. **$p < .01$.

Table 77 indicated that the surgency and effortful control dimensions of temperament together accounted for 29 percent of variance while predicting adaptive skills scores. The negative affectivity on the other hand, increased the percentage of variability accounted for prediction to 40 percent, the value of F ratio was also significant and thus supported the three dimensions of temperament as important predictors of adaptive functioning score in this sample. The difference between values of R-square and adjusted R was observed to be small indicating the satisfactory generalizability of predictive power of temperament dimensions even to other samples.

Discussion.

The current study attempted to assess the adaptive skills of children and to explore the psychosocial correlates of adaptive behaviors in children following typical development, those diagnosed with autism spectrum disorders and or intellectual disabilities. For this purpose, a sample of 437 children was selected and assessed for different demographic variables, adaptive skills and temperament from Lahore city. Majority of the sample comprised boys reflecting the general population trend which showed that the number of boys was relatively higher compared to girls in general population of Pakistan (CIA World Facts, 2012).

When adaptive behavior scores were analyzed with reference to demographic factors the results presented an interesting picture. Majority of the sample belonged to joint family system, and this family system was observed to have inverse relationship with adaptive skills scores. This trend was observed across all three groups. The reason might be that the presence of more family members provides permanent assistance to children in terms of routine tasks. Consequently, due to this constant availability of help, children may not need to carry out and practice the routine chores themselves that were related to adaptive skills development. On the other hand, there are comparatively fewer family members present in nuclear family system, and this situation actually helps children initiate and master many adaptive behaviors. As when no one is available all the time to fix food for the child, family members try to teach many small self help and safety skills so that they can effectively handle the small daily demands.

Siblings are considered social partners and believed to impact each other's development in multiple ways, but the role and behaviors of siblings is said to be dependent on different factors like child characteristics and cultural values and norms (McHale, Updegraff, & Whiteman, 2012). The number of siblings was assumed to be another factor related with adaptive skills. The results of children with ID and ASD supported the hypothesis, whereas, the scores of children with typical development did not support it. Although, review of literature did not reveal much research on role of siblings in adaptive skills attainment in ID and ASD children, findings of ID and ASD group could be supported by the role of siblings in general development. McHale and Susan (1989) compared siblings of intellectually challenged children with siblings of children following typical development. They reported that siblings of children with ID shared more positive emotions and provided more care giving to their sibling with ID in comparison of siblings of children with normal development. Smith, Romski, and Sevcik (2013) studied the communication and quality of sibling relationships in pairs with and without disabilities. They concluded that siblings of children with disabilities were more helping and provided good assistance to their disabled siblings in managing behavior. Perhaps the presence of typically developing children provided ID and ASD children good learning stimulation and frequent modeling of correct forms of adaptive skills might have helped them acquire and practice those behaviors. Another possibility was that siblings at times perceive their typically developing siblings as competitors, exhibit negative emotions towards them and could be less motivating to them. Kaminsky and Dewey (2002) compared the siblings of Down syndrome's and ASD children to siblings of children with typical development. They observed that the siblings of ASD children and Down syndrome had more appreciation of their siblings, having fewer quarrels and competitiveness in relationship with their special sibling as compared to siblings of normally developing children.

Many studies noted family income as a vital demographic variable contributing directly to the developmental process of children (Durkin, Hasan, & Hasan, 1998) as family income is closely associated with providing means of behavioral and cognitive stimulation which in turn is related to high performance on different developmental domains (Nievar & Luster, 2006). However, the present study observed an interesting blend of findings in this regard. Adaptive skills were observed to be negatively associated with family income among children with intellectual disability and ASD, whereas it shared a positive relationship with adaptive skills in typically developing children. No research could be found that observed these two variables in Pakistan, however, the above finding can be related with those reported by Khan, Quadri, & Aziz (2014) that lower family income was positively related with the development of negative behaviors. This finding may reflect the possibility that better income families generally have access to more domestic help (domestic servants) and may provide more assistance to children which in turn provide less stimulation to practice and master different skills as is also reported by Nievar and Luster (2006). Another reason may be a heightened sense of responsibility of parents towards providing special children with more supportive assistance in an attempt to make things easier for them. In contrast to these two groups the children following typical developmental pattern observed to have a positive relationship between adaptive skills scores and family income and which is in line with some previous researches reporting a positive trend between family income and adaptive skills (Durkin et al., 1998).

As far as the parental marital status was concerned, single parents (divorcee and or widower) shown to have inverse relationship with adaptive skills. This pattern was stable in almost all groups. No research was found that directly assessed the relationship between parental marital status and adaptive skills. However, there are some researches that discussed the association between parental marital status and problem behaviors. One such study was conducted by Amato and Cheadle (2008) who concluded that parental marital conflicts and divorce were positively associated with problem behaviors. Bradley and Corwyn (2008) also reported positive association between negative maternal attitude and behavioral problems of children. Problem behaviors and adaptive functioning shared negative relationship, therefore, it could be assumed that parental marital status was associated with development of adaptive functioning. This might be because in stable families the couple not only provided support to each other but also facilitate and assist children in their learning process. Parental education presented a mixed finding, in general father's education was positively correlated with all domains of adaptive skills but home living skills. However, in children with ID and ASD this relationship was inversed. On the other hand, mother's education presented the same pattern of relationship generally and only shared a negative relationship with all adaptive skills domains among children with ID. The possible reason might be same as was discussed in family income. Moreover, parental age observed to have a negative correlation with all domains of adaptive skills and this trend was evident across all groups. The reason might be that the older parents were not as actively participating in the developmental process of their children as young parents due to lack of physical energy or burden of other responsibilities.

Other than the family indicators, some personal demographic indicators were also assumed to be playing part in development of adaptive skills for instance age, gender, presence of behavior problems and cognitive functioning. Though adaptive skills were usually considered to be developing in accordance with chronological age as in previous study of this project and even in typically developing of the current study an age related progression was observed between these two variables (Goldberg et al., 2009). The findings were mixed as these two variables have positive relationship among children with ID and typical development, however, an inverse relationship between adaptive skills and chronological age was observed in children being diagnosed with ASD. The negative association between age and adaptive skills score among ASD children was in line with previous findings presented by many experts reporting negative impact of older age on adaptive functioning in children with ASD (Pugliese et al., 2015). This inverse relationship might be a result of developmental disabilities which repressed the growth in multiple domains of development while the chronological age remains stable. The stability of chronological age against the delayed and or impaired growth across different developmental domains only increased this discrepancy (Dykens, Hodapp & Evans, 2006). When chronological age was used as a criterion to assess the growth in developmental domains among children with ASD, it generally results in reverse pattern compared to children with typical development (Duncan, & Bishop, 2013; Klin et al., 2006). Kanne et al., (2011) also found a negative relationship between adaptive skills scores and age when assessed among children with ASD. There are many researches that either reported lack of association or negative association between adaptive skills scores and chronological age among children with developmental disabilities and physical conditions that lead to compromised growth like brain tumors etc. (Klein-Tasman et al., 2013). An opposite pattern of relationship between age and adaptive skills was noted among children with typical development which was in line with the previous research that studied adaptive functioning in typically developing children (Fombonne, & Achard, 1993; Goldberg et al., 2009). Regardless of the different patterns of association observed among groups, in general the age emerged as a factor indicating mean differences in scores of participants across all domains of adaptive functioning. These results stood in agreement with results of many previous researches which concluded that adaptive skills scores differ across different age groups (Thomas, Kelly, Mattson, & Riley,1998).

The association of behavioral problems with adaptive skills was also explored in this study, as behavioral problems are generally observed to hinder the normal functioning and performance of children (Achenbach,1991). The findings reveal a significant negative relationship between behavioral problems and adaptive skills among both children with autism spectrum disorders and those with intellectual disability. This result was in accordance with the earlier done researches which explored the relationship between these two variables and concluded that the presence of behavior problems was related to low adaptive skills scores among children and adolescents (Gardiner, & Iarocci, 2015).

Gender was studied as another personal demographic indicator of adaptive skills. However, gender was not observed to be related to any differences in adaptive skills scores across groups. It was only the self help domain among typically developed children that revealed the gender differences in scores. This finding was not in accordance with other researches that concluded significant gender differences in adaptive functioning (Bornstein & Hahan, 2007; Oakland, Zhong, & Kane, 2015). But this finding was supported by a study conducted with Indian children which revealed no significant gender differences in adaptive skills scores of children with intellectual disability (Upreti & Singh, 2016).

Intellectual functioning is generally believed to be linked with many developmental dimensions. Adaptive skills and cognitive functioning are generally reported to share a significant positive relationships not only among children with developmental psychopathologies (Woo, & Teoh, 2007) but in children with physical disabilities (Bjoraker, Delaney, Peters, Krivit, & Shapiro, 2006; Peters et al., 2004; Ji, Yao, Chen, Li, & Zhao, 2014) and typical development as well (Goldberg et al., 2009). An interesting pattern of relationships between adaptive skills and cognitive level was found in the different IQ subgroups. In general IQ was observed to share a positive relationship with all domains of adaptive functioning, which was consistent with finding of other researches (Perry, Flanagan , Geier & Freeman, 2009; Bradley et al., 1995). The findings of present phase revealed that adaptive scores shared significant positive correlation with intellectual functioning, the strength of correlation ranged from low to moderate and this finding remained stable across all three groups. Since long, intelligence and adaptive skills considered to be two distinct constructs that only share certain degree of relatedness (Keith et al.,1987). This moderate correlation was the result of the distinct nature of two constructs, that is, adaptive behaviors and intelligence (Tesse et al., 2007).

When the cognitive functioning of children with ID was compared to those of ASD, the difference was significant, which is supported by the previous research that children with ID comparatively have better cognitive functioning than children with ASD (Boltë, & Poustka, 2002; Bishop, Farmer, & Thurm, 2015). The scores of children in ASD group showed relatively stronger correlation with IQ compared to scores of children in ID. This result was observed to be inconsistent compared to the findings of other researches reporting that higher intellectual functioning does not necessarily ensure higher adaptive performance among children with ASD (Mazefsky, Williams, & Minshew, 2008). The discrepancy between adaptive profile scores and IQ was pronounced among children with autism when compared to non autistic children (Bolte & Poutska 2002) including children with intellectual disability (Fenton et al., 2003). The possible reason might be that most of the children in ASD group had been receiving structured behavioral interventions that might had resulted in comparatively better adaptive skills than ASD children not receiving intervention. This argument was also supported by the findings of Eldevik, Hastings, Jahr and Hughes (2012) who compared the children with ASD receiving structured behavioral intervention to children not receiving behavioral intervention in a mainstream preschool and other researches that reported improvement in IQ and adaptive skills scores of autistic children after receiving structured behavior treatment (Eikeseth, Smith, Jahr, & Eldevik, 2007) . The two groups were matched on disability type and other demographic variables like age, cognitive level etc. They concluded that the children who attended structured intervention showed a significant difference in their scores across all domains of adaptive skills compared to children not attending the structured intervention programs.

Temperament is described as significant component directly related and affecting both human functioning and human development (Putnam, Gartstein, & Rothbart, 2008; Schwartz et al., 2004). Adaptive skills when compared to three main domains of temperament showed to have significant positive association with surgency and effortful control but showed negative correlation with negative affectivity, this trend remained same across all groups. This finding was in accordance with the results of other researches (Riggs, Jahromi, Razza, Dillworth-Bart,& Mueller, 2006). Negative affectivity observed to have highest negative correlation with home living skills and this trend was found across all groups. Whereas, surgency and effortful control found to have highest correlations with daily living skills. Self regulation was found to share a significant positive relationship with all domains of adaptive behaviors across groups. This finding was in accordance with findings of previous researches which concluded that self regulation was positively related with multiple indices of adaptive skills from childhood till adulthood (Buckner, Mezzacappa, & Beardslee, 2009). Many studies had reported that temperamental traits based on self regulation and effortful control were predictive of high adaptive functioning among children suffering from intellectual disability (Spinrad et al., 2004), autism (Schwartz et al., 2009) and children following typical developmental pattern (Riggs et al., 2006). The scores of children in ASD group were observed to be significantly high on negative affectivity and lower on self regulation compared to other two groups. The findings of previous researchers supported this result by reporting a similar pattern (Schwartz et al., 2009). Negative affectivity showed the strongest negative correlation with home living skills across all groups. The subsequent strength of correlation with other domains of adaptive skills varied across groups, this variability may be attributable to nature of developmental pattern followed among these groups.

When adaptive skills scores were analyzed across three groups of children, all three groups were significantly different from each other. As expected and mentioned in previous researches, the scores of typically developing children were significantly higher than children with ID (Sadrossadat, Moghaddami & Sadrossadat, 2010) and children with ASD scored lower compared to intellectually challenged children. These findings were in accordance with the results of other researchers concluding that typically developing children usually show better behavioral performance compared to children with physical (Cyrulnik et al., 2008;

Bonita et al., 2013) and developmental disabilities (Zion & Jewey, 2006). The scores of children in ASD group were significantly different than scores of children in ID and typical development groups. The children in ASD had the lowest score on all domains among all three groups and children in typically developing group scored highest on all adaptive behavior domains. In general, these findings were similar with results of the prior studies reporting that children with ID tend to perform significantly better compared to children with ASD on measures of cognitive and adaptive functioning (Perry et al., 2009; Weismer, Lord & Esler, 2010). The adaptive skills of children with diagnosis of ASD and children with normal functioning were significantly different from each other which was supported by the conclusion of Kenworthy, Case, Harms, Martin, & Wallace (2010) that even children with high functioning autism scored significantly lower on adaptive functioning than typically developing children. The children with ASD were believed to perform significantly poor on social skills domain of adaptive skills compared to other domains. However, the present sample did not support this finding; the possible reason might be that most of the children with ASD were receiving regular structured therapy sessions. Research also supported the fact that developmentally delayed children who regularly attend structured treatment programs could show an improvement in their general developmental skills particularly in social skills (Buckley, Bird, Sacks & Archer, 2002).

Apart from exploring the psychosocial correlates of adaptive functioning a forward step was taken to assess the predictive value of some significant demographic variables on the basis of research conducted in western culture. The gender was assumed as a significant predictor but in this particular sample it could not predict adaptive skills, this result was in line with findings of previous researches which explored gender variability and predictors of adaptive skills among intellectually challenged children and siblings of children with cancer reported gender as a non significant predictor of adaptive skills in their sample (Ponkaew, & Sanasuttipun, 2013; Upreti, & Singh, 2016). Likewise, age, parental education and family income also failed to significantly predict the adaptive behavior scores and this was also in accordance with previous findings which inferred same (Persha et al., 2007; Ashford et al., 2016). Cognitive functioning assessed through IQ turned out as a significant predictor of adaptive skills scores in participants of present study and this finding was in accordance with the results of multiple researches reporting IQ as an important predictor of adaptive skills among children with typical development and developmental disabilities (Liss et al., 2001; Kanne et al.,2011). Presence of developmental psychopathology also appeared as a major predictor of adaptive skills. This result was consistent with the data of earlier researches stating that presence and severity of intellectual disability and autistic symptomatology significantly predicted adaptive functioning (Perry et al., 2009).

Summary

Many researchers consider adaptive skills a pertinent dimension of development influencing not only normal human functioning but also development and prognosis of various developmental psychopathologies (Klinger, Klinger, Mussey, Thomas, & Powell, 2015). The present research was an attempt to assess adaptive skills and to explore related psychosocial correlates and predictors in children. This research was conceptualized in two main phases. Phase – I was focused on developing an indigenous adaptive behaviors scale for children and developing its psychometric characteristics. Phase- II was aimed to assess adaptive behaviors and explore its association with significant psychosocial factors among children following different patterns of development.

Due to absence of standardized measure of adaptive functioning for children in Pakistan, the first phase was aimed at developing an indigenous measure to assess adaptive skills of children. Standard procedures were employed to develop the indigenous AB scale (Giesler, Forster, Bille, & Fabry, 2011) and strong efforts were made to use the set of procedures frequently mentioned in literature to establish psychometric characteristics of the indigenous tool (Carter, Briggs-Gowman, Jones & Little, 2003). After developing the initial pool of items, the next consideration was to assess whether the indigenously developed adaptive behavior scale own the typical features considered characteristic of the adaptive skill construct. The evidence of validity in present research was built on findings of content validity analysis (Alonso et al., 2010; Luckasson, 2002), construct validity and criterion validity. The standard formula of ICVI was used to calculate content validity (Haynes et al., 1995; Sealy et al., 2016) and total 264 items were selected out of 397 items on the basis of

ICVI ratio. Next step was to assess the criterion validity. Examining the latent means of adaptive behavior scores across gender and age made score invariance evident for almost all sub-domains of adaptive behavior scale. As expected, most sub-domains revealed differences in mean level scores across age and gender that supported criterion validity (Rojahn, Matson, Lott, Esbensen & Smalls, 2001). This method was also employed in many studies previously to evaluate criterion related validity (Marteleto & Pedromonico, 2005). The statistically significant results not only indicated adequate criterion validity but also showed the strength of indigenously developed scale to measure various pertinent characteristics of adaptive construct (Schalock,1999). Construct validity was established through factor structure, convergence and divergence of adaptive skill scores. The factorial structure of the scale was established through factor analysis as it was reported as one of the strongest method to test construct validity (Fayers & Machin, 2000). The analysis of multifactor models helped choosing the 4 factor structure as the final structure for newly established scale. This convulsion was based on multiple criteria mentioned in literature such as Eigen values, scree plot, total variances explained by factors and theoretical relevance (Field, 2009). Another evidence supporting the factor structure was that all items shared medium to very strong positive correlation with the total score, and items showed comparatively higher correlation with the total score of the respective subscale in which they were placed and relatively weak correlation with total score of other subscales supporting the validity of the selected factor structure (Marnat, 2009; Piland, Motl, Guskiewicz, Mccrea, and Ferrara, 2006) and was in line with the previous research findings that reported significant high correlation in all the various domains of adaptive behaviors (Alonso et al., 2010). This was also supported by another evidence which primarily was used to support the convergent validity. This characteristic was often established by assessing the degree of relatedness between scores of two independent measures based on similar theoretical orientation (Anastasi,1997; Barbuto & Wheeler, 2006; Luo et al., 2010). Therefore, the scores on newly developed adaptive behavior scale were compared with the scores of CABS another adaptive behavior measure developed in a western country for children. The findings revealed positive correlation ranging from 0.39 to 0.89 between scores of the two adaptive behavior measures. Instruments measuring similar constructs are not likely to always generate excellent correlation, and moderate correlation was taken as a reflection of variations in test content, differences in item presentation and cultural changes in societies in which two measures were developed (Cicchetti, 1994) which was also the case in current research. The moderate to high positive correlation between scores of the two adaptive behavior instruments indicated good evidence of convergent validity (Cicchetti, 1994). One popular technique for establishing discriminant validity is to use the matched group approach (Cicchetti, 1994) where experts assess the instruments' ability to differentially identify the members of each group based on their differing characteristics like age, gender and disability status etc. (Bildt et al., 2005). The present project assessed this feature by comparing the scores of children with typical development with scores of those with developmental disabilities. The result revealed that two groups had significant mean differences in scores of all domains of adaptive skills and successfully discriminated participants of both groups based on their scores and performance pattern on adaptive behavior scale. The other popular method for evaluating discriminant validity was also employed which involved comparing the scores on indigenous adaptive behavior measure with scores of CBCL (Barbuto & Wheeler, 2006) which was frequently used to assess behavior problems in children and adolescents. The results revealed that scores of CBCL shared significantly negative and very low correlation with scores of adaptive behaviors. These findings were very much in accordance with literature which concluded that instruments based on different theoretical assumption should produce different scores (Anastasi, 1997; Barbuto & Wheeler, 2006). The convergence of scores within the domain and divergence of the scores between domains also supports the convergent and discriminant validity of the newly developed scale (Barbuto & Wheeler, 2006; Bildt et al., 2005). All the measures of construct validity including factorial structure, convergent and divergent indicated good evidences which supported the construct validity of the newly developed adaptive behavior scale (Strauss, & Smith, 2009).

After collecting sufficient evidences for validity, the next step was to explore the reliability of adaptive behavior scale (Kline, 2015; Peneva et al., 2003). Both the type of reliability index used and the size of the coefficient were considered to assess reliability (Nunhually & Bernstein,1994). The values of reliability coefficient for present AB scale were found to fall in the fair to excellent clinical range (Cicchetti & Sparrow, 1990), contributing to the strengths of the measure in terms of stability (Bildt et al.,2005). Some of the reliability values were noted to be higher than 0.95, which might be considered very high by some. However, many experts (Tavakol, & Dennick, 2011) had described these high values adequate for measures with large number of items and multifactor nature. Experts had also suggested that the reliability coefficient of diagnostic instruments could be as high as 0.95 or above (Nunhually & Bernstein,1994; Pasta, Suhr, 2009) which justify those high values. After determining the primary psychometric features next central concern was to establish reliable cut off scores for newly developed scale. ROC curve, AUC criteria and estimates based on sensitivity and specificity were used to determine cut off scores for subscales and composite score (Emmons & Alfonso, 2005) as these are reported to be valid criteria to select cut off scores (Brown, et al., 1993). In short, the validity and reliability for the indigenously adaptive behavior scale could be seen as corroborated through consistent and mutually supportive findings observed across multiple analyses of different procedures employed in phase-I.

The second phase of this research was to assess adaptive skills in children along with significant correlates. Temperament was selected as a significant correlate of adaptive functioning literature identified it as a significant predictor of academic and general functioning and developmental psychopathologies among children and adolescents (Rettew, & McKee, 2005; Rothbart, Ahadi & Hershey, 1994; Smith & Prior, 1995). Lack of availability of standardized temperament measures in Pakistan for children of 5 through 11 years of age directed the search towards temperament tools developed and standardized in western countries. Finally, the temperament instruments based on models of Rothbart (1984) were selected to be used. These tools were chosen specifically for their well established psychometric features and secondly for their wide use across cultures (Klein, Putnam & Linhares, 2009; Ye, Ming & Rothbart, 1988) including Iran, Saudi Arabia and Turkey that share important religious and cultural ties with Pakistan. Therefore, it was assumed that these measures had a potential to be used for assessment of Pakistani children.

According to experts, measurement instruments should be translated and adapted according to particular socio cultural demands of a specific group to provide reliable information. The failure to do so was said to lead to factual mistakes like misinterpretations and false inferences about a particular group (Byrene et al., 2012). In the light of this, it was decided to translate and adapt both measures of temperament. The cross cultural literature indicate presence of many well established methodological approaches for adaptation and translation of instruments, still the literature is marked with a great variation in the use of these approaches (Johnson, 2006). Present research tried to avoid making significant mistakes during translation and adaptation process (Juniper, 2009). A standard synthesized approach of instrument translation and adaptation reported frequently in literature (International Test Commission, 2010) was preferred to be used in the present study (Hambleton, Merenda, & Spielberger, 2005; Van de Vijver and Leung ,1997). The current research employed a two pronged approach of translation and adaptation of CBQ-T and TMCQ scales involving forward and backward translation procedures, employing committee approach, taking assistance from professional translators and pilot study as these procedures are frequently supported by experts to be used for technically sound translations (Beck, Bernal, & Forman, 2003). The main focus of the translation and adaptation was to use easily comprehendible language, culturally relevant idioms and contextual behavioral examples with which people could easily relate without changing the actual content. As these components play a pertinent role in instrument translation and later application (Borsa et al., 2012; Hambleton, & Patsula,1998). Some of the idioms and speech expressions of original temperament scales were specific to American culture, so instead of simply deleting those items it was decided to replace those words with culturally adequate words to increase the experiential equivalence without compromising the conceptual meaning (Guillemin et al., 1993). The blended methodology for instrument translation and adaption helped establishing a culturally relevant version of CBQ-T and TMCQ forms. Evaluation of the translated instruments on a sample of target population was the next step after translation and synthesis. The complex task of developing culturally relevant translations of psychological instruments is many folds and requires strong evidences of semantic and measurement equivalence of the tool (Beaton et al., 2000), cultural fit and psychometric properties of the translated version (Sousa, & Rojjanasrirat, 2011) to ensure adequacy (Borsa et al., 2012; International Test Commission, 2010).Therefore after completing translation process, psychometric properties were assessed.

The reliabilities for CBQ-T and TMCQ were found to be in acceptable range (Andreu et al., 2008). All the preliminary findings aimed to establish primary psychometric characteristics, however, results showed some differences compared to original questionnaires. Borsa, Damasio and Bandeira (2012) reported that the values of reliability and validity of translated versions may differ from the original instrument due to the background differences in samples on whom both versions are administered. This provide justification for the results observed in the present research. As far as the validity indicators were concerned, content and construct validity indices were established for both measures as these analyses considered essential for translated tools (Helena, Rohlf & Krahé, 2015; Rubio, Berg-Weger, Tebb, Lee, & Rauch, 2003). All these preliminary analyses assessing reliability and validity supported CBQ-T and TMCQ Udru versions as suitable tools to be used in the main study of this research.

The last study of phase II assessed adaptive skills and explored its multiple personal and familial demographic correlates including age, gender, disability status, IQ, family income, parental age, marital status etc.

Gender was assumed to be a significant predictor of adaptive functioning, as adaptive behaviors usually grew out of social role expectations that vary across gender (Bornstein, & Hahan, 2007). Contrary to expectations, findings of present study did not support those reported in western countries (Grigorenko, & Sternberg, 2001), however, was supported by some other researches (Treadwell, Flannery-Schroeder, & Kendall,1995) particularly those conducted in India(Upreti & Singh, 2016) and Veitnam (Vinh, 2014).

When adaptive behaviors of all three groups were compared, children with ASD received scores significantly lower than other two groups. This was supported by findings of many researchers who reported that children with ASD exhibited significantly higher deficits in adaptive behaviors compared to non autistic children (Volkmar et al., 1987; Panerai, Tasca, Ferri,Arrigo & Elia, 2014). It is generally observed that children with ID and ASD follow a pattern and pace of development which is slightly different from children with typical development (Brereton, Tonge & Einfeld,2006) even children with ID and ASD have many developmental variations compared to each other (APA, 2013; Bertelli et al., 2016; Zion, & Jenvey, 2006).

The IQ was another related correlate observed to be relatively lower in children with ASD compared to other two groups which was in line with previous researches (Panerai et al., 2014). In present research, intellectual functioning was noted to have significant positive correlation with adaptive skills, the strength of correlation was observed from weak to moderately strong. This was in line with the findings of many previous studies **(Keith et al., 1987)** that showed the similar pattern of relationship (Bjoraker, Delaney, Peters, Krivit, & Shapiro , 2006). According to researchers, this positive association between these two variables was found evident even among children with physical disabilities (Kushalnagar, Krull, Hannay, Mehta, & Oghalai, 2007) and normal development (Grigorenko, & Sternberg, 2001) all supporting the pattern of findings observed in the present study.

Generally, adaptive behaviors were believed to change in relation to progression in age and this was considered an important characteristic of adaptive functioning. According to the results of the main study, adaptive behavior scores of children with intellectual disability and typical development showed a positive significant relationship with age, however, the children with autism showed a reverse pattern of relationship between age and adaptive behaviors. Some previous researches particularly in children with severe developmental disabilities also reported lack of association (Brown et al., 1993), negative or no association between age and adaptive functioning (Ashford et al., 2014; Vinh, 2014) particularly in ASD (Bishop, Farmer, & Thurm, 2015) and other developmental problems (Kramer, Crittenden, DeSantes,& Cowan,1997). Some researchers also indicated an interesting dimension of relationship between age and adaptive behaviors by reporting that children with developmental disabilities observed to attain some age related adaptive skills during infancy and early childhood, however, their sample evidently showed a no gain or decline in adaptive behavior attainment from middle childhood through adolescence (Dykens et al., 2006). One possibility might be that the severity of disability increases with age and hindered not only the acquisition of skills but also represses the learning process, which was then reflected in the lower performance on different domains of development regardless of the chronological age. The specific observation of relationship between adaptive behavior scores and age couold be supported by the results of Akram, and Batool (2018) who reported significant negative relationship between age and learning new behaviors (Bailey, Hatton, Mesibov, Ament, & Skinner, 1998; Kumar, Singh, & Akhtar, 2009).

In addition to personal variables, there were many familial factors that were believed to directly or indirectly influence one's development. From the familial factors, family style was taken as an important variable. Most of the participants in the present research belonged to joint family system which is still a popular and preferred family setup for many (Sabah, & Gilani, 2010). The present research contradicted the popular belief of advantages of joint family system (Shakeel & Johar, 2014) by reporting an inverse relationship of joint family system with adaptive skill scores. One possible reason might be that the presence and availability of more family members did not let the child experience many behaviors as their needs were fulfilled by elder family members even in the absence of parents (Sahar, & Muzaffar, 2017). Cultural, social and religious believes usually make family members to provide a less able member with strong assistance which hamper the acquisition of adaptive behaviors in many ways, which might have led to inverse correlation between these two variables. As it was reported in a research conducted by Taverna, Bornstein, Putnick, and Axia (2011) that some cultures intentionally support interdependence in children and this behavioral trait directly affects the acquisition and quality of adaptive behaviors in children.

On the other hand, presence of both parents and number of siblings observed to have positive relationship with adaptive behaviors in general. There was a possibility that presence of both parents provided a certain sense of emotional comfort (Cairney, Boyle, Offord & Racine, 2003; Jackson, Preston & Franke, 2010) to the child and stable home environment that were closely associated with development of adaptive functioning (Glaser et al., 2003). The present results could also be supported by the findings of other studies concluding that parental involvement and support was linked with higher levels of adaptive functioning (Weiss, Sullivan, & Diamond, 2003) and better developmental outcomes (Sabah, & Gilani, 2010) in children with (Haider, & Khan, 2015) and without developmental disabilities (Blacher & McIntyre, 2005; Calkins, Smith, Gill & Johnson, 1998; Manning, 2003). Another related variable was number of siblings which was observed to be positively associated with adaptive behaviors in children with ID and ASD, whereas, the relationship was negative in typical development group. One reason might be that typically developing siblings usually share rivalry and competitiveness, whereas, siblings of children with developmental and physical problems were reported to be more supportive (Umberson, 1987) positively predicting adaptive functioning (Beardslee, Schultz, & Selman, 1987). Another reason might be that presence of typically developing sibling provided good sample of behavior to be imitated by children with ID and ASD as was concluded by Azmitia and Hesser (1993). The findings observed among children with typical developmental groups could be supported by results of Akram and Batool (2018) who reported that the higher number of siblings had significant inverse effects on the development of positive traits and behaviors in adolescents.

Previous work (Leerkes, Paradise, O'Brien,Calkins, & Lange, 2008) presented temperament as a strong predictor of adaptive behaviors (Izard, Schultz, Fine, Younstrom, & Ackerman, 2000) and global functioning (Healey, Brodzinsky, Bernstein, Rabinovitz, & Halperin, 2009), therefore, it was included as a study variable. The present study revealed a pattern reported in previous work (Smith & Prior, 1995) that surgency and effortful control domains of temperament shared positive relationship with all domains of adaptive behaviors (Buckner, Mezzacappa, & Beardslee, 2009) particularly among children with ID and ASD (Schawrtz et al., 2009). Negative affectivity of temperament is frequently reported to be inversely associated with functional behaviors (Muris,& Ollendick, 2005), experts often relate this with a wide array of non functional behaviors (Asl, Sighari, Zahra, Pournaghi, & Ghertasi, 2015; Foley, McClowry, & Castellanos, 2008). Inverse relationship was observed between negative affectivity and adaptive behaviors in current research which was supported by results of previous studies (Blair, Denham, Kochanoff, & Whipple, 2004; Vachaa, 2003). Negative affectivity also shared inverse association even with self regulation and effortful control which was in line with previous data (Bradley,2008) reporting that three dimensions of temperament were distinct and surgency and effortful control had inverse correlation with negative affectivity (Nakagawa, Sukigara, Miyachi & Nakai, 2016; Rothbart et al., 2000). It was observed to be highest in children with ASD from all three groups which was noted to be consistent with results of studies (Bostrom, Broberg & Hwang, 2010) reporting that levels of negative affectivity were often high among children and adolescents with ASD (Schawrtz et al., 2009).

As far as the predictors of adaptive functioning were considered, gender and family income failed to predict adaptive behaviors in current data. However, severity of disability and IQ emerged to be significant predictors of adaptive functioning in the current sample. In the main study of present research both intellectual functioning and severity of disability strongly predicted the adaptive functioning and it was in accordance with previous findings (Perry et al., 2009) reporting that intellectual functioning (Puig et al., 2013) and severity of disability in early years strongly predicted adaptive functioning outcomes (Charman et al., 2010; Malhi & Singh, 2015). Temperament also proved to be a significant predictor of adaptive behaviors in current sample. Researchers had reported that the combination of high intellectual functioning and positive temperamental traits strongly predicted better adaptive functioning (Mervis, & Klein-Tasman, 2000) and the findings of the present research also supported this. Hauser-Cram et al., (2001) studied a group of children with developmental disabilities and concluded that type of disability, self regulation on part of children and quality of interaction between mother and child were strong predictor of adaptive behavior trajectories. This finding also supported the results of main study that identified positive temperamental dimensions and type of disability as strong predictors of adaptive behaviors.

Conclusion

Adaptive behaviors play a significant role in an individuals' functioning affecting developmental process particularly during childhood and adolescence. The findings of this project present indigenously developed adaptive behavior scale, CBQ-T and TMCQ Urdu versions as reliable measures to be used for assessment of children in Pakistan. The present research concludes that personal variables like age, intellectual functioning level, specific developmental pattern along with familial variables like family system, parental marital status and number of siblings are significantly associated with the attainment and quality of adaptive functioning. These variables should be taken into account while assessing adaptive behaviors, planning treatment and management programs for children with developmental disabilities particularly intellectual disability and autism spectrum disorders.

Limitations and Recommendations

Despite all the care taken, the current research has some limitations, one of which was sample size for factor analysis. Although, the data of current research fulfilled the primary requirements of factor analysis, a larger sample might have added more strength to the procedure. Therefore, it is strongly recommended to use a larger sample for factor analysis. Confirmatory factor analysis could not be performed due to time constraint and security issues due to which a large sample required for CFA could not be employed. The main reason behind this was the strict security policy for elementary and middle schools implemented after mass shooting incident at Army public school, Peshawar in 2014. Due to security concerns the schools initially remained closed and then they were very reluctant to let an outsider enter the school premises even for research purposes. Even when schools allowed to collect data there was a time issue as school administration was not in comfortable to made students miss their academic work. All these problems made it very hard for collecting large data set required even for exploratory factor analysis. To perform confirmatory factor analysis on 206 items a large data set was required completely independent of the data used for EFA, which was hard at that time.   However, performing confirmatory factor analysis for adaptive behavior and temperament scales would have been more beneficial to explore and confirm the latent structure of the interments. Some research in future can specifically focus to overcome this limitation by running confirmatory factor analysis.

One of the short comings of this project was it's non diverse sample, which was taken mainly from the city of Lahore and two nearby small cities, it would have been more interesting to take sample from at least one city of each province. However, this type of large scale study could not be practically possible for a lone researcher relying solely on her personal resources. Future researchers can extend this basic work to children of other areas of the country. Another limitation was that the percentage of boys in current study outnumbered girls. More representation of girls is strongly suggested to be taken in future studies in this area. Parenting is an important factor considered significantly associated with children's development. Future researchers can also assess parenting styles and explore the relationship between parenting styles and adaptive functioning.

The researcher could not establish standard normative scores for adaptive behaviors scale due to resource constraints. Future studies should aim to develop proper norms for adaptive behavior scale on a large sample. Age, grade, developmental group and gender wise norms can be established by future researchers.

This project only presents the preliminary findings regarding the psychometric properties of adaptive behavior and temperament scales. Although, these preliminary investigations provide promising results, further studies employing larger samples and advanced analyses should be conducted to evaluate these scales.

Primarily due to time and cost restraints, the researcher could not assess cognitive functioning of children with typical development, future researches in this area can also evaluate the exact cognitive level of children with typical development.

Researchers can also examine the association of various psychosocial factors with different dimensions of temperament. Moreover, Urdu temperament scales can be used in researches to examine the applicability of this scale with a larger sample of parents.

Implications

1. The scales used in this study would be helpful for clinical professionals and researchers to evaluate the temperament and adaptive skills of children and will provide easy exploration of these dimensions of child development.

2. Present project would facilitate researchers to understand the adaptive skills of children and their temperament and to carry out more refined researchers in these developmental areas.

3. The findings of this project would be helpful for clinical professional, teachers and researchers to understand the dynamics of adaptive functioning and the role of a range of variables that can influence the temperament and adaptive functioning.

4. The findings can be useful for teachers and clinical professionals in designing more relevant IEPs and assessing the adequacy of treatment programs.

5. Two important instruments to assess children's temperament namely TMCQ and CBQ-T were adapted, translated and validated to use in this research. These scales can be used for research and clinical assessment purposes in future.

REFERENCES

Abramovitch, R., Stanhope, L., Pepler, D., & Corter, C. (1987). The influence of Down's Syndrome on sibling interaction. The *Journal of Child Psychology and Psychiatry, 28*, 865–879.DOI: 10.1111/j.1469-7610.1987.tb00675.x.

Achenbach,T.M., & Edelbrock, C. (1983). Manual for the child behavior checklist and revised child behavior profile. Burlington, VT: University of Vermont, Department of Psychiatry.

Achenbach, T.M. (1991). Integrateive guide for the 1991 CBCL/4-18, YSR and TRF profiles. Burlington: University of Vermont, Department of Psychiatry.

Achenbach, T.M. (2005). Advancing assessment of children and adolescents: Commentary on evidence-based assessment of child and adolescent disorders. *Journal of Clinical Child and Adolescent Psychology,34*, 541-547.

Achenbach, T.M., & Ruffle, T.M. (2000). The child behavior checklist and related forms for assessing behavioral/ emotional problems and competencies. *Pediatrics in Review,21*, 265-271.

Adams, G.L. (2000). CTAB-R and NABC-R technical manual. Seattle, WA: Educational Achievement Systems.

Aertssen, W.F.M., Ferguson, G.D., & Smits-Engelsman, B.C.M.(2016). Reliability and structural and construct validity of the functional strength measurement in children aged 4 to 10 years. *Physical Therapy, 96*, 888-897.

Ahadi, S.A., Rothbart, M. K., & Ye, R. (1993). Children's temperament in the US and China: Similarities and differences. *European Journal of Personality, 7*, 359 – 377.

Akram, M., & Batool, Z. (2018). Effect of parental conflict on adolescents personality development in Pakistan. *Journal of Applied Environmental and Biological Sciences, 8* (6), 44 – 49.

Allana, S., Ali, T., Khowaja, K., Khan, A.H., & Moser, D.K. (2013). Validity and Reliability Testing: Urdu translated modified response to symptoms questionnaire. *Journal of the College of Physicians and Surgeons Pakistan, 23,* 383 – 387.

Allen, R.M., Cortazzo, A.D., & Adamo, C. (1970). Factors in an adaptive behavior check list for use with retardates. *Training School Bulletin, 67,* 144-157.

Allen-Meares, P. (2008). Assessing the adaptive behavior of youths: Multicultural responsivity. Social Work, 53, 307 -316.

Allen, R.M., Cortazzo, A.D., & Adamo, C. (1970). Factors in an adaptive behavior check list for use with retardates. Training School Bulletin, 67, 144-157. A

Alonso, I. G., Anuncibay, R.F.,& Hawrylak, M.F. (2010). Adaptation of the ABS-S:2 for use in Spain with children with intellectual disabilities. *Journal of Policy and Practice in Intellectual Disabilities, 7, 221–230.*

American Association on Mental Retardation. (1992). Mental retardation: Definition, classification, and systems of support (9th ed.). Washington, DC: American Association on Mental Retardation.

American Association on Mental Retardation. (2002). Mental retardation: Definition, classification, and systems of support (10th ed.). Washington, DC: American Association on Mental Retardation.

American Psychiatric Association. (2000). Diagnostic and statistical manual of mental disorders (text revision). Washington DC: American Psychiatric Association Press.

American Psychiatric Association. (2013). *Diagnostic and statistical manual of mental disorders (5thed.).* Arlington, VA: American Psychiatric Publishing Company.

Amato, P.R., & Cheadle, J.E. (2008). Parental divorce, marital conflict and children's behavior problems: A comparison of adopted and biological children. *Social Forces, 86,* 1139-1161.

Annastasi, A. (1997). Psychological testing. New York: Macmillan Publishing Company.

Anastasi, A., & Urbina, S. (1997). *Psychological testing* (7th ed.). New York: Macmillan.

Anderson, D.K., Oti, R.S., Lord, C., & Welch, K.(2009). Patterns of growth in adaptive social abilities among children with autism spectrum disorders. *Journal of Abnormal Child Psychology,37,* 1019–1034. doi:10.1007/s10802-009-9326-0.

Andreu,Y., Galdón, M.J., Dura, E., Ferrando, M., Murgui, S., García, A., & Ibáñez, E.(2008). Psychometric properties of the Brief Symptoms Inventory-18 (BSI-18) in a Spanish sample of outpatients with psychiatric disorders. *Psicothema,20,* 844-850.

Archer, R.P., Maruish, M., Imhof, E.A., & Piotrowski, C. (1991). Psychological test usage with adolescent clients: 1990 survey findings. *Professional Psychology: Research and Practice, 22,* 247-252.

Arias, B., Verdugob, M.A., Navasb, P., & Gomezc, L.E. (2013). Factor structure of the construct of adaptive behavior in children with and without intellectual disability. *International Journal of Clinical and Health Psychology,13,* 155-166.

Ashford, J.M., Netson, K.L., Clark, K.N., Merchant, T.E., Santana, V.M., Wu, S., & Conklin, H.M. (2014). Adaptive functioning of childhood brain tumor survivors following conformal radiation therapy. *Journal of Neurooncology,118,* 193–199. doi:10.1007/s11060-014-1420-7.

Asl, A.N., Sighari, D.A., Zahra, J., Pournaghi, A. F., & Ghertasi, O. S. (2015). The Influence of Parenting Style and Child Temperament on Child-Parent-Dentist Interactions. *Pediatric Dentistry, 37,* 342-347.

Azmitia, M.,& Hesser, J. (1993). Why siblings are important agents of cognitive development: A comparison of siblings and peers. *Child Development,64,* 430 – 444. DOI: 10.1111/j.1467-8624.1993.tb02919.x

Baghooli, H., Toeiserkani, M., & Chavooshi, B. (2009). Vineland adaptive behavior scale for people with mental retardation, emotional disorders, and behavioral problems. *Iranian Rehabilitation Journal,7,* 1-18.

Bailey, A., Palferman,S., Heavey, L.,& Le Couteur, A. (1998). Autism: The phenotypes in relatives. *Journal of Autism and Developmental Disorders, 28,* 369–392. doi:10.1023/A:1026048320785.

Bailey, D.B., Hatton, D.D., & Skinner, M. (1998). Early developmental trajectories of males with fragile X syndrome. *American Journal on Mental Retardation, 103,* 29-39

Bailey DB, Hatton DD, Mesibov GB, Amnet N, Skinner M. (2000). Early development, temperament and functional impairment in autism and fragile X syndrome. *Journal of Autism and Development Disorders, 30,* 49–59.

Baird, G., Charman, T., Cox, A., Baron-Cohen, S., Swettenham, J., Wheelwright, S., & Drew, A. (2001). Screening and surveillance for autism and pervasive developmental disorders. *Archives of Disease in Childhood, 14,* 468-475.

Bal, V. H., Kim, S., Cheong, D., & Lord, C. (2015). Daily living skills in individuals with autism spectrum disorder from 2 to 21 years of age. *Autism, 19,* 774–784.

Barbuto, John E. & Wheeler, Daniel W. (2006). Scale Development and Construct Clarification of Servant Leadership. *Faculty Publications: Agricultural Leadership, Education & Communication Department.* Paper 51. http://digitalcommons.unl.edu/a glecfacpub/51.

Barkley, R. A. (Ed.). (2014). *Attention-deficit hyperactivity disorder: A handbook for diagnosis and treatment* (2nd ed.). New York: Guilford Publications.

Barnes, S. K., & Burchard, M. S. (2009). Developing a scale to assess self-efficacy for response to intervention practices in schools. *NERA Conference Proceedings 2009.* Paper 14. http://digitalcommons.uconn.edu/nera_2009/14.

Baughman, A.L., Bisgard, K.M., Edwards, K.M., Guris, D., Decker, M.D., Holland, K., Meade, B.D., & Lynn, F. (2004). Establishment of diagnostic cutoff points for levels of serum antibodies to pertussis toxin, filamentous hemagglutinin and fimbriae in adolescents and adults in the United States. *Clinical and Diagnostic Laboratory Immunology, 11*, 1045-1053. DOI: 10.1128/CDLI.11.6.1045-1053.2004

Baumgartner, T.A. (2009). Tutorial: Calculating Percentile ranks and percentile norms using SPSS. *Measurement in Physical Education and Exercise Science,13*, 227 – 233.

Bates, M. J. (1986). Subject access in online catalogs: A design model. *Journal of the American Society for Information Science, 37*, 357-368.

Bates, J. E., Wachs, T. D., & Emde, R. N. (1994). Toward practical uses of biological concepts of temperament. In J. E. Bates & Y. D. Wachs (Eds.), *Temperament: Individual differences at the interface of biology and behavior* (pp. 275-306). Washington, D.C.: American Psychology Association.

Bean, G.A., & Roszkowski, M.J. (1982). Item domain relationships in the adaptive behavior scale. *Applied Research in Mental Retardation,3*, 359 – 367.

Beardslee, W. R., Schultz, L. H., Selman, R. L. (1987). Level of social-cognitive development, adaptive functioning, and *DSM-III* diagnoses in adolescent offspring of parents with affective disorders: Implications of the development of the capacity for mutuality. *Developmental Psychology, 23*, 807-815.

Beaton, D.E., Bombardier, C., Guillemin, F., & Ferraz, M.B. (2000). Guidelines for the process of cross-cultural adaptation of self-report measures. *Spine, 15*, 3186 – 3191.

Beavers, A.S., Lounsbury, J.W., Richards, J.K., Huck, S.W., Skolits, G.J., & Esquivel, S.L. (2013). Practical Considerations for Using Exploratory Factor Analysis in Educational Research. *Practical Assessment, Research and Evaluation, 18*,ISSN 1531-7714.

Beck, C.T., Bernal, H., Forman, R.D. (2003). Methods to document semantic equivalence of a translated scale. *Research in Nursing Health, 26*, 64 – 73.

Belsky, J. (1999). Interactional and contextual determinants of attachment security. In: Cassidy J, & Shaver, P.R. (eds) *Handbook of attachment: theory, research, and clinical applications*. Guilford, New York pp. 249–264.

Benda,C.E. (1969). *Down's syndrome:Mongolism and its management*. Grune & Stratton.

Benda, C. E., & Strassmann, G. S. (1965). The Thymus in mongolism. *Journal of Mental Deficiency Research, 9*, 109-117.

Biederman, J., Milberger, S., Faraone, S. V., Kiely, K., Guite, J., Mick, E., & Reed, E. (1995).Family-environment risk factors for attention-deficit hyperactivity disorder: A test of Rutter's indicators of adversity. *Archives of general psychiatry,52*, 464-470.

Bertelli, M.O., Munir, K., Harris, J., Salvador- Carulla, L.(2016). Intellectual developmental disorders: reflections on the international consensus document for redefining mental retardation-intellectual disability in ICD-11. *Advances in Mental Health and Intellectual Disabilities, 10*, 36 – 58.

Bildt, A, Kraijer, D., Sytema, S., and Minderaa, R. (2005). The psychometric properties of the Vineland adaptive behavior scales in children and adolescents with mental retardation. *Journal of Autism and Developmental Disorders,35*, 53 – 62.

Bishop, S.L., Farmer, C., & Thurm, A. (2015). measurement of nonverbal IQ in autism spectrum disorder: Scores in young adulthood compared to early childhood. *Journal of Autism and Developmental Disorders, 45*, 966 – 974.

Bjoraker, K.J., Delaney, K., Peters, C., Krivit, W., & Shapiro, E.G. (2006). Long-term outcomes of adaptive functions for children with mucopolysaccharidosis I (Hurler syndrome) treated with hematopoietic stem cell transplantation. *Journal Developmental and Behavioral Pediatrics, 27*, 290 – 296.

Blacher, J., & McIntyre, L.L.(2005). Syndrome specificity and behavioural disorders in young adults with intellectual disability: cultural differences in family impact. DOI: 10.1111/j.1365-2788.2005.00768.x. http://onlinelibrary.wiley.com/doi/10.1111/j.1365-2788.2005.00768.x/full

Blair, K. A., Denham, S.A., Kochanoff, A., & Whipple, B. (2004). Playing it cool: Temperament, emotion regulation, and social behavior in preschoolers. *Journal of School Psychology, 42*, 419 – 443.

Blair, C., & Peters, R. (2003). Physiological and neurocognitive correlates of adaptive behavior in preschool among children in head start. *Developmental Neuropsychology,24,479- 497.*

Boateng, G.O., Neilands, T.B., Frongillo, E.A., Melgar-Quinonez, H. R., & Young, S.L. (2018). Best practices for developing and validating scales for health, social, and behavioral research: A primer. *Frontiers in Public Health, 6.* doi: 10.3389/fpubh.2018.00149

Bohlin, G., Hagekull, B., & Lindhagen, K. (1981). Dimensions of infant behavior. *Infant Behavior and Development,4*, 83-96.

Boltë, S., & Poustka, F. (2002). The relation between general cognitive level and adaptive behavior domains in individuals with autism with and without co-morbid mental retardation. *Child Psychiatric and Human Development, 33*,165–172.

Bornstein, M.H., & Hahan, C.S. (2007). Infant childcare settings and the development of gender-specific adaptive behaviors. *Early Child Development and Care,177*, 15-41.

Borsa, J.C., Damasio, B. F., & Bandeira, D.R. (2012). Cross cultural adaptation and validation of psychological instruments: some considerations. *Paideia, 22*, 423-432.

Boström, P., Broberg, M., & Hwang, C.P. (2010). Different, difficult or distinct? Mothers' and fathers' perceptions of temperament in children with and without intellectual disabilities. *Journal of Intellectual Disability Research, 54*, 806 – 819. doi: 10.1111/j.1365-2788.2010.01309.x

Boyle, C.A., Yeargin-Allsop, M., Doernberg, N.S., Holmgreen, P., Murphy, C.C., and Schendel, D.E. (1996). Prevalence of selected developmental disabilities in children 3-10 years of age: The metropolitan Atlanta developmental disabilities surveillance program, 1991. *Morbidity and Mortality Weekly Report. CDC Surveillance Summaries, 45*, 1-14.

Bradley, R.H.(2008). Infant temperament, parenting and externalizing behavior in first grade: A test of the differential susceptibility hypothesis. *Journal of Child Psychology and Psychiatry, 49*, 124 – 131.

Bradley, R.H., & Corwyn, R.F. (2008). Infant temperament, parenting, and externalizing behavior in first grade: a test of the differential susceptibility hypothesis. *The Journal of Child Psychology and Psychiatry, 49*, 124 – 131.

Bradley-Johnson, S. (2001). Cognitive assessment for the youngest children: A critical review of tests. *Journal of Psychoeducational Assessment,19*, 19–44.

Bryant, B.R., Bryant, D.P., & Chamberlain, S. (1999). Examination of gender and race factors in the assessment of adaptive behavior. In R.L. Schalock, editor; and D.L. Braddock, editor. (eds.), Adaptive behavior and its measurements: Implications for the field of mental retardation (pp. 141-160). Washington, DC: American Association on Mental Retardation.

Brereton, A.V., Tonge, B.J., & Einfeld, S.L. (2006). Psychopathology in children and adolescents with autism compared to young people with intellectual disability. *Journal of Autism and Developmental Disorders,36*, 863 – 870.

Bristol, M., & Schopler, E.(1984). A developmental perspective on stress and coping in families of autistic children. In: Blacher, J., Ed. Severely handicapped children and their families (pp 91-141). New York: Academic Press.

Brockley, J.A. (1999). History of mental retardation: An essay review. *History of Psychology, 2*, 25-36.

Brown, J. D. (1996). *Testing in language programs*. Upper Saddle River, NJ: Prentice Hall

Regents.

Brown, J. D. (2000). What is construct validity? *JALT Testing and Evaluation SIG

Newsletter, 4*, 8-12.

Brown, J.D. (2009). Choosing the type of rotation in PCA and EFA. Shiken: *JALT Testing

and Evaluation SIG Newsletter, 13*, 20-25.

Brown, R.T., Kaslow, N. J. , Doepke, K., Buchanan, I., Eckman, J., Baldwin, K., Goonan, B.

(1993). Psychosocial and family functioning in children with sickle cell syndrome

and their mothers. *Journal of the American Academy of Child & Adolescent

Psychiatry, 32*, 545-553. https://doi.org/10.1097/00004583-199305000-00009.

Bruininks, R., McGrew, K., & Maruyama, G.(1988). Structure of adaptive behavior in

samples with and without mental retardation. *American Journal of Mental

Retardation,93,* 265-272.

Bruininks, R.H., Woodcock, R.W., Weatherman, R.F., & Hill, B.K. (1996). *SIB-R: Scales of

independent behavior-Revised*. Chicago: Riverside Publishing.

Bruininks, R.H., Woodcock, R.W., Weatherman, R.F., & Hill, B.K. (2000). *Scales

of independent behavior - revised*. Itasca, IL: Riverside Publishing.

Buckley, S.J., Bird, G., Sacks, B., & Archer, T. (2002). A comparison of mainstream and

special education for teenagers with Down syndrome: implications for parents and

teachers. *Down Syndrome News and Update,2*, 46-54. doi:10.3104/updates.166

Buckner, J.C., Mezzacappa, E., & Beardslee, W.R. (2009). Self-regulation and its relations to

adaptive functioning in low income youths. *American Journal of

Orthopsychiatry,79*,19-30. doi: 10.1037/a0014796.

Buss, A. H., & Plomin, R. (1975). *A Temperament Theory of Personality Development.* Wiley,New York.

Buss, A. H., & Plomin, R. (1984). *Temperament: Early developing personality traits.* Hillside, NJ: Erlbaum.

Byrne B. M., Shavelson R. J., Muthén B. (1989). Testing for the equivalence of factor covariance and mean structures: The issue of partial measurement equivalence. *Psychological Bulletin, 105*, 456-466.

Cabrera-Nguyen, P. (2010). Author guide lines for reporting scale development and validation results in the journal of the society for social work and research. *Journal of the Society for Social Work and Research, 1,* 99 – 103.

Cairney, J., Boyle, M., Offord, D.R., & Racine, Y. (2003). Stress, social support and depression in single and married mothers. *Social Psychiatry and Psychiatric Epidemiology, 38*, 442 – 449.

Calkins, S.D., Smith, C. L., Gill, K.H. Johnson, M.C. (1998). Maternal interactive styles across context: Relational to behavioral, emotional and physical regulation during toddlerhood. *Social Development,7*, 350 – 369.

Campbell, D. T., & Fiske, D. W. (1959). Convergent and discriminant validation by the multitrait-multimethod matrix. *Psychological Bulletin.56*, 81 – 105.

Campbell, G. M. (2005). Diagnostic assessment of Asperger's disorder: A review of five third-party rating scales. *Journal of Autism and Developmental Disorders,35*, 25–35.

Capaldi, D.M., & Rothbart, M. K. (1992). Development and validation of an early adolescent temperament measure. *Journal of Early Adolescence,12*, 153- 173.

Carter, A.S., Briggs-Gowman, M.J., Jones, S.M., & Little, T.D.(2003). The infant-toddler social and emotional assessment (ITSEA): Factor structure, reliability and validity. *Journal of Abnormal Child Psychology,31*, 495-514.

Carter, A.S., Volkmar, F.R., Sparrow,S.S., Wang, J., Lord, C., Dawson, G., ... Schopler, E. (1998). The Vineland adaptive behavior scales: Supplementary norms for individuals with autism. *Journal of Autism and Developmental Disorders, 28,287 – 302.*

Centers for Disease Control and Prevention. (2014). *Autism Spectrum Disorder.* Centers for Disease Control and Prevention.

Charman, T., Pickles, A., Simonoff, E., Chandler, S., Loucas, T., & Baird, G.(2010). IQ in children with autism spectrum disorders: data from the Special Needs and Autism Project (SNAP). *Psychological Medicine, 41*, 619 - 627. doi:10.1017/S0033291710000991.

Chess, S., & Korn, S. (1970). Temperament and behavior disorders in mentally retarded children. *Archives of General Psychiatry, 23*, 122-130.

Chess, S., & Thomas, A. (1990). The New York longitudinal study (NYLS): the young adult periods. *The Canadian Journal of Psychiatry, 35*, 557-561.

Central Intelligence Agency. (2012). The World Fact Book: Pakistan. New York: Central Intelligence Agency.

Cicchetti,D.V. (1994). Guidelines, criteria and rules of thumb for evaluating normed and standardized assessment instruments in psychology. *Psychological Assessment,6*, 284-290.

Clark, L.A., Watson, D. (1995). Constructing validity: Basic issues in objective scale development. *Psychological Assessment, 7*, 309–319.

Calzada, E. J., Brotman, L.M., Huang, K.Y., Bat-Chavae, Y., & Kingston, S. (2009). Parent Cultural Adaptation and Child Functioning in Culturally Diverse, Urban Families of Preschoolers. *Journal of Applied Developmental Psychology, 30*, 515- 524.

Capaldi, D. M., & Rothbart, M. K. (1992). Development and validation of an early adolescent temperament measure. *The Journal of Early Adolescence, 12*, 153-173.

Cortina, J.M. (1993). What is coefficient alpha? An examination of theory and applications. *Journal of Applied Psychology, 78*, 98 – 104.

Costello, A.B., and Osborne, J.W. (2005). Best practices in exploratory factor analysis : four recommendations for getting the most from your analysis. *Practical Assessment Research and Evaluation, 10,*

Craig, E.M., & Tasse, M.J. (1999). Cultural and demographic group comparisons in adaptive behavior. In R.L. Schalock, and D.L. Braddock (Eds.), Adaptive behavior and its measurements: Implications for the field of mental retardation (pp. 119- 140). Washington, DC: American Association on Mental Retardation.

Croft, C., Brown, R.F., Thorsteinsson, E.B., & Noble, W. (2013). Development of the tinnitus response scales: Factors analyses, subscale reliability and validity analyses. *International Tinnitus Journal, 1*, 45-56.

Cronbach, L.J. (1990). *Essentials of psychological testing* (5th ed.). New York: Harper and Row.

Cronbach, L. J., & Meehl, P.E. (1955). Construct validity in psychological tests. *Psychological Bulletin, 52*, 281- 302.

Cyrulnik,S. E., Fee, R.J., Batchelder, A., Kiefel, J., Goldstein, E., & Hinton, V.J.

    (2008).Cognitive and adaptive deficits in young children with Duchenne muscular

    dystrophy . *Journal of the International Neuropsychological Society*, 14, 853–861.

    Doi:10.10170S135561770808106X

Delemarre-van deW aal HA. (1993). Environmental factors influencing growth and pubertal

    development. *Environmental Health Perspective, 101*, 39-44.

Denton, C.A., Ciancio, D.J., & Fletcher, J.M. (2006). Validity, reliability and utility of the

    observation survey of early literacy achievement. *Reading Research Quarterly, 41*, 8

    – 34.

DeVellis, R.F. (1991). *Scale development: Theory and application*. California:Sage

    Publications, Inc.

DeVellis, R. F. (2003). *Scale development: Theory and applications (2nd ed.)*Thousand

    Oaks: Sage.

DeVon, H.A., Block, M.E., Moyle-Wright, P., Ernst, D.M., Hayden, S.J., Lazzara, D.J., …..

    Kostas-Polston, E. (2007). A psychometric toolbox for testing validity and reliability.

    Journal of Nursing Scholarship,39, 155-164.

Ditterline, J., Banner,D., Oakland, T., & Becton, D. (2008). Adaptive behavior profiles of

    students with disabilities. *Journal of Applied School Psychology, 24*,191-208. **DOI:**

    10.1080/15377900802089973

Doll, E.A. (1935). A generic scale of social maturity. *American Journal of*

    Orthopsychiatry,5, 180-188.

317

Drahota, A., Wood, J.J., Sze, K. M., & Dyke, M.V. (2011). Effects of cognitive behavioral therapy on daily living skills in children with high functioning autism and concurrent anxiety disorders. *Journal of Autism and Developmental Disorders, 4*, 257–265.

Duncan, A.W., & Bishop, S.L. (2013).Understanding the gap between cognitive abilities and daily living skills in adolescents with autism spectrum disorders with average intelligence. *Autism.*Advance online publication. 10.1177/1362361313510068

Durkin, M. S., Hasan, Z. M., & Hasan, K. Z. (1998). Prevalence and correlates of mental retardation among children in Karachi, Pakistan. *American Journal of Epidemiology, 147*, 281-288.

Dykens, E.M., Hodapp, R.M., & Evans, D.W. (2006). Profiles and development of adaptive behavior in children with Down syndrome. *Down Syndrome Research and Practice, 9*, 45-50. doi:10.3104/reprints.293

Eikeseth, S., Smith, T., Jahr, S.E., & Eldevik, S. (2007). Outcome for children with autism who began intensive behavioral treatment between ages 4 and 7. *Behavior Modification, 31*, 264 – 278.

Eisen, S. V., Normand, S., Belanger, A. J., Spiro, A., & Esch, D. (2004). The Revised Behavior and Symptom Identification Scale (BASIS-R): Reliability and Validity. *Medical Care, 42*, 1230-1241.

Eldevik, S., Hastings, R.P., Jahr, E., & Hughes, J.C. (2012). Outcomes of behavioral intervention for children with Autism in mainstream pre-school settings. *Journal of Autism and Developmental Disorders,42*, 210–220. DOI 10.1007/s10803-011-1234-9

Emmons, M.R., & Alfonso, V. C. (2005). A critical review of the technical characteristics of

current preschool screening batteries. *Journal of Psychoeducational

Assessment,23,*111-127.

Eristi, B., & Akdeniz, C. (2012). Development of a Scale to Diagnose Instructional

Strategies. *Contemporary Educational Technology, 3,* 141-161.

Evans, L.D., & Bradley-Johnson, S. (1988). A review of recently developed measures of

adaptive behavior. *Psychology in Schools, 25,* 276 – 287.

Evans, D., & Rothbart, M. K. (2001). *A hierarchal model of temperament and the Big Five.*

Manuscript submitted for publication.

Evans, D. E., & Rothbart, M. K. (2007). Developing a model for adult temperament. *Journal

of Research in Personality, 41,* 868-888.

Eysenck, H. J., & Eysenck, M. W. (1987). *Personality and individual differences: A natural

science approach.* New York: Plenum.

Farrokhzad, S., Nedjat, S., Kamangar, F., Kamail, M., Malekzadeh, R., & Pourshams, A.

(2014). Validity and reliability of a questionnaire designed to assess risk factors of

pancreatic cancer in Iran. *Archives of Iranian Medicine,17,* 102 – 105.

Fawcett, T.(2006). An introduction to ROC analysis. *Pattern Recognition Letters, 27,* 861-

874.

Fayers, P.M., & Machin, D. (2000). *Quality of life: Assessment, analysis and interpretation.*

Chichester: John Wiley & Sons Ltd.

Fenton, G., D'Ardia, C., Valente, D., Del Vecchio, I., Fabrizi, A., & Bernabei, P. (2003).

Vineland adaptive behavior profiles in children with autism and moderate to severe

developmental delay. *Autism, 7,* 269–287.

Feinstein, A. (2012). *A Historical Perspective on Autism*. Encyclopedia on early child

   development. www. Child-encyclopedia.com/sites/files/experts/en/572/

Field, A., (2005). *Discovering statistics using SPSS* (2nd ed.). New York: SAGE

   publications, Inc.

Fisher, M., & Meyer, L.H.(2002). Development and social competence after two years for

   students enrolled in inclusive and self contained educational programs. *Research and

   Practice for Persons with Severe Disabilities, 27*, 165-174.

Flanagan, D. P., McGrew, K. S., & Oritz, S.O. (2000). *The Wechsler intelligence scales and

   Gf-Gc theory: A contemporary approach to interpretation*. Needham Heights, MA:

   Allyn & Bacon

Flanagan, D. P., & Ortiz, S. O. (2001). *Essentials of cross-battery assessment.* New York:

   John Wiley & Sons, Inc.

Flonkowski, C.M. (2008). Sensitivity, specificity, receiver operating characteristic curve and

   likelihood ratios: communicating the performance of diagnostic tests. *Clinical

   Biochemistry Review Supplement, 29*, 83 – 87.

Floyd, F.J., Purcell, S.E., Richardson, S.S., & Kupersmidt, J.B. (2009). Sibling relationship

   quality and social functioning of children and adolescents with intellectual disability.

   American Journal on Intellectual and Developmental Disabilities, 114, 110-127.

Floyd, F.J., & Widaman, K.F. (1995). Factor analysis in the development and refinement of

   clinical assessment instruments. *Psychological Assessment,7*, 286 – 299.

Foley, M., McClowry, S.G., & Castellanos, F.X. (2008). The relationship between attention

   deficit hyperactivity disorder and child temperament. *Journal of Applied

   Developmental Psychology,29*, 157–169.

Fombonne, E., & Achard, S. (1993). The Vineland adaptive behavior scale in a sample of

normal French children: A Research Note. *The Journal of Child Psychology and

Psychiatry, 34*, 1051–1058.

Forness, S.R., Keogh, B.K., MacMillan, D.L., Kavale, K.A., &Gresham, F.M. (1998). What

is so special about IQ? The limited explanatory power of cognitive abilities in the real

world of special education. *Remedial and Special Education , 19*, 315-322.

Furr, R.M. (2010). *Scale construction and psychometrics for social and personality

psychology*. London: Sage Publication.

Gardiner, E. & Iarocci., G.(2015). Family quality of life and ASD: The role of child adaptive

functioning and behavior problems. *Autism Research, 8*, 199–213. DOI:

10.1002/aur.1442

Giesler, M., Forster, J., Biller, S., & Fabry, G. (2011). Development of a questionnaire to

assess medical competencies: reliability and validity of the questionnaire. *GMS

Zeitschrift für Medizinische Ausbildung, 28*, 1-15.

Gillespie-Lynch, K., Sepeta, L., Wang, Y., Marshall, S., Gomez, L., Sigman, M., & Hutman,

T. (2012). Early Childhood Predictors of the Social Competence of Adults with

Autism. *Journal of Autism and Developmental Disorders, 42*, 161 – 174.

Gersten, R. Chard, D. & Baker, S. (2000). Factors enhancing sustained use of research-based

instructional practices. *Journal of Learning Disabilities, 33,* 445- 457.

Goldberg ,M.R., Dill, C.A.,Shin, J,Y., & Nhan, N.V. (2009). Reliability and validity of the

Vietnamese Vineland Adaptive Behavior Scales with preschool-age children.

Research in Developmental Disabilities, 30, 592–602.

http://www.jstor.org/stable/584926 .

Grant, J. S., & Davis, L.L. (1997). Selection and use of content experts for instrument development. *Research in Nursing Health, 20*, 269 – 274.

Greenspan, S.I. (1979). Intelligence and adaptation: An integration of psychoanalytic and Piagetian developmental psychology. Psychological Issues (Monograph 47/68). New York: International Universities Press.

Grigorenko , E.L., & Sternberg, R.J. (2001). Analytical, creative, and practical intelligence as predictors of self-reported adaptive functioning: A case study in Russia. *Intelligence, 29*, 57–73. https://doi.org/10.1016/S0160-2896(00)00043-X

Guillemin, F., Bombardier, C., & Beaton, D. (1993). Cross cultural adaptation of health related quality of life measures: Literature review and proposed guidelines. *Journal of Clinical Epidemiology ,46*, 1417-1432.

Goldsmith, H. H., Buss, K. A., & Lemery, K. S. (1997). Toddler and childhood temperament: Expanded content, stronger genetic evidence, new evidence for the importance of environment. *Developmental Psychology,33*, 880- 891.

Goldstein, S., & Barkley, R. A. (1998). ADHD, hunting, and evolution:"Just so" stories. *ADHD Report, 6*, 1-4.

Gotham, K., Pickles, A., & Lord, C. (2012). Trajectories of autism severity in children using standardized ADOS scores. *Pediatrics, 130*(5), 1278–1284.

Gray, J. A. (1987). Perspectives on anxiety and impulsivity: A commentary. *Journal of Research in Personality, 21*, 493-509.

Gunnar, M. R. (1990). The psychobiology of infant temperament. *Individual differences in infancy: Reliability, stability, prediction*, 387-409.

Haider, S. & Khan

Hall, H. R. (2008). The relationships among adaptive behaviors of children with autism

spectrum disorder: Their family support networks, parental stress, and parental

coping" (2008). Theses and Dissertations (ETD). Paper 344. http://dx.doi.org/

10.21007/etd.cghs.2008.0123.

Hall, C.R., & Hughes, J.N. (2007). An examination of the convergent and discriminant

validity of the strengths and difficulties questionnaire. *School Psychology Quarterly,*

3, 380 – 406.

Halladay, A.K., Bishop, S., Constantino , J.N., Daniels, A.M., Koenig, K., Palmer, K., ...

Szatmari, P. (2015). Sex and gender differences in autism spectrum disorder:

summarizing evidence gaps and identifying emerging areas of priority. *Molecular*

Autism , 6, 29 – 36. DOI 10.1186/s13229-015-0019-y

Hambleton, R.K. (2006). Chapter 1: Issues, designs, and technical guidelines for adapting

tests into multiple languages and cultures. In: Hambleton, R.K., Merenda, P.F., &

Spielberger, C.D. (2005/6). *Adapting educational and psychological tests for cross*

cultural assessment. Mahwah NJ: Lawrence Erlbaum Associates

Hambleton, R. K., Merenda, P. F., & Spielberger, C.D. (Eds.). (2005). *Adapting educational*

and psychological tests for cross-cultural assessment. Mahwah, New Jersey:

Lawrence Erlbaum.

Hambleton, R. K., & Patsula, L. (1998). *Adapting tests for use in multiple languages and*

cultures. Social Indicators Research, 45, 153-171.

Hanley, J.A., & McNeil, B.J. (1982). The meaning and use of the area under a receiver

operating characteristic (ROC) curve. *Radiology, 143*, 29 – 36.

Harrington, R.G. (1985). Review of the Batelle developmental inventory. In J. Keyser, & R.C. Sweetland (eds.), Test Critiques (Vol. 2, pp. 72-82). Austin, TX: Pro-Ed.

Harrison, P.L. (1987). Research with adaptive behavior scales. *Journal of Special Education, 21*, 37-68.

Harrison, P.L., & Oakland, T. (2000). ABAS: adaptive behavior assessment system. San Antonio, TX: Psychological Corporation.

Hart, B. (2000). A natural history of early language experience. *Topics in Early Childhood Special Education ,20*, 28-32.

Hauser-Cram,P., Warfield, M. E., Shonkoff, J. P., Krauss, M. W., Upshur, C. C., &Sayer, A. (1999). Family Influences on Adaptive Development in Young Children with Down Syndrome. *Child Development, 70*, 979-989.

Hauser-Cram, P., Warfield, M.E., Shonkoff, J.P., Krauss, M.W., Sayer, A., Upshur, C.C., & Hodapp, R.M. (2001). Children with Disabilities: A Longitudinal Study of Child Development and Parent Well-Being. *Monographs of the Society for Research in Child Development, 66*,115-126.

Haynes, S.N., Richard, D.C.S., & Kubany, E.S. (1995). Content validity in psychological assessment: A functional approach to concepts and methods. *Psychological Assessment, 7*, 238-247.

Hays, P. A. (2001). Addressing cultural complexities in practice: A framework for clinicians and counsellors. Washington, DC: American Psychological Association.

Health, C. P., & Obrzut, J. E. (1986). Adaptive behavior: Concurrent validity. *Journal of Psychoeducational Assessment, 4*, 53-59.

Healey, D. M., Brodzinsky, L. K., Bernstein, M., Rabinovitz, B., & Halperin, J. M.(2009).

Moderating effects of neurocognitive abilities on the relationship between

temperament and global functioning. *Child Neuropsychology*,9, 1-12.

Doi:10.1080/09297040902984490.

Hearth, C. P., & Obrzut, J. E. (1986). Adaptive behavior: Concurrent validity. *Journal of*

Psychoeducational Assessment, 4, 53-59.

Heber, R. (1961). Modifications in the manual on terminology and classification in mental

retardation. *American Journal of Mental Deficiency , 65,* 499-500.

He, P., Chen, G., Wang, Z., Guo, C., & Zheng, X. (2017). The role of parental education in

child disability in China from 1987 to 2006. *Plos One, 12* (10),

e0186623. https://doi.org/10.1371/journal.pone.0186623

Helena L.Rohlf , H.L.,& Krahé, B.(2015). Assessing anger regulation in middle childhood:

Development and validation of a behavioral observation measure. *Frontiers in*

Psychology, 6:453. doi: 10.3389/fpsyg.2015.00453

Herschkowitz, N., Kagan, J., & Zilles, K. (1997). Neurobiological bases of behavioral

development in the first year. *Neuropediatrics, 28,* 296-306.

Hill, B.K. (1999) Adaptive and maladaptive behavior scales. Available: http://

www.isd.net/bhill/icap.htm

Hilton, A., & Skrutkowski, M. (2002). Translating instruments into other languages:

Development and testing processes. *Cancer Nursing: International Journal for*

Cancer Care , 25, 1-7.

Hofman, S. G., & Kashdan,T.B.(2010). The affective style questionnaire: Development and

psychometric properties. *Journal of Psychopathology and Behavior Assessment,32*,

255-263.

Hollander, E. (2004). Fluoxetine for repetitive behaviors and Valproate for irritability in

autism. In Hepburn, S. L., & Stone, W. L. (2006). Using Carey Temperament Scales

to assess behavioral style in children with autism spectrum disorders. *Journal of*

autism and developmental disorders, 36, 637-642.

Holman, J.G., and Bruininks, R.H. (1985). Assessing and training adaptive behaviors. In

K.L. Lakin,& R.H. Bruininks, editor. (Eds.), *Strategies for achieving*

community integration of developmentally disabled citizens (pp. 73-104). Baltimore,

MD: Paul H. Brooks.

Holroyd, J., & McArthur, D. (1976). Mental retardation and stress on the parents: A contrast

between Down's syndrome and childhood autism. *American Journal of Mental*

Deficiency, 80, 431–438.

Hubert, N. C., Wachs, T. D., Peters-Martin, P., & Gandour, M. J. (1982). The study of early

temperament: Measurement and conceptual issues. *Child Development,* 571-600.

Huq, M.N., & Tasnim, T. (2008). Maternal education and child healthcare in

Bangladesh. *Maternal Child Health Journal,12,* 43–51. DOI 10.1007/s10995-

007-0303-3.

Hussein, H., Taha, G.R.A., & Almanasef, A. (2011). Characteristics of autism spectrum

disorders in a sample of Egyptian and Saudi patients: Transcultural cross sectional

study. *Child Adolescent Psychiatry Mental Health* , *5,* 34-41.

Ibrahim, S. H., & Bhutta, Z. (2013). Prevalence of early childhood disability in a rural district of Sind, Pakistan. *Developmental Medicine and Child Neurology,*357 – 363. DOI: 10.1111/dmcn.12103

Ittenbach, R.F., Spiegel, A.N., McGrew, K.S., & Bruinninks, R.H. (1992). Confirmatory factor analysis of early childhood ability measures within a model of personal competence. Educational Psychology Papers and Publications, 179.

Izard, C.E., Schultz, D., Fine,S.E., Younstrom,E., & Ackerman, B.P. (2000). Temperament, cognitive ability, emotion knowledge, and adaptive social behavior. *Imagination, Cognition and Personality, 19*, 305 –330.

International Test Commission. (2005). ITC guidelines for translating and adapting tests. Geneva, Switzerland: ITC.

Jackson, A.P., Preston, K.S.J., & Franke, T.M. (2010). Single parenting and child behavior problems in kindergarten. *Race and social Problems, 2*, 50 – 58.

Jacobson, J.W., & Mulick, J.A. (1996). Manual of diagnosis and professional practice in mental retardation. Washington, DC: American Psychological Association.

James T. Croasmun, J. T., & Ostrom, L. (2011). Using Likert-Type Scales in the Social Sciences. *Journal of Adult Education, 40* (1), 19-22.

Jew, C.L., Green, K.E., & Kroger, J.K. (1999). Development and validation of a measure of resiliency.*Measurement and Evaluation in Counseling and Development,32*,75–89.

Ji, C., Yao, D., Chen, W., Li, M., & Zhao, Z. (2014).Adaptive behavior in Chinese children with Williams syndrome. *Pediatrics, 14*, 82 - 90. http://www.biomedcentral.com/1471-2431/14/90

Johnson, T.P. (2000). Methods and frameworks for cross cultural measurement.

Medical Care, 44, S17 – S20.

Johnson, B. D., Franklin, L. C., Hall, K., & Prieto, L. R. (2000). Parent training

through play: Parent-child interaction therapy with a hyperactive child. *The Family*

Journal, 8, 180 -186.

Jung, C. G. (1921). General description of the types. *Psychological Types. CW, 6.*

Juniper, E.F. (2009). Modification, translation and adaptation of questionnaires: Should

copyright laws be observed? *Quality of Life Research,* Doi: 10.1007/s11136-008-9440-4.

Kaminsky, L., & Dewey,D. (2002). Psychosocial adjustment in siblings of children with

autism. *Journal of Child Psychology and Psychiatry, 43,* 225 – 232.

Kamphaus, R.W. (1987). Conceptual and psychometric issues in the assessment of adaptive

behavior. *Journal of Special Education, 21,* 27-35.

Kamphaus, R.W., Petoskey, M.D., & Rowe, E.W. (2000). Current trends in psychological

testing of children. *Professional Psychology: Research and Practice, 31,* 155-164.

Kane, M.T. (2001). Current concerns in validity theory. *Journal of Educational*

Measurement,38, 319– 342.

Kane, M. T. (2006). Validation. In R. L. Brennan (Ed.), Educational measurement (4th ed.).

Westport, CT: Praeger.

Kanne, S.M., Gerber, A.J., Quirmbach, L.M., Sparrow, S.S., Cicchetti, D.V., & Saulnier,

C.A. (2011). The role of adaptive behavior in autism spectrum disorders: Implications

for functional outcome. *Journal of Autism and Developmental Disorder, 41,* 1007–

1018 DOI 10.1007/s10803-010-1126-4

Kasari, C., & Sigman, M. (1997). Linking parental perceptions to interactions in young

children with autism. *Journal of Autism and Developmental Disorders, 27,* 39-57.

Katz,G., & Lazcano-Ponce, E. (2008). Intellectual disability: definition, etiological factors,

classification, diagnosis, treatment and prognosis. *Salud Publica de Mexico, 50*, 132 –

141.

Kazdin, A.E., (Ed.). (2003). Methodological issues and strategies in clinical research (3rd

ed.). Washington D.C: Americans Psychological Association.

Keith, T. Z., Fehrmann, P.C., Harrison, P.L., & Pottebaum,S.M. (1987). The relation between

adaptive behavior and intelligence: Testing alternative explanations. *Journal of

School Psychology, 25*, 31 – 43.

Kelly, Y., Sacker, A., Schoon, I., & Nazroo, J. (2006). Ethnic differences in achievement of

developmental milestones by 9 months of age: The millennium cohort study.

Developmental Medicine & Child Neurology, 48, 825-830.

Kenworthy, L.,Case, L., Harms, M.B., Martin, A., & Wallace, G.L. (2010). Adaptive

behavior ratings correlate with symptomatology and IQ among individuals with high-

functioning autism spectrum disorders. *Journal of Autism and Developmental

Disorders, 40*,416–423. DOI 10.1007/s10803-009-0911-4

Khan, M., Quadri, S.M. A., & Aziz, S. (2014). Association of family structure and its

enviroenment with aggressive behavior of children in a rural community. *Journal of

Child and Adolescent Behavior, 2(125)*. DOI:10.1472/jcalb.1000125.

Kita, Y., & Hosokawa, T. (2011). History of Autism Spectrum disorders: Historical

controversy over the diagnosis. Tohoku University Graduate School of Education

Graduate *School of Education Annual Report,59/2*, 147-164.

Klein, V.C., Putnam, S.P., & Linhares, M. B. M. (2009). Assessment of temperament in

children: translation of instruments to Portuguese (Brazil) Language. *Interam Journal

of Psychology,43*, 552-557.

Klein-Tasman, B. P., Colon, A.M., Brei,N., Fluit, F.V., Casnar,C.L., Janke, K.M., ...

Walker, J.A. (2013). Adaptive behavior in young children with neurofibromatosis

type 1. *International Journal of Pediatrics Volume , 7,* 56 – 64.

http://dx.doi.org/10.1155/2013/690432

Klin, A., Pauls, D., Schultz, R., & Volkmar, F. (2005). Three Diagnostic Approaches

to Asperger Syndrome: Implications for Research. *Journal of Autism and

Developmental Disorders, 35* (2). DOI: 10.1007/s10803-004-2001-y

Klin, A., Saulnier, C.A., Sparrow, S.S., Cicchetti, D.V., Volkmar, F.R., & Lord, C.

(2007).Social and communication abilities and disabilities in higher functioning

individuals with autism spectrum disorders: The Vineland and the ADOS. *Journal of

Autism and Developmental Disorders,37,*748–59.

Kline, P. (2000). *Handbook of psychological testing* (2nd ed.). London. Routledge.

Kline, P. (2002). *An easy guide to factor analysis*. London: Routledse.

Kneil, A., and Kneil, C. (2006). Ghana adaptive behavior scales: An assessment tool to

measure competence in daily life of Ghanian children.

Kojkowski, N.M., Hileman, C.M., & Mundy, P.C.. (2009). Temperament as a predictor of

symptomotology and adaptive functioning in adolescents with high-functioning

autism. *Journal of Autism and Developmental Disorder, 39,* 842–855.

doi:10.1007/s10803-009-0690-y

Kotelnikova, Y., Olino, T.M., Klein, D.N., Mackrell, S.V.M., & Hayden, E.P. (2016). Higher and lower order factor analyses of the temperament in middle childhood questionnaire. *Assessment,1*,1–12. DOI: 10.1177/1073191116639376

Kramer, J .H., Crittenden, M. R., DeSantes, K., & Cowan, M. J. (1997). Cognitive and adaptive behavior 1 and 3 years following bone marrow transplantation. *Bone Marrow Transplantation,19*, 607-61 7.

Kochanska, G., Murray, K. T., & Harlan, E. T. (2000). Effortful control in early childhood: Continuity and change, antecedents, and implications for social development. *Developmental psychology, 36*, 220.

Koller, H., Richardson, S. A., Katz, M., & McLaren, J. (1983). Behavior disturbance since childhood among a 5-year birth cohort of all mentally retarded young adults in a city. *American Journal of Mental Deficiency,7,*128-137.

Konstantareas, M. M., & Homatidis, S. (1989). Assessing child symptom severity and stress in parents of autistic children. *Journal of Child Psychology and Psychiatry, 30*, 459-470.

Konstantareas, M. M., & Stewart, K. (2001). Affect regulation and temperament in children with pervasive developmental disorder. In *Society for Research in Child Development Conference, Minneapolis, MN.*

Konstantareas, M.M., & Stewart, K . J. (2006). Affect regulation and temperament in children with autism spectrum disorder. *Journal of Autism and Developmental Disorder, 36*, 143 – 154.

Kumar,I., Singh, A.R., & Akhtar, S. (2009). Social development of children with mental retardation. *Indian Psychiatry Journal,18*, 56–59. doi: 10.4103/0972-6748.57862

Kushalnagar, P., Krull, K., Hannay, J., Mehta, P., & Oghalai, J. (2007). Intelligence, parental depression, and behavior adaptability in deaf children being considered for cochlear implantation. *Journal of Deaf Studies and Deaf Education, 12*, 335 – 349.

Lancaster, G. A., Dodd, S., & Williamson, P. R.. (2004).Design and analysis of pilot studies: Recommendations for good practice. *Journal of Evaluation in Clinical Practice,10*, 307–312.

Lambert, N.M., Nihira, K., & Leland, H. (1993). AAMR Adaptive Behavior Scale (ABS-S:2): School (2nd ed.). Austin, TX: Pro-Ed.

Leerkes, E. M., Paradise, M., O'Brien, M., Calkins, S. D., & Lange, G. (2008). Emotion and cognition processes in preschool children. *Merrill-Palmer Quarterly, 54*, 102–124.

Leibowitz, G. (1991). Organic and biophysical theories of behavior. *Journal of Developmental and Physical Disabilities, 3*, 201-243.

Lemery, K. S., Essex, M. J., & Smider, N.A. (2002). Revealing the Relation between Temperament and Behavior Problem Symptoms by Eliminating Measurement Confounding: Expert Ratings and Factor Analyses. *Child Development,73*, 867-882.

Leonard, H., Petterson, B., Bower, C., & Sanders, R. (2003). Prevalence of intellectual disability in western Australia. *Pediatric and Perinatal Epidemiology, 17*, 58 - 67

Lerner, J. W. (1976). *Children with learning disabilities: theories, diagnosis, teaching strategies*. Houghton Mifflin School.

Lindahl, K. M. (1998). Family process variables and children's disruptive behavior problems. *Journal of Family Psychology, 12*, 420-428.

Liss,M., Harel, B., Fein, D., Allen, D., Dunn, M., Feinstein, C., ... Rapin, I. (2001).

    Predictors and correlates of adaptive functioning in children with developmental

    disorders. *Journal of Autism and Developmental Disorders, 31,* 98 – 106.

Loevinger J. (1957). Objective tests as instruments of psychological theory: Monograph

    supplement 9. Psychological Reports, 3, 635–694. Doi: 10.2466/pr0.1957.3.3.635

Lord, C., Cook, E.H., Leventhal, B.L., & Amaral, D.G. (2000). Autism Spectrum Disorders.

    Neuron, 28, 355–363.

Luckasson, R. L. (2002). Definition, classification, and systems of support: Workbook.

    Washington, DC: American Association on Mental Retardation.

Luo, W., Gui, X., Wang, B., Zhang, W., Ouyang,Z., Guo, Y.,……..,Ding,M. (2010). Validity

    and reliability testing of the Chinese (mainland) version of the 39 item Parkinson's

    disease Questionnaire. *Journal of Zhwjiang University Science, 11,* 531 – 538.

MacDonald, M., Lord, C., & Ulrich, D. (2013). The relationship of motor skills and adaptive

    behavior skills in young children with autism spectrum disorders. *Research in Autism*

    *Spectrum Disorders,1,*1383-1390.

MacMillan, D.L., Gresham, F.M., Siperstein, G.N., and Bocian, K.M. (1996). The labyrinth

    of I.D.E.A.: School decisions on referred students with subaverage general intelligence.

    American Journal on Mental Retardation, 101, 161-174.

Mahmood, T. (2010). Validation of procedures for identification of the children with specific

    learning difficulties in mainstream classrooms. *Bulletin of Education and Research, 32,*

    93-101.

Malhi, P., & Singhi, P. (2015). Adaptive behavior functioning in children with autism. *The*

    Indian Journal of Pediatrics, 82, 677 – 681.

Mandic-Maravic, V., Pejovic-Milovancevic, M., Mitkovic-Voncina, M., Kostic, M., Aleksic-Hil, O., Radosavljey-Kircanski, J.,……Lecic-Tosevski, D. (2015). Sex differences in autism spectrum disorders: Does sex moderate the pathway from clinical symptoms to adaptive behavior? *Scientific Reports, 5,* 211 -230.

Manohari, S.M., Raman, V., & Ashok, M.V. (2013).Use of Vineland Adaptive Behavior Scales – II in Children with Autism - An Indian Experience. *Journal of Indian Association of Child Adolescents Mental Health, 9, 5-12.*

Marnat, G. G. (2003). Handbook of psychological assessment. Hoboken, NJ: John Wiley & Sons.

Marnat, G. G. (2009). Handbook of psychological assessment. Hoboken, NJ: John Wiley & Sons.

Marteleto,F., & Pedromônico, M. (2005). Validity of autism behavior checklist (ABC): Preliminary study. *Revista Brasileira Psiquiatria, 27,* 295-301.

Martin, R. P., & Bridger, R. C. (1999). The temperament assessment battery for children revised. *Athens, GA: University of Georgia, School Psychology Clinic.*

Mash, E.J., & Terdal, L.G. (Eds.). (1997). Assessment of childhood disorders (3rd ed.). New York: Guilford Press.

Mathias, J. L., & Nettelbeck, R. (1992). Validity of Greenspan's model of adaptive and social intelligence. *Research in Developmental Disabilities, 13,* 113–129.

Matson, J. L., Rivet, T. T., Fodstad, J. C., Dempsey, T., & Boisjoli, J. A. (2009). Examination of adaptive behavior differences in adults with autism spectrum disorders and intellectual disability. *Research in Developmental Disabilities, 30* ,1317–1325.

Maulik, P.K., & Darmstadt, G.L. (2007). Childhood disability in low- and middle-income countries: Overview of screening, prevention, services, legislation, and epidemiology. *Pediatrics, 120*, 51- 56.

Maulik,P.K., Mascarenhas, M.N., Mathers, C.D., Dua, T., & Saxena, S. (2011). Corrigendum to "Prevalence of intellectual disability: A meta-analysis of population-based studies. *Research in Developmental Disabilities,32*, 419 – 436.

Mazefsky, C. A., Williams, D. L., & Minshew, N. J. (2008). Variability in adaptive behavior in Autism: Evidence for the importance of family history. *Journal of Abnormal Child Psychology, 36*,591–599.

McCarthy, J., Hemmings, C., Kavariti, F., Dworsynski, K., Holt, G., Bouras, N., & Tsakanikos, E. (2010). Challenging behavior and co-morbid psychopathology in adults with intellectual disability and autism spectrum disorders. *Research in Developmental Disabilities, 31*, 362–366.

McConaughy, S.H., & Achenbach,T.M. (1988). Practical guide for the child behavior checklist and related materials. Burlington, VT: University of Vermont Department of Psychiatry.

McDermott, S., Durkin, M.S., Schupf, N., & Stein, Z.A. (2007). *Epidemiology and Etiology of Mental Retardation.* In Jacobson, J.W., Mulick, J .A., & Rojahn, J. New York: Springer Science and Business Media.

McDevitt, S. C., & Carey, W. B. (1996). Manual for the behavioral style questionnaire. *Scottsdale, AZ: Behavioral-Developmental Initiatives.*

McGrew, K.S., and Bruininks, R.H. (1989). The factor structure of adaptive behavior. *School Psychology Review, 18*, 64-81.

McGrew, K.S., & Bruininks, R.H. (1990). Defining adaptive and maladaptive behavior within a model of personal competence. *School Psychology Review, 19*, 53-73.

McHale, S., M., Updegraff, K.A., & Whiteman, S.D. (2012). Sibling relationships and influences in childhood and adolescence. *Journal of Marriage and Family, 1*, 913 – 930.

McHale, S. M., Updegraff, K.A., & Whiteman, S.D. (2012). Sibling relationships and influences in childhood and adolescence. *Journal of Marriage and Family, 74*, 913–930.

Memari, A.H., Shayestehfar, M., Mirfazeli, F.S., Rashidi, T., Ghanouni, P., & Hafizi, S. (2013). Cross-cultural adaptation, reliability and validity of the autism treatment evaluation checklist in Persian. *Iranian Journal of Pediatrics, 23*, 269- 275.

Menolascino, F. J. (1965). Psychiatric aspects of mental retardation in children under eight. *American Journal of Orthopsychiatry, 35*, 852.

Mervis, C.B., & Klein-Tasman, B.P. (2000). Williams syndrome: Cognition, personality and adaptive behavior. *Mental Retardation And Developmental Disabilities Research Reviews, 6,* 148–158.

Messick, S. (1995). Validity of psychological assessment: Validation of inferences from persons' responses and performances as scientific inquiry into score meaning. *American Psychologist, 50,* 741–749. doi:10.1037/0003-066x.50.9.741

Meyers, C.E., Nihira, K., & Zetlin, A. (1979). The measurement of adaptive behavior. In N.R. Ellis (ed.), Handbook of mental deficiency: Psychological theory and research. Hillsdale, NJ: Lawrence Erlbaum Associates.

Myers, I. B., & Myers, P. B. (1980). *Gifts differing: Understanding personality type.* Palo Alto, CA: Consulting Psychological Press.

Mirza, I. Tareen, A., Davidson, L.L., & Rahman, A. (2009). Community management of

intellectual disabilities in Pakistan: a mixed methods study. *Journal of Intellectual*

Disability Research, 53,559-70.

Mordre, M., Groholt, B., Knudson, A.K., sponheim, E., Mykletun, A., & Myhre, A.M.

(2012). Is long-term prognosis for pervasive developmental disorder NOS different from

prognosis for autistic disorder? Findings from a 30-year follow-up study. *Journal of*

Autism and Developmental Disorders, 42, 920 – 928.

Morris, A. S., Silk, J. S., Steinberg, L., Sessa, F. M., Avenevoli, S., & Essex, M. J. (2002).

Temperamental vulnerability and negative parenting as interacting predictors of child

adjustment. *Journal of Marriage and Family, 64*, 461-471.

Muris, P., & Ollendick, T.H. (2005). The role of temperament in the etiology of child

psychopathology. *Clinical Child and Family Psychology Review, 8*, 271 - 289.

DOI:10.1007/s10567-005-8809-y

Mushquash, C.J., &Bova, D.L.(2007). Cross-cultural assessment and measurement issues.

Journal on Developmental Disabilities,13,50-65.

Mulick, J. A., Hammer, D., & Dura, J. R. (1991). Assessment and management of antisocial

and hyperactive behavior. *Handbook of mental retardation*, 397-412.

Mylonas, K. & Furnham, A. (2013). Bias in terms of culture and a method for reducing it: An

eight-country explanations of unemployment scale study. *Education and Psychological*

Measurement, 74, 77-96. doi.org/10.1177/0013164413502669.

Nakagawa, A., Sukigara, M., Miyachi, T., & Nakai, A.(2016). Relations between

temperament, sensory processing, and motor coordination in 3-year-old children.

Frontier in Psychology,7,623-636. oi: 10.3389/fpsyg.2016.00623.

Nakamura, B.J., Ebesutani, C., Bernstein, A., & Chorpita, B.F. (2009). A psychometric

analysis of the child behavior checklist DSM-oriented scales. *Journal of Psychological

and Behavioral Assessment,31*, 178 – 189.

Netemeyer, R. G., Bearden, W. O., & Sharma, S. (2003). *Scaling procedures: Issues and

applications*. Thousand Oaks, CA: Sage Publications.

Newborg, J. (2005). *Battelle developmental inventory* (2nd ed.). Itasca, IL: Riverside

Publishing.

Newborg, J., Stock, J.R., Wnek, L., Guidubaldi, J., & Svinicki, J.G. (1984). Battelle

Developmental Inventory. Allen, TX: DLM Teaching Resources.

Nievar, M.A., & Luster, T. (2006). Developmental processes in African American families:

An application of McLoyd's theoretical model. *Journal of Marriage and Family, 68*,

320-331.URL: http://www.jstor.org/stable/3838903

Nihira, K., Leland, H., & Lambert, N.M. (1993). AAMR Adaptive behavior scales residential

and community (ABS-RC:2). Austin, TX: Pro-Ed.

Nihira, K., Webster, R., Tomiyasu, Y., & Oshio, C. (1998). Child-environment relationships:

a cross-cultural study of educable mentally retarded children and their families. *Journal

of Autism and Developmental Disabilities,18*, 327 -341.

Nunnally, J. C., & Bernstein, I. H. (1994). *Psychometric theory* (3rd ed.). New York:

McGraw-Hill.

Nygaard, E., Smith, L., & Torgersen, A. M. (2002). Temperament in children with Down

syndrome and in prematurely born children. *Scandinavian Journal of Psychology, 43*,

61-71.

Oakland, T., & Harrison, P.L. Eds. (2008). *Adaptive behavior assessment system-II:*

clinical use and interpretation. London: Elsevier.

Oakland,T.D., Zhong, N.H. , & Kane. H.D. (2015). Gender differences in adaptive behavior among children and adolescents: Evidence from the USA. *Mankind Quarterly,56.2*, 208-225.

Obuchowski, N.A. (2003). Receiver operating characteristic curves and their use in radiology. *Radiology,1* , 3-8.

Ochoa, S.H., Powell, M.P., & Robles-Pina, R. (1996). School psychologists' assessment practices with bilingual and limited-English-proficient students. *Journal of Psychoeducational Assessment, 14*, 250-275.

Oehler-Stinnett, J. (1989). Review of the Battelle developmental inventory. In J.C. Conoley, and J.J. Kramer (eds.), The tenth mental measurements yearbook (pp. 10- 75). Lincoln, NE: Buros Institute of Mental Measurements.

Osa, N., Ezpeleta, L., Domenech, J.M., Navarro, J.B., & Losilla, J.M. (1997). Convergent and discriminant validity of the structured diagnostic interview for children and adolescents. *Psychology in Spain, 1,* 37– 44.

Osdol, B. M. V., & Carlson, L. (1972). Developmental Hyperactivity. *Mental retardation, 10*,18-32.

Panerai,S., Tasca, D., Ferri, R., Arrigo, V.G., & Elia,M. (2014). Executive functions and adaptive behavior in autism spectrum disorders with and without Intellectual disability. *Psychiatry Journal* .doi.org/10.1155/2014/941809.

Paniagua, F. A. (1994). *Assessing and treating culturally diverse clients: A practical guide.* Thousand Oaks, CA: SAGE Publications, Inc.

Park, S.H., Goo, J.M., & Jo, C.H. (2004). Receiver operating characteristic curve: Practical review for radiologists. *Korean Journal of Radiology,5*, 11 – 18.

Parsian, N., & Dunning, T. (2009). Developing and validating a questionnaire to measure sipirituality: A Psychometric process. *Global Journal of Health Sciences, 1*, 2-11.

Paternite, C. E., Loney, J., & Roberts, M. (1995). External validation of oppositional disorder and attention deficit disorder with hyperactivity. *Journal of Abnormal Child Psychology, 23,* 453–471.

Paternite, C. E., Loney, J., & Roberts, M. A. (1996). A preliminary validation of subtypes of DSM-IV attention-deficit/hyperactivity disorder. *Journal of Attention Disorders, 1,* 70–86.

Pellicano, E. (2012). The development of executive function in autism. *Autism Research and Treatment, 8,* doi:10.1155/2012/146132.

Peneva, I., Yordzhev, K., & Ali, A.S. (2013). The adaptation and translation of psychological test as a necessary condition for ensuring the reliability of scientific research. *The international Journal of Engineering Science and Innovative Technology,2*, 557 – 560.

Perry, A., Flanagan, H.E., Dunn- Geier, J., & Freeman, N.L. (2009). Brief report: The Vineland adaptive behavior scales in young children with autism spectrum disorders at different cognitive levels. *Journal of Autism and Developmental Disorders,39*,1066-1078.

Persha, A., Arya, S., Nagar, R.K., Behera, P., Verma, R.K., & Kishore, M. T. (2007). Biological and psychological predictors of developmental delay in persons with intellectual disability: Retrospective case-file study. *Asia Pacific Disability Rehabilitation Journal, 18*, 93 – 100.

Peshawaria,R.& Venkatesan,S. (1992). Behavioural assessment scales for Indian children with mental retardation BASIC-MR. Secuderabad, India.

Peters,S.U., Goddard-Finegold, J., Beaudet, A.L.,Madduri,N., Turcich,M., & Bacino, C.A. (2004). Cognitive and adaptive behavior profiles of children with Angelman Syndrome. *American Journal of Medical Genetics,128*,110–113.

Phillips, J., Minjarez, M., Mercier, E., Feinstein, C., & Hardan, A.Y. Autism Spectrum Disorders 15 chapter. In Steiner, H. Eds. (2011). Handbook of Developmental Psychology. New Jersey: World Scientific Publishing Co. Ltd.

Pien, D., & Rothbart, M. K. (1980). Incongruity humour, play, and self-regulation of arousal in young children. *Children's Humour*, 1-26.

Piland, S. G., Motl, R.W., Guskiewicz, K..M., Mccrea, M., & Ferrara, M.S. (2006). Structural validity of a self-report concussion-related symptom scale. *Medicine and Sciences in Sports and Exercise, 38*, 27–32.

Pintea, S., & Moldovan, R. (2009). The receiver-operating characteristic (ROC) analysis: fundamentals and applications in clinical psychology. *Journal of Cognitive and Behavioral Psychotherapies, 9*, 49 – 66.

Pittman J & Bakas T. (2010). Measurement and instrument design *Journal of Wound, Ostomy and Continence Nursing,37*, 603-607.DOI:10.1097/WON.0b013e3181f90a60

Platt, L.O., & Kamphaus, R, W., Cole, R. W., & Smith, C. L. (1991). Relationship between adaptive behavior and intelligence: Additional evidence. *Psychological Reports, 68*, 139 – 145.

Polit, D.F., & Beck, C.T. (2006). The content validity index: Are you sure you know what's being reported? Critique and recommendations. *Research in Nursing and Health, 29,* 489-497.

Polit, D.F., & Beck, C.T. (2012). *Nursing research: Generating and assessing evidence for nursing practice* (9th ed.). Philadelphia, USA: Wolters Klower Health, Lippincott Williams & Wilkins.

Ponkaew, W., & Sanasuttipun, W. (2013). Factors predicting adaptive behaviors in siblings of children with cancer. *Journal of Nursing Science, 31,* 71 -81.

Posner, M.I., Rothbart, M.K., & Sheese, B.E. (2007). Attention genes. *Developmental Science, 10,* 24–29.

Preacher, K.J., & MacCallum, R.C. (2003). Repairing Tom Swift's electric factor analysis machine. *Understanding Statistics,2,* 13 – 43.

Pribram, K. H., & McGuiness, D. (1992). Brain systems involved in attention and para attentional processing. *Annals of New York Academy of Science, 658,* 65-92.

Prior, M. R., Sanson, A. V., & Oberklaid, F. (1989). The Australian temperament project.

Pugliese, C.E., Anthony, L.E., Strang, J.F., Dudley, K., Wallace, G.L., & Kenworthy, L. (2015). Increasing adaptive behavior skill deficits from childhood to adolescence in autism spectrum disorder: Role of executive function. *Journal of Autism and Developmental Disorders, 45,* 1579–1587. doi:10.1007/s10803-014-2309-1.

Puig, O., Calvo, R., Rosa, M., Serna, E.D., Lera-Miguel, S., Sánchez-Gistau, V., & Castro-Fornieles, J.(2013). Verbal memory and IQ predict adaptive behavior in children and adolescents with high-functioning autism spectrum disorders. *Journal of Intellectual Disability - Diagnosis and Treatment,1,* 22-27.

Putnam, S.P., Gartstein, M.A., & Rothbart, M.K. (2008). Homotypic and heterotypic

continuity of fine-grained temperament during infancy, toddlerhood, and early childhood.

Infant and Child Development, 17, 387–405.

Putnam, S.P., & Rothbart, M.K. (2006). Development of short and very short forms of the

children's behavior questionnaire. *Journal of Personality Assessment,87*,103– 113.

Rauf, N.K., Haq, A., Aslam, N., & Anjum, U. (2014). Characteristic symptoms and adaptive

behaviors of children with autism. *Journal of College of Physicians and Surgeons

Pakistan, 24*, 658- 662. doi: 09.2014/JCPSP.658662.

Rende, R. D. (1993). Longitudinal relations between temperament traits and behavioral

syndromes in middle childhood. *Journal of the American Academy of Child & Adolescent

Psychiatry, 32*, 287-290.

Reschly, D. J., Myers, T. G., & Hartel, C. R. (Eds.). (2002). Mental retardation: Determining

eligibility for social security benefits. Washington, DC: National Academy Press.

Rettew, D.C., & McKee, L. (2005). Temperament and its role in developmental

psychopathology. *Harvard Review of Psychiatry, 13,* 14–27.

doi:10.1080/10673220590923146.

Richmond, B. O., & Kicklighter, R. H.(1980). Children's Adaptive Behavior Scale. Atlanta,

GA: Humanics.

Riggs, N.R., Jahromi, L.B., Razza, R.P., Dillworth-Bart, J.E., & Mueller, U. (2006).

Executive function and the promotion of social-emotional competence. *Journal of

Applied Developmental Psychology ,27*, 300–309.

Rodrigue, J.R., Morgan, S.B., & Geffken, G.R. (1991). A comparative evaluation of adaptive

behaviors

Rojahn, J., Matson, J.L., Lott, D., Esbensen, A.J., & Smalls, Y. (2001). The behavior problems inventory: An instrument for the assessment of self-injury, stereotyped behavior, and aggression /destruction in individuals with developmental disabilities. *Journal of Autism and Developmental Disorders, 31,* 577 – 588.

Rosenthal, M.M. (1999). Out of home child care research: A cultural perspective. *International Journal of Behavioral Development, 23*, 477 – 518.

Rothbart, M. K. (1981). Measurement of temperament in infancy. *Child Development, 52,* 569 - 578.

Rothbart, M. K. (2007). Temperament, development, and personality. *Current Directions in Psychological Science, 16*, 207 – 212.

Rothbart, M.K., Ahadi, S.A., & Evans, D. E. (2000). Temperament and personality: Origins and outcomes. *Journal of Personality and Social Psychology, 78,*122–135.

Rothbart, M.K., Ahadi, S.A., & Hershey, K.L. (1994). Temperament and Social Behavior in Childhood. *Merrill-Palmer Quarterly, 40,* 21 -39.

Rothbart, M.K., Ahadi, S.A., Hershey, K.L., & Fisher, P. (2001).Investigations of temperament at three to seven years: The Children's Behavior Questionnaire. *Child Development., 72,*1394–1408.

Rothbart, M.K., & Bates, J.E. (2006). Temperament. In W. Damon, R. Lerner, & N. Eisenberg (Eds.), Handbook of child psychology: Vol. 3. Social, emotional, and personalitydevelopment (6th ed., pp. 99 166). New York: Wiley.

Rothbart, M.K., & Derryberry, D. (1981). Development of individual differences in temperament. In M.E. Lamb & A. Brown (Eds.), Advances in developmental psychology (Vol. 1, pp. 37-86). Hills dale, NJ: Erlbaum.

Rothbart, M. K., & Derryberry, D. (2002). Temperament in children. *Psychology at The Turn of the Millennium, 2*, 17-35.

Rothbart, M. K., & Hanson, M. J. (1983). A caregiver report comparison of temperamental characteristics of Down Syndrome and normal infants. *Developmental Psychology, 19*, 766-780.

Rothbart, M. K., & Jones, L. B. (1998). Temperament, self-regulation, and education. *School Psychology Review, 27*, 479.

Rothbart, M. K. & Mauro, J. A. (1990). Questionnaire approaches to the study of infant temperament. In J. W. Fagen & J. Colombo (Eds.), *Individual differences in infancy: Reliability, stability and prediction*. Hillsdale, NJ: Erlbaum.

Rothbart, M. K., & Posner, M. I. (1985). Temperament and the development of self-regulation. In *The neuropsychology of individual differences* (pp. 93-123). Springer US.

Rothbart, M.K., & Sheese, B.E. (2007). Temperament and emotion regulation. In J.J. Gross (Ed.), Handbook of emotion regulation (pp. 331-350). New York: Guilford.

Rubio, D.M., Berg-Weger, M., Tebb, S.S., Lee, S., & Rauch, S. (2003). Objectifying content validity: conducting a content validity study in social work research. *Social Work Research, 27*, 94-105.

Sabah, S., & Gilani, N. (2010). Household chaos and its association with maternal education, family system and children's academic achievement in Pakistani culture. *Pakistan Journal of Psychological Research,25* (1), 19 – 30.

Sahar, N., & Muzaffar, N. (2017). Role of family system, positive emotions and reseilience in social adjustment among Pakistani adolescents. *Journal of Educational Health and Community Psychology,6* (2), 46-58.

Sadrossadat, L., Moghaddami, A., & Sadrossadat, S.J. (2010). A comparison of adaptive behaviors among mentally retarded and normal individuals: A guide to prevention and treatment. *International Journal of Preventive Medicine, 1,* 34 -38.

Saigal, S., Rosenbaum, P., Stoskopf, B., Hoult, L., Furlong, W., Feeny, D.,& Hagan, R. (2005). Development, reliability and validity of a new measure of overall health for pre-school children. *Quality of Life Research, 14,* 243-257

Sanson, A., Prior, M., Garino, E., Oberklaid, F., & Sewell, J. (1987). The structure of infant temperament: Factor analysis of the Revised Infant Temperament Questionnaire. *Infant Behavior and Development, 10,* 97-104.

Sattler, J.M. (2001). *Assessment of children* (4th ed.). San Diego, CA: Jerome Sattler, Publisher, Inc.

Schalock, R.L. (Ed.). (1999). *Adaptive behavior and its measurement: Implications for the field of mental retardation.* Washington, DC: American Association on Mental Retardation.

Schalock, R. L., Borthwick-Duffy, S. A., Bradley, V. J., Buntinx, W. H. E., Coulter, D. L., Craig, E. M., ... Yeager, M. H. (2010). *Mental retardation: Definition, classification, and systems of supports (11th ed.).* Washington, DC: American Association on Intellectual and Developmental Disabilities.

Schatz, J., & Hamdan-Allen, G. (1995). Effects of age and IQ on adaptive behavior domains for children with autism. *Journal of Autism and Developmental Disorders, 25,* 51-60.

Schaughency, E., & Fagot, B.I. (1993). The prediction of adjustment at age 7 from

activity level at age 5. *Journal of Abnormal Child Psychology, 21*, 29 – 50.

Scheerenberger, R. (1983). A history of mental retardation: A quarter century of

progress.Baltimore, MD: Paul H. Brookes.

Schell, L.M. (19 97).Culture as a stressor : A revised model of biocultural interaction.

American Journal of Physical Anthropology, 102, 67-78.

Schotte, C. K. W., Maes, M., Cluydts, R., De-Doncker, D., & Cosyns, P. (1997). Construct

validity of the Beck Depression Inventory in a depressive population. *Journal of Affective

Disorders, 46,* 115–125. doi:10.1016/s0165-0327(97)00094-3.

Schwartz, C.B., Henderson, H.A., Inge, A.P., Nicole, E., Coman, D.C., Spinrad, ...

Kupanoff, K . (2004). The relation of children's everyday nonsocial peer play behavior

to their emotionality, regulation, and social functioning. *Developmental Psychology, 40,*

67–80. [PubMed: 14700465]

Schwartz, C.B., Henderson, H.A., Inge, A.P., Zahka, N.E., Coman, D.C., Kojkowski, N.M., .

. . . Mundy, P.C. (2009). Temperament as a predictor of symptomotology and adaptive

functioning in adolescents with high-functioning autism. *Journal of Autism and

Developmental Disorders, 39*, 842–855.

Schwebel, D. C., & Plumert, J. M. (1999). Longitudinal and concurrent relations among

temperament, ability estimation, and injury proneness. *Child development, 70*, 700-712.

Sealy, M.J., Nijholt, W., Stuiver, M.M., Berg, M.M., Roodenburg, J.L.N., Schans, C.P.,

.....Jager-Wittenaar, H. (2016). Content validity across methods of malnutrition

assessment in patients with cancer is limited. *Journal of Clinical Epidemiology, 76*, 125-

136.

Selikowitz, M. (1992). Health problems and health checks in school-aged children with

Down syndrome. *Journal of Pediatrics and Child Health, 28*, 383-386.

Shakeel, A., Johar, A. (2014). Parent's perception on children's intellectual disability: A case

study of Khyber Pakhtunkhwa, Pakistan. *Internal Journal of Rehabilitative Sciences, 3*,

31- 38.

Shiner, R., & Caspi, A. (2003). Personality differences in childhood and adolescence:

Measurement, development, and consequences. *Journal of Child Psychology and

Psychiatry, 44*, 2-32.

Shiraev, E. B. & Levy, D. A. (2010). Cross-cultural psychology: Critical thinking and

contemporary applications (4th ed.). Boston: Pearson/Allyn Bacon.

Sidani, S., Guruge, S., Miranda, J., Ford-Gilboe, M., & Varcoe, C. (2010). Cultural

adaptation and translation of measures: an integrated method. *Research in Nursing and

Health, 33*,133-143.

Sigman,M., & Ruskin, E. (1999).Continuity and change in the social competence of children

with autism, Down syndrome, and developmental delays. *Monographs of the Society for

Research in Child Development, 64*,256.

Singh, G. (2006). Determination of Cutoff Score for a Diagnostic Test. *The Internet Journal

of Laboratory Medicine, 2*, https://print.ispub.com/api/0/ispub-article/9884

Silverman, I. W., & Ippolito, M. F. (1995). Maternal antecedents of delay ability in young

children. *Journal of Applied Developmental Psychology, 16*, 569-591.

Simms, L.J. (2008). Classical and modern methods of psychological scale construction.

Social and Personality Psychology Compass, 2, 414-433.

Simonds, J., & Rothbart, M. K. (2004). The temperament in middle childhood questionnaire (TMCQ): A computerized self report measure of temperament for ages 7-*10*. Poster session presented at the Occasional Temperament Conference, Athens, Greece.

Simonds, J., & Rothbart, M. K. (2006). Temperament in Middle Childhood Questionnaire. *Manuscript in preparation*.

Singh, G. (2006). Determination of cutoff score for a diagnostic test. *The Internet Journal of Laboratory Medicine, 2,*21-26.

Siperstein, G.N., & Leffert, J.S. (1997). Comparison of socially accepted and rejected children with mental retardation. *American Journal on Mental Retardation, 101*, 339-351.

Sikora, D. M., Vora, P., Coury, D. L., and Rosenberg, D. (2012). Attention-Deficit/ Hyperactivity Disorder Symptoms, Adaptive Functioning, and Quality of Life in Children With Autism Spectrum Disorder. *Pediatrics,130*, 91 - 97.

Slabach, E. H., Morrow, J., & Wachs, T. D. (1991). Questionnaire measurement of infant and child temperament: Current status and future directions.

Smith, A. L., Romski, M. A., & Sevcik, R.A. (2013) .Examining the role of communication on sibling relationship quality and interaction for sibling pairs with and without a developmental disability. *American Journal on Intellectual and Developmental Disabilities: September, 118*, 394-409.

Smith, G.T. (2005). On construct validity: Issues of method and measurement. *Psychological Assessment, 17*, 396 – 408.

Smith, J., Prior, M. (1995). Temperament and stress resilience in school-age children: A within-families study. *Journal of the American Academy of Child & Adolescent Psychiatry, 34*, 168 – 179.

Smith, T., Eikeseth, S., & Lande, H. (2006). The Vineland Adaptive Behavior Scale in a Sample of Norwegian Second-Grade Children: A Preliminary Study. *Tidsskrift for Norsk Psykologforening, 43*, 2–5.

Songa, S.H., Kima, H. R., Chunb, K.A., & Kima, Y.T. (2014). Vocabulary characteristics of children with high and low functioning autism and intellectual disabilities. *Communication Sciences and Disorders, 19* (4):423-429.

Sousa,V.D.,Rojjanasrirat,W. (2011). Translation, adaptation and validation of instruments or scales for use in cross cultural health care research: A clear and user friendly guidelines. *Journal of Evaluation in Clinical Practice, 17*,268- 274.

Sparrow, S.S., Balla, D.A., & Cicchetti, D.V. (1984). Vineland adaptive behavior scales. Circle Pines, MN: American Guidance Service.

Sparrow, S.S., & Cicchetti, D.V. (1985). Diagnostic uses of the Vineland Adaptive Behavior Scales. *Journal of Pediatric Psychology, 10*, 215-225.

Sparrow, S. S., Balla, D. A., & Cicchetti, D. V. (2005). Vineland Adaptive Behavior Scales Second Edition Survey Forms Manual. AGS Publishing.

Spector, J.E. (1999). Precision of age norms in tests used to assess preschool children. *Psychology in the Schools, 36*, 459-471.

Spinrad, T.L., Eisenberg, N., Harris, E., Hanish, L., Fabes, R.A., Kupanoff K, . (2004).The relation of children's everyday nonsocial peer play behavior to their emotionality, regulation, and social functioning. *Developmental Psychology,40*,67–80.

Squires, A., Aiken, L.H., Heede, K.V., Sermeus, W., Bruyneel, L., Lindqvist, R.,....Brozstek,

T. (2012). A systematic survey instrument translation process for multi-country,

comparative health workforce studies. *International Journal of Nursing Studies, 50,* 264

– 273.

Steiner, H. (Ed.). (2011). Handbook of developmental psychiatry. Singapore: World

Scientific Co.

Strauss, M. E., & Rourke, D. L. (1978). A multivariate analysis of the Neonatal Behavioral

Assessment Scale in several samples. *Monographs of the Society for Research in Child

Development, 43,* 81-91.

Strauss, M.E., & Smith, G.T. (2009). Construct Validity: Advances in Theory and

Methodology. *Annual Review of Clinical Psychology, 27,* 1–25.

doi:10.1146/annurev.clinpsy.032408.153639.

Stelmack, R. M., & Stalikas, A. (1991). Galen and the humour theory of temperament.

Personality and Individual Differences, 12, 255-263.

Stinnett, T.A. (1997). AAMR Adaptive Behavior Scale-School: Test review. *Journal of

Psychoeducational Assessment, 15,* 361-372.

Susan, M. M., & Wendy, G. C. (1989). Sibling relationships of children with disabled and

nondisabled brothers and sisters. *Developmental Psychology, 25,* 421-429.

http://dx.doi.org/10.1037/0012-1649.25.3.421.

Tabachnick, B.G., & Fidell, L.S. (2013). *Using multivariate statistics* (6th ed.). Upper Saddle

River, NJ: Pearson Allyn & Bacon.

Tan, M., Reich, J., Hart, L., Thuma, P. E., & Grigorenko, E.L. (2011). Examining Specific

Effects of Context on Adaptive Behavior and Achievement in Rural Africa: Six Case

Studies from Southern Province, Zambia. *Journal of Autism and Developmental Disorders*,44, 271-282. doi: 10.1007/s10803-012-1487-y .

Tasse´, M.J., & Havercamp, S.M. (2006). The Role of Motivation and Psychopathology in Understanding the IQ–Adaptive Behavior Discrepancy. *International Review of Research in Mental Retardation, 31*, 231-253.

Tasse´, M. J., Schalock, R.L., Balboni, G., Bersani, H., Borthwick-Duffy, S.A., Spreat, S., ... Zhang, D. (2012). The construct of adaptive behavior: Its conceptualization, measurement, and use in the field of intellectual disability. *American Journal of Intellectual and Developmental Disabilities, 117*, 291–303. DOI: 10.1352/1944-7558-117.4.291.

Tavakol, M., & Dennick, R. (2011). Making sense of cronbach's alpha. *International Journal of Medical Education, 2*, 53-55. ISSN: 2042-6372. DOI: 10.5116/ijme.4dfb.8dfd

The National Institute of Mental Health.(2016). *Autism spectrum disorder*. https://www.nimh.nih.gov/health/topics/autism-spectrum-disorders-asd/index.shtml

Thomas, A., Chess, S., Birch, H.G., Herzig, M.E., & Korn, S. (1963). *Behavioral individuality in early childhood*. New York: New York University Press.

Thomas, A., Chess, S., & Birch, H.G. (1968). *Temperament and behavior: Disorders in children*. New York: New York University Press.

Thomas, A., & Chess, S. (1977). Temperament and development. New York: Bruner/Mazel.

Thomas, A., & Chess, S. (1989). Temperament and personality. In G. A. Kohnstamm, J. E., Bates, & M. K. Rothbart (Eds.), *Temperament in childhood* (pp. 249-261). New York: John Wiley.

Thomas, A., & Chess, S. (1996). Temperament: theory and practice. *New York, NY: Brunner & Mazel.*

Thomas,S.E., Kelly, S.J., Mattson, S.N., & Riley, E.P. (1998). Comparison of social abilities of children with Fetal Alcohol Syndrome to those of children with similar IQ scores and normal controls. *Alcoholism Clinical and Experimental Research,22,*528-533. DOI: 10.1111/j.1530-0277.1998.tb03684.x

Thompson, F.R., McGrew, K.S., & Bruininks, R.H. (1999). Adaptive and maladaptive behavior: Functional and structural characteristics. In R.L. Schalock (ed.), Adaptive behavior and its measurement: Implications for the field of mental retardation (pp. 15-42). Washington, DC: American Association on Mental Retardation

Tombokan-Runtukahu, J., Nitko, A. J. (1991). Translation, cultural adjustment, and operationalization of the construct of adaptive behavior. Unpublished doctoral dissertation, Regional Office of Education and Culture Department, North Sulawesi Province, Indonesia.

Tonge, B., & Brereton, A. (2011). Autism spectrum disorders. *Australian Family Physician, 40,* 672 – 677.

Traverna, L., Bornstein, M.H., Putnick, D.L., & Axia, G. (2011). Adaptive behaviors in young children: A unique cultural comparison in Italy. *Journal of Cross Cultural Psychology, 42,* 445 – 465.

Treadwell, K. R.H.,Flannery-Schroeder, E.C., & Kendall, P.C. (1995). Ethnicity and gender in relation to adaptive functioning, diagnostic status, and treatment outcome in children from an anxiety clinic. *Journal of Anxiety Disorders,9,* 373-384.

Tubman, J.G. (1993). Family risk factors, parental alcohol use, and problem behaviors among school-age children. *Family Relations, 42*, 81-86.

Umberson, D. (1987). Family status and health behaviors: Social control as a dimension of social integration. *Journal of Health and Social Behavior, 28*, 306-319.

Upreti, R., & Singh, R.(2016). A study of differences in adaptive behavioral skills of mentally challenged children with gender. *International Journal of Humanities and Social Sciences, 5*, 87-94.

Vachaa, B.(2003). Poster 26: Temperament characteristics and adaptive behavior of school-aged children with myelomeningocele and shunted hydrocephalus. *Archives of Physical Medicine and Rehabilitation, 84*, E9.

Valdivia, R. (1999) The implications of culture on developmental delay.URL http://ericec.org/digests/e589.html

Van de Vijver, F. J. R., & Leung, K. (1997). *Methods and data analysis for cross-cultural research.* Thousand Oaks, CA: Sage.

Van de Vijver, F. J. R., & Tanzer, N.K. (1997). Bias and equivalence in cross cultural assessment: An overview. *European Review of Applied Psychology, 47*, 263 – 279.

Vaughn, B. E., & Bost, K. K. (1999). Attachment and temperament: redundant, independent, or interacting influences on interpersonal adaptation and personality development? In: Cassidy J, Shaver PR (Eds). Handbook of attachment: theory, research, and clinical applications. Guilford Press, New York pp. 198–225.

Vinh, N. T. (2104). Assessing adaptive behavior of children with Down Syndrome in

Vietnam by Vineland adaptive behavior scale II. Proceedings of the 7th International Conference on Educational Reform (ICER 2014), Innovations and Good Practices in Education: Global Perspectives. 327-334.

Volkmar, F.R., & McPartland, J.C. (2014). From Kanner to DSM-5: Autism as an evolving diagnostic concept. *Annual Review of Clinical Psychology, 10*:193–212

Volkmar, F.R., & Pauls, D. (2003). Autism. *Lancet, 362*, 1133-1141.

Volkmar, F.R., Sparrow, S.S., Goudreau, D., Cicchetti, D.V., Paul, R., & Cohen, D.J. (1987). Social deficits in autism: An operational approach using the Vineland adaptive behavior scales. *Adolescent Psychiatry,26*, 156-161

Volkmar, F.R., Szatmari, P., & Sparrow, S.S.(1993).Sex differences in pervasive developmental disorders. *Journal of Autism and Developmental Disorders, 23*,579–591.

Wachs, T.D., Bishry, Z., Sobhy, A., McCabe, G., Galal, O., & Shaheen, F. (1993). Relation of rearing environment to adaptive behavior of Egyptian toddlers. *Child Development, 64*, 586-604.

Walls, R.T., & Werner, T.J. (1977). Vocational behavior checklists. *Mental Retardation, 15*, 30-35.

Walters, A.V. (2010). Developmental Delay – Causes and Investigation. *Pediatric Neurology, 10* (2), 32 – 34.

Watkins, C.E., Campbell, V.L., Nieberding, R., & Hallmark, R. (1995). Contemporary practice of psychological assessment by clinical psychologists. *Professional Psychology: Research and Practice, 26*, 54-60.

Watkins, M.W., Ravert, C.M., & Crosby, E.G. (2002). Normative Factor Structure of the AAMR adaptive behavior scale- school, second edition. *Journal of Psychoeducational Assessment, 20,* 337-345.

Weiss, J. A., Sullivan, A. & Diamond, T. (2003). Parent stress and adaptive functioning of individuals with developmental disabilities. *Journal on Developmental Disabilities, 10,* 129 - 136.

Weismer, S.E., Lord, C., & Esler, A.(2010). Early language patterns of toddlers on the autism spectrum compared to toddlers with developmental delay . *Journal of Autism and Developmental Disorders, 40,* 1259–1273. doi:10.1007/s10803-010-0983-1.

Wells, K., Condillac, R., Perry, A. , & Factor, D.C. (2010). A comparison of three adaptive behavior measures in relation to cognitive level and severity of autism. *Journal on Developmental Disabilities, 15,* 55-63.

White, J. D. (1999). Review Personality, temperament and ADHD: a review of the literature. *Personality and individual differences, 27,* 589-598.

Widaman, K.F., & McGrew, K.S. (1996). The structure of adaptive behavior. In J.W. Jacobson, & J.A. Mulick (Eds.), Manual of diagnosis and professional practice in mental retardation (pp. 97-110). Washington, DC: American Psychological Association.

Widaman, K.F., Stacy, A.W., & Borthwick-Duffy, S.A. (1993). Construct validity of dimensions of adaptive behavior: A multitrait-multimethod evaluation. *American Journal on Mental Retardation, 98,* 219-234.

Windle, M., & Lerner, R. M. (1986). Reassessing the dimensions of temperamental individuality across the life span: The Revised Dimensions of Temperament Survey (DOTS-R). *Journal of Adolescent Research, 1,* 213-229.

Wing, L. (1997). Syndromes of autism and atypical developmental disorders. In: Volkmar FR, Paul R, Klin A, Cohen D, editors. Handbook of autism and pervasive developmental disorders. New York: John Wiley.

Wing, L., & Potter, D. (2000). The epidemiology of autistic spectrum disorders: Is the prevalence rising? *Mental Retardation and Developmental Disabilities Reviews, 8,* 151 – 161.

Wise, S., & Sanson, A. (2000). Child care in cultural context: Issues for new research. *Research Paper No. 22,December.*Melbourne: Australian Institute of Family Studies.

Woo, P. J., & Teoh, H.J. (2007). An investigation of cognitive and behavioural problems in children with attention deficit hyperactive disorder and speech delay. *Malaysian Journal of Psychiatry September,16,* 49 - 58.

World Health Organization. (1992). International classification of diseases No. 10: Classification of mental and behavioural disorders. Geneva: WHO.

World Health Organization. (2011). The international statistical classification of diseases and related health problems-10th revision (2010th ed.). Geneva: WHO.

World Health Organization. (2013). Process of Translation and adaptation of instruments. Geneva: WHO.

Yaghmaie, F. (2003). Content validity and its estimation. *Journal of Medical Education, 3,* 25-27.

Ye, R., Ming, S., & Rothbart, M.K. (1988).A longitudinal study of infant temperament: Cross cultural comparisons of Chinese and American infants. *Psychological Progress and Education, 4,* 6–10.

Yong, A. G., & Pearce, S. (2013). A beginner's guide to factor analysis: Focusing on exploratory factor analysis. *Tutorials in Quantitative Methods for Psychology, 9,* 79–94.

Yunus, A., Mushtaq, S.K., & Qaiser, S. (2012). Peer pressure and adaptive behavior learning: A study of adolescents in Gujrat city. *International Journal of Asian Social Science, 2,*1832 - 1841.

Zhang, J., Wheeler, J. J., & Richey, D. (2006). Cultural validity in assessment instruments for children with autism from a Chinese cultural perspective. *International Journal of Special Education, 21,* 109—114.

Zheng, W., Hou, F., & Schimmele, C.M. (2008). Family structure and children's psychosocial outcomes. *Journal of Family Issues,29,* 1600 – 1624. DOI: https://doi.org/10.1177/0192513X08322818

Zhao, X., Zhang, Q., Shan, Y., Zhang, H., & Guo, L. (2002). A study on the influence factors for social adaptive behavior of children. *Journal of West China University of Medical Sciences,33,* 259-61.

Zigler, E., Balla, D.A., & Hodapp, R.M. (1984). On the definition and classification of mental retardation. *American Journal of Mental Deficiency , 89,* 215-230.

Zion, E., & Jenvey, V.B. (2006). Temperament and social behaviour at home and school among typically developing children and children with an intellectually disability. *Journal of Intellectual Disability Research,50,* 445 – 456.

Appendices

Appendix

<u>Description of Adaptive Behavior Domains</u>

1. **Communication:** Interacting with others, talking, writing, using the phone. Skills include the ability to comprehend and express information through symbolic behaviors (e.g., spoken words, written word, graphic symbols, sign language) or non symbolic behaviors (e.g., facial expression, body movement, touch gesture). Specific examples include the ability to comprehend and/or receive a request, an emotion, a greeting, a comment, a protest, or rejection.

2. **Self-Care:** Skills involved in eating, dressing, hygiene, toileting, grooming.

3. **Home-Living:** Skills related to functioning within a home, which include caring for clothes, housekeeping, property maintenance, food preparation, cooking, budgeting, home safety and daily scheduling. Related skills include orientation and behavior in the home and nearby neighborhood, communications of choices and needs, social interaction and application of functional academics in the home.

4. **Social:** Skills related to social exchanges with other individuals, including initiating, interacting and terminating interaction with others; receiving and responding to pertinent situational cues; recognizing feelings; providing positive and negative feedback; regulating ones behavior; being aware of peers and peer acceptance; gauging the amount and type of interaction with others; assisting others; forming and fostering of friendship and love; coping with demands from others; making choices; sharing, controlling impulses; conforming conduct to laws and rules. Getting along with others, being aware of other people's feelings, forming relationships.

5. **Community Use:** skills related to the appropriated use of community resources, including travelling within community, shopping at stores and markets, obtaining services in community (doctor, dentist, and setting up utilities), attending mosque, using public transportation and public facilities such as schools, libraries, parks and recreational areas. Related skills include behavior in the community, communication of choices and needs, social interaction and application of functional academics

6. **Self-Direction:** Skills related to making choices about how to use one's time, following a schedule, seeking assistance when needed, resolving problems confronted in familiar and novel situations, deciding what to do in new situations, demonstrating appropriate assertiveness and self advocacy skills.

7. **Health and Safety:** Making choices about what to eat, illness identification, prevention and treatment, basic first aid, avoiding danger, basic safety considerations (e.g., following rules and laws, using seat belts, crossing streets, interacting with strangers, seeking assistance).

8. **Functional Academics:** Cognitive abilities and skills related to learning at school that also have direct application in one's life e.g., reading, writing, computation skills, telling time. The focus is not on grade-level academic achievement but, rather, on the acquisition of academic skills that are functional in terms of independent living.

9. **Leisure:** The development of a variety of leisure and recreational interests (i.e., self-entertainment and interaction) that reflect personal preferences and choices, and if the activity will be conducted in public, age and cultural norms. Using available time when not working or in school, choosing age appropriate activities. Skills include choosing and self – initiating interests, using and enjoying home and community leisure and recreational activities alone or with others, playing socially with others, taking turns, terminating or refusing leisure or recreational activities.

10. **Work:** Skills related to holding a part time or full time job in the community, in terms of specific job skills appropriate work-related attitudes and social behaviors, completion of tasks, persistent effort/stamina and taking criticism.

<u>Picture Booklet for Adaptive Behavior Scale.</u>

Communication Item 4

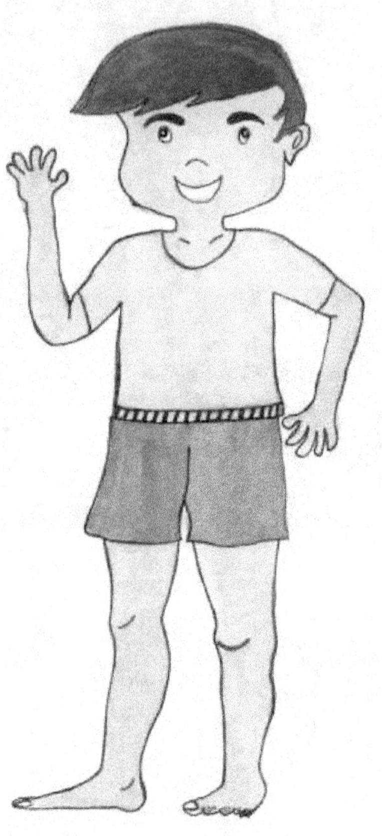

<u>**Communication Item 32**</u>

a b c d e f g h i j k l m n o p q r s t u
v w x y z

A B C D E F G H I J K L M N O P Q R
S T U V W X Y Z

ا ب پ ت ٹ ث ج چ

ح خ د ڈ ذ ر ڑ ز ژ

س ش ص ض ط ظ ع

غ ف ق ک گ ل م ن

و د ی ے

<u>**Work Item 1 and 10**</u>

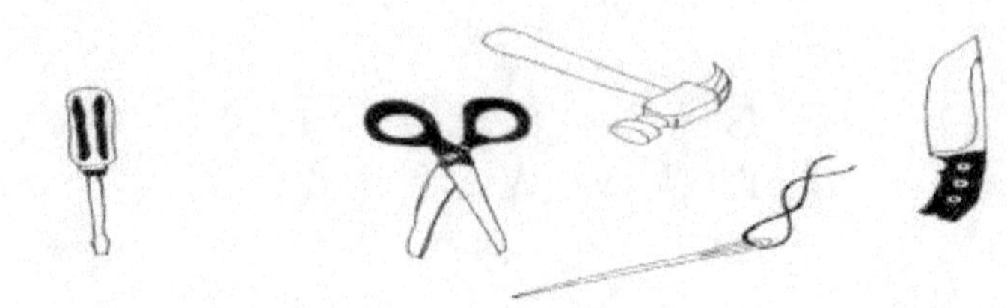

<u>**Home Living Item 2**</u>

Home Living Item 2

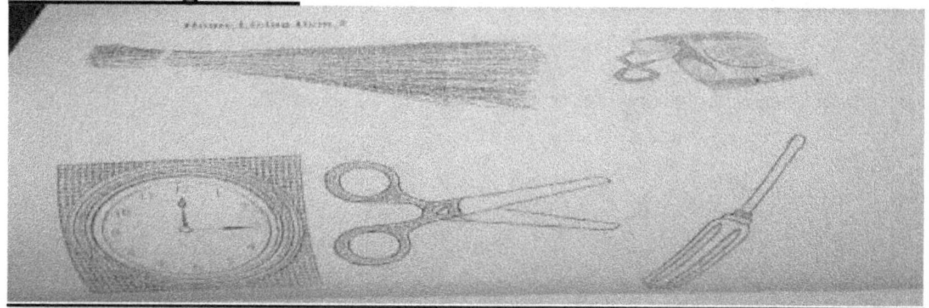

Home Living Item 29

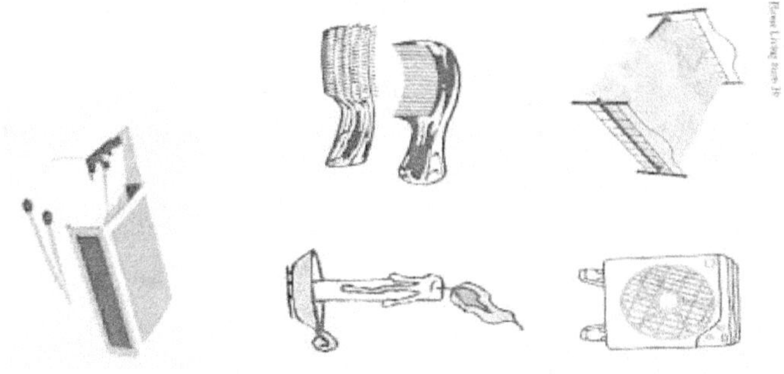

Functional Academic Skills Item 2

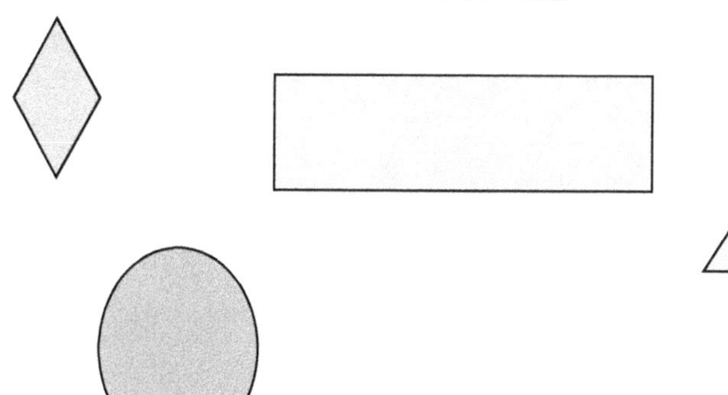

Functional Academic Skills Item 2

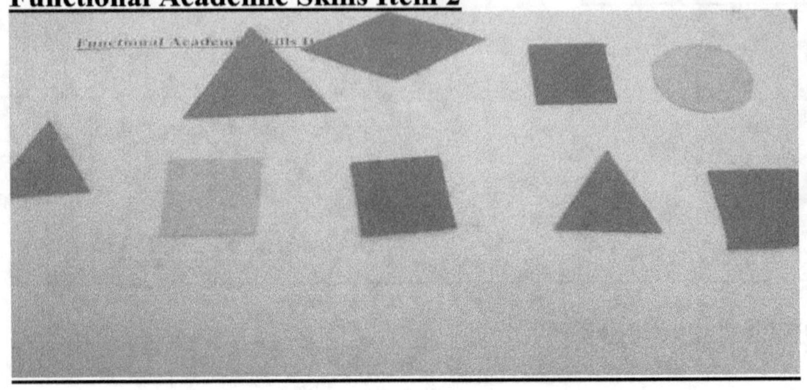

Worksheets for Functional Academic Skills

Item 5

کار	بلی
عید	ماں
کتا	شہر
سیب	ناک
جنگ	رات
فون	پچ
شہر	فوج
گھر	باغ

2 + 3 =

4 + 5 =

7 + 3 =

5 + 1 =

8 + 2 =

2 + 6 =

1 + 6 =

4 + 3 =

1 + 3 =

5   9   20   66   48

11   97

32   14   69   75   0

سکول   درخت

بس   کتاب

پھول

Functional Academic Skills Item 16

Calendar   November 2013

Sunday	Monday	Tuesday	Wednesday	Thursday	Friday	Saturday
					1	2
3	4	5	6	7	8	9
10	11	12	13	14	15	16
17	18	19	20	21	22	23
24	25	26	27	28	29	30

Functional Academic Skills Item 17

Functional Academic Skills Item 19

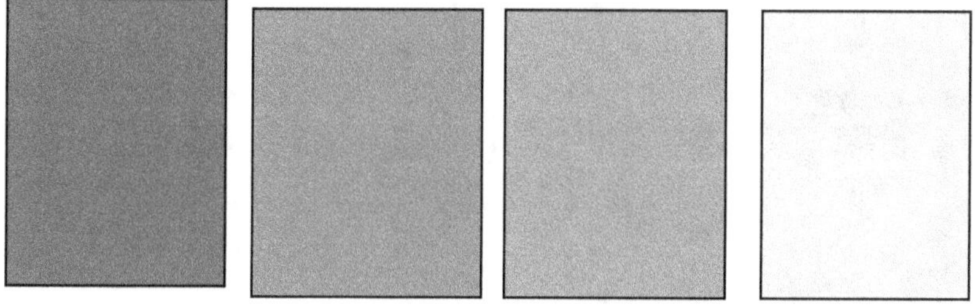

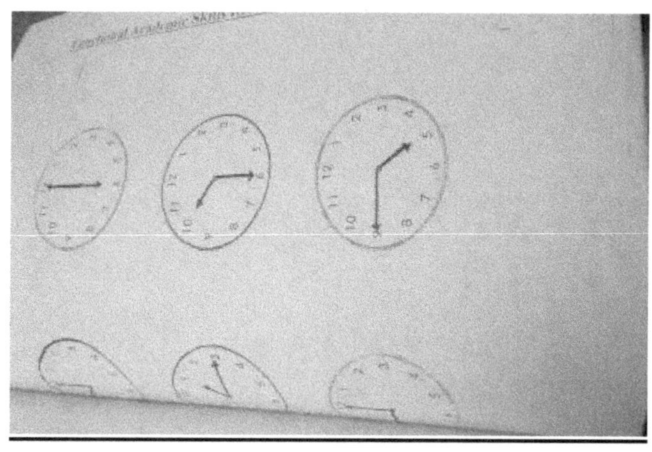

Sample Reinforcers

<u>Sample picture of maze</u>

Maze with Broader Lines

Motor Skills - Item 25

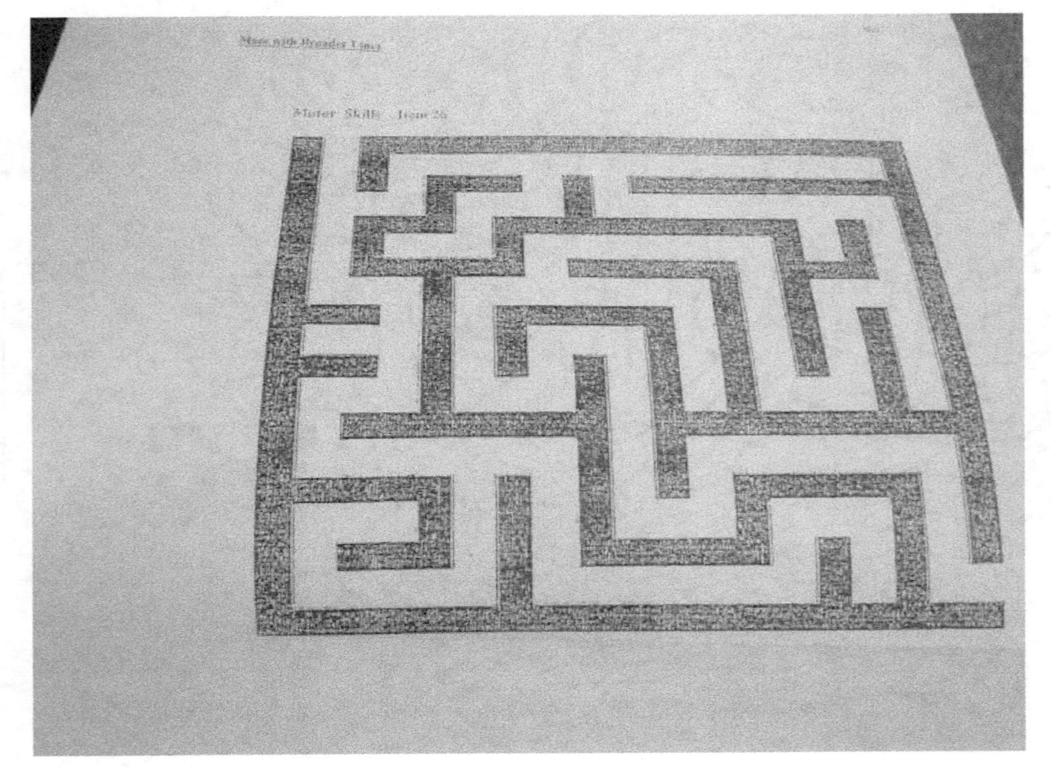

Adaptive Behavior Domains

1. **Communication:** Interacting with others, talking, writing, using the phone. Skills include the ability to comprehend and express information through symbolic behaviors (e.g., spoken words, written word, graphic symbols, sign language) or non symbolic behaviors (e.g., facial expression, body movement, touch gesture). Specific examples include the ability to comprehend and/or receive a request, an emotion, a greeting, a comment, a protest, or rejection.

2. **Self-Care:** Skills involved in eating, dressing, hygiene, toileting, grooming.

3. **Home-Living:** Skills related to functioning within a home, which include caring for clothes, housekeeping, property maintenance, food preparation, cooking, budgeting, home safety and daily scheduling. Related skills include orientation and behavior in the home and nearby neighborhood, communications of choices and needs, social interaction and application of functional academics in the home.

4. **Social:** Skills related to social exchanges with other individuals, including initiating, interacting and terminating interaction with others; receiving and responding to pertinent situational cues; recognizing feelings; providing positive and negative feedback; regulating ones behavior; being aware of peers and peer acceptance; gauging the amount and type of interaction with others; assisting others; forming and fostering of friendship and love; coping with demands from others; making choices; sharing, controlling impulses; conforming conduct to laws and rules. Getting along with others, being aware of other people's feelings, forming relationships.

5. **Community Use:** skills related to the appropriated use of community resources, including travelling within community, shopping at stores and markets, obtaining services in community (doctor, dentist, and setting up utilities), attending mosque, using public transportation and public facilities such as schools, libraries, parks and recreational areas. Related skills include behavior in the community, communication of choices and needs, social interaction and application of functional academics

6. **Self-Direction:** Skills related to making choices about how to use one's time, following a schedule, seeking assistance when needed, resolving problems confronted in familiar and novel situations, deciding what to do in new situations, demonstrating appropriate assertiveness and self advocacy skills.

7. **Health and Safety:** Making choices about what to eat, illness identification, prevention and treatment, basic first aid, avoiding danger, basic safety considerations (e.g., following rules and laws, using seat belts, crossing streets, interacting with strangers, seeking assistance).

8. **Functional Academics:** Cognitive abilities and skills related to learning at school that also have direct application in one's life e.g., reading, writing, computation skills, telling time. The focus is not on grade-level academic achievement but, rather, on the acquisition of academic skills that are functional in terms of independent living.

9. **Leisure:** The development of a variety of leisure and recreational interests (i.e., self entertainment and interaction) that reflect personal preferences and choices, and if the activity will be conducted in public, age and cultural norms. Using available time when not working or in school, choosing age appropriate activities. Skills include choosing and self – initiating interests, using and enjoying home and community leisure and recreational activities alone or with others, playing socially with others, taking turns, terminating or refusing leisure or recreational activities.

10. **Motor:** Gross and fine motor skills that are considered essential to attain for all children during middle childhood

11. **Work:** Skills related to holding a part time or full time job in the community, in terms of specific job skills appropriate work-related attitudes and social behaviors, completion of tasks, persistent effort/stamina and taking criticism.

Items Sent for ICVI Ratings

Communication			
Interacting with others, talking, writing, using the phone. Skills include the ability to comprehend and express information through symbolic behaviors (e.g., spoken words, written word, graphic symbols, sign language) or non symbolic behaviors (e.g., facial expression, body movement, touch gesture). Specific examples include the ability to comprehend and/or receive a request, an emotion, a greeting, a comment, a protest, or rejection.	Construct Relevance	Cultural relevance	Repetition
1 Uses 4 to 8 words sentences			
2 Points to at least five part of his body ("mouth", "ear", "nose", "hand", "knee")			
3 Listens to a story for 5 minutes			
4 Understands simple instructions such as "open the door", "get your bag", and "show me your pencil"			
5 Enjoys tracing or copying letters			
6 Points to 5 common objects ("ball", "spoon", "knife", "cup", "book") in the test booklet (page) on request			
7 Sits down when signaled to do so (can stretched arm with open hand pointing down)			
8 Responds to a finger put on closed lips to indicate be quiet			
9 Gets up when signaled to do so (outstretched arm with open hand raised and moving upward)			
10 Tells the names of familiar people (at least four names)			
11 How old are you			
12 Describes action in a picture (page of the test booklet)			
13 After listening to a one-page story (page) child can answer specific questions with "yes" and "no"			
14 Prints simple words (writes legibly first name or a few familiar words of three or four letters not using copying)			
15 Uses pencil for writing (write dozen or more simple words with correct spellings. Does so on own initiative or from dictation, but not from copy)			
16 Name something that you can eat; you can drink; you can ride ; you can eat			
17 Follows instructions requiring an action and an object			
18 Carries out a series of three related directions			
19 Tells familiar story without pictures reproducing essential elements (for example sequence of actions, solution and final ending)			
20 Starts a conversation of interest with others			

21	Makes telephone calls – (Uses phone for practical purposes, that is, looks up numbers, places calls and carries on purposive conversations effectively)
22	Name three kind of animals who have 4 legs
23	What do these words mean Automobile; elevator; trouble; dangerous
8	Can jump rope by self
9	Cuts a piece of paper with scissors
10	Hits ball with bat or stick
11	Picks up objects from ground while running
12	Rides bicycle
13	Can catch a small ball from 3 yards distance even if it means running to catch it
14	Uses pencil or crayon for drawing (draws with pencil or crayon and produces simple but recognizable forms such as man, house, tree, animal, landscape)
15	Stands on one foot eyes open
16	Uses skates, sled, wagon – (takes care of self unsupervised outside of own yard in use of skates, led, wagon, velocipede, skooter and similar play vehicles involving small hazard)
17	Stands on tiptoes with eyes closed for at least 5 seconds
18	Cuts a star out of a piece of paper with scissors following the drawn lines (copy star from test booklet, page 2)
19	Bears weight one knee - half kneeling position
20	Puts small objects in a box using thumb and index finger
21	Can jump with both feet into the air
22	Can walk for 15 minutes without pause ("How long does it take to walk to your house from school?") *
23	Can hop on one foot at least 3 time without losing his balance
24	Can run on difficult terrain (hills, holes in the ground) without falling
25	Can draw a straight line with the use of a ruler
26	Can open and lock a padlock
27	Can fold a piece of paper and put it into an envelope
28	Can thread a needle with an average size opening
29	Walks backward on a line
30	Can draw simple but recognizable pictures e.g., a man, a woman, an animal, landscape
31	Walks and bounces a ball
32	Can jump on a step or stone block alternating each foot at least 20 times
33	Can flip bottle caps so they fall on each other

| 34 | Can trace a path in maze with a pencil without touching the borders (copy maze from test booklet , page 1) | | | |
| 35 | Manages kite | | | |

Home Living

Skills related to functioning within a home, which include caring for clothes, housekeeping, property maintenance, food preparation, cooking, budgeting, home safety and daily scheduling. Related skills include orientation and behavior in the home and nearby neighborhood, communications of choices and needs, social interaction and application of functional academics in the home.

#		Construct Relevance	Cultural Relevance	Repetition
1	Mend cloth for minor problems			
2	Can concentrate on a task for at least 5 minutes (rate picture drawing)			
3	What do you use this for Broom ; Towel ; clock ; telephone Broom ; Screw driver ; clock ; scissor			
4	Does small errands in familiar surroundings ("Fetch me a chair!")			
5	Concentrates for 15 minutes on a given task (observe child's behaviour in academic skills!)			
6	Cleaning the house, dusting, washing clothes, (girls)			
7	Can light a candle and places it in a safe place			
8	Makes his own bed and changes the sheets regularly ("Who makes your bed?")*			
9	Can use a stove without danger for heating food or water ("Are you allowed to use a stove for heating something without someone else watching over you?")			
10	Washes own clothing ("Can you wash your own clothing and did you wash the clothing you are wearing?")*			
11	Participates in organized games like cricket ("Do you play cricket with others?")*			
12	Avoids danger of pointed and sharp objects ("How many times have you hurt yourself with a razor blade or a can opener?") *			
13	Knows the value of coins			
14	Can put coins in order of their value			
15	Exchanges an amount of coins in another (five 1 rupee coins into 5 rupee coin)			
16	"I have 100 rupees and buy bread for 50. Please give me my change"			
17	Uses pointed objects (knives, scissors, needles) safely (to be observed with motor skill tasks 9,13,23)			
18	Washes and irons clothing ("Who washed and ironed the clothing you are wearing?")*			
19	Drying the clothes			
20	Ironing the clothes			

21	Avoids dangers of electrical objects ("Show me how to pull put the plug!") (Child pulls it out by seizing the plug and not tugging on the cable of the extension cord)
22	Putting things in right order at home
23	Cleaning the room
24	Ensuring discipline in house (elder siblings)
25	Can cook a simple meal like porridge ("Tell me what you can cook alone without anyone helping you!") *
26	Avoiding fights when they are given responsibilities (elder ones)
27	Can understand time concepts like yesterday, today, and tomorrow. (Name the days of week and reads time from clock/ reads calendar and clock adequately)
28	Can begin to understand time and the days of the week
29	Can complete basic food preparation (e.g., make sandwich, heat soup)
30	Following time table
31	Taking care of younger siblings
32	Making time table for younger siblings to study and play
33	Helping the younger siblings to study / explaining the subject matter or taking tests
34	Buying edibles from the market (boys)
35	Keep an eye on household items and preparing the list when something is finished or required.
36	Taking care of household items
37	Checking doors and locks and keeping an eye on their younger siblings
38	Fulfilling the responsibilities given to them
39	Helping parents to plan budget in house (elder ones)
40	Managing the kitchen especially girls around 10-12 years of age
41	Making breakfast and lunch for themselves and their siblings
42	Washing dishes
43	Helping mother preparing in meal
44	Preparing cereals
45	Helping mother in weekly menu
46	Cooking instant foods
47	Hemming
48	What do you use to make bread
49	Setting the table
50	Button the shirt (stitch the button)
51	Show picture of knife; spoon; fork; plate; glass and ask the child to name each
52	Show card and ask for time indicated 9:00 ; 10:30 ; 1:15

		Construct Relevance	Cultural Relevance	Repetition
53	What would you do if your house is caught on fire and nobody was home but you?			
54	Can differentiate between different cereals (daals)			
55	Can Clean daal n rice independently			

Community Skills
Skills related to the appropriated use of community resources, including travelling within community, shopping at stores and markets, obtaining services in community (doctor, dentist, and setting up utilities), attending mosque, using public transportation and public facilities such as schools, libraries, parks and recreational areas. Related skills include behavior in the community, communication of choices and needs, social interaction and application of functional academics

		Construct Relevance	Cultural Relevance	Repetition
1	"Can you find your way home from school alone?" *			
2	Keep space from others			
3	Stay in queue Waiting for turn in queue			
4	Leaving seat for elders, greeting familiar people (travelling)			
5	Keep quiet in mosques, libraries			
6	Keep the place clean			
7	Keeping the things on their right place especially in library and shopping centre			
8	Do not misbehave with others			
9	Following the rules and regulation			
10	Be on time / punctual (mosque and school).			
11	Seek permission before entering class			
12	Knows the name of his town, his neighborhood, his street and house			
13	Participates in leisure time activities with friends without being accompanied by adults ("Who takes you out to play?")			
14	Knows the correct price of at least 3 objects (matches .pencil ,orange)			
15	Crosses the roads in the neighborhood looking to both sides and waiting for passing cars before crossing (let the child demonstrate!)			
16	Can buy small objects locally ("Show me some small things you have bought yourself in local shops")			
17	Collects trash and disposes of on request (instruct and observe!)			
18	Taking care of baggage while travelling			
19	Going to the Doctor and expressing problems			
20	Use of public transport with an elder member			
21	Going to a cinema			
22	Knowledge of traffic signals			
23	Knowledge of public bathroom signs			
24	Visiting fast food chains			
25	Where could you find the phone number of the police or sheriff			

26	If you move into a new neighborhood or school name three things you could do to make new friends
27	Why grownups need to work
28	Why do we need to have laws
29	Where do you get your car worked on? (If answer is at home ask:) If a stranger in town has trouble with his car, where would he get it fixed?
30	Why do we need to have police
31	Where does a nurse usually works?
32	What should you say if someone gives you a piece of candy
33	What should you do if a little kid called you a bad name?
34	W hat should you do if you found a purse on the ground with two hundred rupees in it
35	Name three games you can play with other children on the play ground
36	How old do you have to be to Vote ; Get a good Job ; Drive a car
37	Where should you go to post a letter or a parcel
38	Where should you go if you need to borrow a book for few days

Items of Adaptive Behavior Scale

	Communication
1	Points to at least five part of his body ("mouth", "ear", "nose", "hand", "knee")
2	Understands simple instructions such as "open the door", "get your bag", and "show me your pencil"
3	Can identify and tell alphabets
4	Points to 5 common objects ("ball", "spoon", "knife", "cup", "book") in the test booklet (page) on request
5	Understands and responds to non verbal gestures (For example, sits down when signaled to do so, responds to a finger put on closed lips to indicate be quiet)
6	How old are you
7	Tells the names of familiar people (at least four names)
8	Describes action in a picture (page of the test booklet)
9	After listening to a one-page story child can answer specific questions with "yes" and "no"
10	Prints simple words by using pencil for writing (writes legibly first name or few simple familiar words of three or four letters with correct spellings not using copying)
11	Use pencil to write (Write one or more simple meaningful word with correct spellings, and does this without looking at the word)
12	Name something that you can eat; you can drink; you can ride ; you can eat
13	Follows three related instructions
14	Tells familiar story without pictures reproducing essential elements (for example sequence of actions, solution and final ending)
	Makes telephone calls – (Uses phone for practical purposes, that is, looks up numbers, places calls and carries on purposive conversations effectively)
16	Name three kind of animals who have 4 legs
17	What do these words mean Terrorist; stranger; martyr; dangerous; obedient; future.
18	Tells address
19	Tells telephone number
20	Points to 10 body parts in the test booklet (page) on request ("Where is the "nose", "arm", "hand", "knee", "thumb", "foot", "eye", "ear", "hair", "elbow"?")
21	Follows a sequence of three or more related instructions both verbal and written ("Stand up", "open the book" and "put it on the chair")
22	Responds to someone nodding his head "yes" or "continue" (to be observed during assessment)

23	Names 20 well known objects (animal fruits clothing etc) in the test booklet ,Speaks clearly without substituting sounds
24	Knows the names of his area/ neighborhood, his city, his province, and the Prime Minister of Pakistan
25	When asked uses the past & the future tense in the sentence "the girl runs to school"
26	Can carry on a conversation with another person for at least 10 minutes using average vocabulary for his age group (rate your own discussion with the child)
27	Describes what happened in the mosque on Friday or in church on Sunday in a logical order
28	Can write a paragraph to clearly convey an idea
29	Uses swear words or "bathroom words" to get attention
30	Enjoys riddles and jokes
31	Can understand and use comparative terms like big, bigger, or biggest
32	Knows some alphabets and numbers
33	Understand & points categories (like these are all animals, these are toys)
34	Understands these prepositions before and after; above/ below; in and on
35	Saying prayers or singing national anthem in school
36	Greeting others by saying salam and shaking hands

Self Care Skill

1	Reciting Bismillah before eating.
2	Washes hands and face
3	Uses correct utensils for food (Which one do you drink out of ; Which one do you eat custard with)
4	Bathes self except for back, neck and ears
5	Uses knife or spoon for spreading soft toppings on toast or rooti
6	Buckles and unbuckles belt on dress, pants or shoes
7	Dresses self completely, including all front fastenings except ties
8	Brushes teeth with tooth brush or maswaq
9	Hangs up cloths on hanger.
10	Why do you take bath/ shower
11	Serves self at table and passes serving dishes
12	Prepares own sandwich
13	Peels and cuts Vegetables and fruits into portions
14	Can toast chapatti or bread on tawa
15	Manners for eating not talking while eating, making noises, filling hands with the food, Waiting for elders to start, finishing the plate/food.
16	Selects appropriate clothing according to temperature and occasion

	Socialization
1	Involves in let's pretend plays (Imitates adult roles)
2	Is afraid of being caught doing something he's not supposed to
3	What would you say if you bump into someone without meaning to
4	Asks permission to use objects belonging to others
5	States feelings about self: mad, happy, love
6	Takes care of others belongings ("If you use some ones book, how do you treat it?")*
7	What would you do if your best friend asked you for an answer during a test
8	Can recognize feelings (Show child card and ask to identify emotions). A boy who lost his basket ball would feel _____________ A girl who lost her doll would feel _______________
9	Is happy or proud if he has achieved something or even without praise from others (judge by observing reaction on motor tasks)
10	Makes sure not to loose his things ("When did you last loose something that belongs to you? What was it? How often does this happens?")
11	Says "please", "thank you" and "sorry"
12	Helps others if necessary ("Can you tell me when you last helped someone? What did you do? Do you do this often?)
13	Can cooperate in a group without quarreling ("Do you often get into fights with other children when you are in a group?")
14	Gives borrowed objects back without being reminded (did the child give back the pencil and scissors for the assessment procedure without being reminded?)
15	Knows quranic verses, popular songs, and school rhymes, and sings with others ("Please sing me a hymn or a song you learned at school!")
16	Tries to meet expectation in different situations such as being a "friend", "visitor", "pupil", or "host" ("How do you behave if you are some one's friend? If you are a visitor? A host? A pupil in school?")
17	Follows school rules or other standards of conduct ("How often in the last month have you been punished for not doing what you were told?")
18	Respects the given time limits for recreation or break time at school or work ("How often in the last month have you been late after break time?")
19	Does his share of the work ("At home, do you do as much work as your brothers and sisters? What exactly do you do? How often do you do this?")
20	Uses names of others
21	Has more than one friend
22	Not overly dependent on others
23	Shows interest in the ideas of others
24	Congratulates others when something good happens
25	Wants to avoid being reprimanded Can be talked into doing things that others want

26	Understands that something that others are asking him to do could get him into trouble
27	Can identify when he is being put down or made fun of
28	Cannot recognize hidden intentions of others

Self Direction

1	Follows classroom rules
2	Completes routine classroom tasks in the given amount of time
3	Control anger or hurt feelings when denied his/her own way
4	Keeps working on the assigned task even when difficult
5	Avoiding fights when they are given responsibilities
6	Tells his/ her gender
7	Apologizes for mistakes or errors
8	Likes to make own decisions when allowed to
9	Can print name
10	What number do you dial to call rescue services
11	What should you do if you lose your reading book
12	Scheduling time dividing it into rest, studies, recitation of Quran and leisure.
13	Saying no to activities or things against their will
14	Where could you find a doctor
15	Knows the method of WUZU fully.
16	What should you do if you get lost in (name child's home or nearest town)
17	Knows all the recitations and method of prayer fully.
18	Knows the timings of all prayers and knows the significance of religious festivals
19	Handles himself (his/her emotions) during argument
20	Proposes solution in group conflicts (such as sticking to the rules of the game) ("If your brothers and sisters quarrel when playing together, what do you do?")
21	Follows advice given by elders ("What was the last time an elder person gave you advice? What did he say? Did you follow his advice?")on
22	Excuses himself for false and unjust accusations ("If you have said something wrong about some one, what do you do?")
23	Can accept criticisms and suggestions without becoming angry or annoyed (observe reactions to your suggestions or criticism during assessment) * SD
24	Can defend himself in a calm way if unfairly treated ("If someone says you have stolen something and you didn't do it – how do you explain?")

1	"Can you find your way home from school alone?"
2	Waiting for turn in queue
3	Leaving seat for elders, greeting familiar people
4	Ensuring discipline in mosques and libraries (remaining quiet)
5	Keep the place clean
6	Keeping the things on their right place especially in library and shopping centre
7	Do not misbehave with others
8	Seek permission before entering class
9	Participates in leisure time activities with friends without being accompanied by adults ("Who takes you out to play?")
10	Knows the correct price of at least 3 objects (matches .pencil ,orange)
11	Collects trash and disposes of on request (instruct and observe!)
12	Taking care of baggage while travelling
13	Going to the Doctor and expressing problems
14	Using public transport with a family member
15	Visiting fast food chains and goes to a cinema
16	Knows traffic signals
17	Use of public transport with an elder member
18	If you move into a new neighborhood or school name three things you could do to make new friends
19	Why grownups need to work
20	Where do you get your car worked on? (If answer is at home ask:) If a stranger in town has trouble with his car, where would he get it fixed?
21	Why do we need to have police
22	Crosses the roads in the neighborhood looking to both sides and waiting for passing cars before crossing (let the child demonstrate!)
23	Why do we need to have laws.
24	Where does a nurse usually works?
25	What should you say if someone gives you a piece of candy
26	Name three games you can play with other children on the play ground
27	What would you do if you find a purse on ground having 500 rupees in it.
28	How old do you have to be to Vote ; Get a good Job ; Drive a car
29	Where should you go to post a letter or a parcel
30	Where should you go if you need to borrow a book for few days
31	Handles school equipment carefully.
32	Goes to local store to make small / explicit purchases (pays proper amount and gets correct change)

1	Follows safety rules on playground
2	Shows caution around dangerous activities
3	Asks to see School Nurse or other adult when ill or hurt
4	Conscious about interacting with strangers/ not taking something to eat from them
5	Why do you brush your teeth
6	Had number of emergency services 911, 1122 or family relatives to call in case of emergency.
7	Follow the traffic rules while crossing the street
8	Expressing pain and discomfort
9	Avoiding physical contact with strangers
10	Discriminating between family, friends and strangers
11	Where could you buy cough medicine or prescription for medicine from the doctor
12	Is left to care for self and others – (Is sometimes left alone or on own responsibility for hour or more at home or at work and is successful in looking after own immediate needs or those of others who may be left in his care.)
13	Avoids danger of pointed and sharp objects ("How many times have you hurt yourself with a razor blade or a can opener?")
14	Avoids dangers of electrical objects ("Show me how to pull put the plug!") (Child pulls it out by seizing the plug and not tugging on the cable of the extension cord)

Work

1	What do you use to hit nail (show picture from booklet)
2	Helps at little household tasks (helping to set up or clear table, feeding pets, dusting, picking up things; running errands)
3	Uses tools and utensils – (Makes some practical use of a simple tools or utensils, such as hammer, saw, screw driver, knife, household or sewing utensils, garden tools). Which one do you use to hit the nail – Knife ; Hammer; Scissor
4	Does routine household tasks (Helps effectively at simple tasks about house which recur routinely and for which some continuous responsibility is assumed, such as dusting, arranging, cleaning, washing dishes, setting or clearing table, making bed etc)
5	Regular and punctual in school
6	Cooperative with others
7	Does simple creative work (Makes useful articles or does simple repair or productive work; cooks; bakes; or sew in small ways; does simple

	gardening; raises pets; makes minor purchases; carrying newspaper; taking care of children)
8	Works patiently
9	Works consistently
10	Ask the use of things given in booklet

Leisure

1	Plays with toys or other objects alone or with others
2	Shows interest in the activities of others
3	Invites a peer to join a game
4	Tries a new activity to learn something new.
5	Playing alone like computer games
6	Plays competitive exercise games (engages in competitive active play in small groups of three or four of like age, e.g., tag, hide and seek, hopscotch, jumping rope, marbles, tops, statue)
7	Interested in magic and tricks.
8	Making partners and carry leisure activity with them
9	Refuse to play with the friend who do not follow the rules of the game
10	Learns a new game, sport, or other activity easily.
11	Ending the game if someone is cheating
12	Can keep score when playing certain games
13	Reads for own entertainment or information practical, such as sign boards, comic strips, movie titles, simple stories, elementary news items, library books, adventure stories etc
14	Wants to attend activities happening in the city
15	Likes making plans and following them
16	Participates in preadolescent plays – (Boy engages in group cooperative baseball, football, basketball, hokey etc; Girls engage in dramatic play symbolizing domestic or social situations, such as playing house, school, doctor-nurse and shopping etc)

Functional Academic Skills

1	Indicate the right number of objects up to 10 ("Show me 2,5,7, and 9 bottle caps!")
2	Can distinguish between "round" and "rectangular" objects (bottle and matchbox and eraser)

3	Understands the difference between yesterday, today and tomorrow ("What happened yesterday? Where will you go tomorrow? What did you do today?")
4	Can name all the days of the week in the correct order
5	Reads three simple words and identifies the corresponding picture in the test booklet, page (such as "apple", "cat" or "table")
6	Counts from 1 to 20 (1 to 10 and 10 to 20)
7	Reads own name
8	Can copy a word made up of three/ four letters ("cat, goat", "pencil","night", "phone", "plane") [in test booklet]
9	Can order objects according to color (bottle caps: red, blue, green)
10	Adds numbers up to 10 (8+2, 7+3, 4+3, 2+5, 1+6)
11	Names the daytime (morning, noon, night) and gives the corresponding activities (awakening, mealtimes, going to bed)
12	Can read five simple printed words: "house", "school", "road", "tree", "lorry"
13	Can respond correctly to the question: "What day and date do we have today?"
14	Writes simple sentences of three or four words (Ahmed goes to school, Ayesha reads a book, mother cooks a meal)
15	Show coins worth Rs. 1, 2 and 5, ask child to name each
16	Locates important dates on calendar
17	Can read 10 words: "teacher", "chocolate", "cow", "taxi", "police", "shoes", "wedding", "shop" etc.
18	May be able to copy simple designs and shapes
19	Knows basic colors like red, yellow, blue, green, orange
20	capable of remembering address and phone number
21	Draws pictures that represent animals, people, and objects
22	Can place objects in order from shortest to tallest
23	Understands that Urdu books are read from right to left, English books are read from left to right, top to bottom
24	Reading signs/ directions.
25	Can write important messages
26	Able to learn difference between left and right Correctly tells right and left side – Touch your right ear with your left hand/ Show me your right hand – now touch your left ear
27	Understands "more," "less," and "same"
28	Can make list of important items needed at home.
29	Can write down all the expenditure after shopping and make calculations
30	Tells time accurately. Show card and ask for time indicated 9:00 ; 10:30 ; 1:15
31	Show rupees 20, 50 and 100, ask child to name each and identify which worth more and least
32	Reading warning signs on edibles, products and medicine

1	Can concentrate on a task for at least 5 minutes (rate picture drawing)
2	What do you use this for Broom ; Towel ; clock ; telephone Broom ; Screw driver ; clock ; scissor
3	Does small errands in familiar surroundings ("Fetch me a chair!")
4	Takes care of guests in absence of adult family members
5	Helps in cleaning the house, dusting, washing clothes, (girls)
6	Can light a candle and places it in a safe place
7	Makes his own bed and changes the sheets regularly ("Who makes your bed?")
8	Can use a stove without danger for heating food or water ("Are you allowed to use a stove for heating something without someone else watching over you?")
9	Washes and irons own clothing ("Can you wash your own clothing and did you wash the clothing you are wearing?") ("Who washed and ironed the clothing you are wearing?")
10	Exchanges an amount of coins in another (five 1 rupee coins into 5 rupee coin)
11	Putting things in right order at home
12	"I have 100 rupees and buy bread for 50. Please give me my change"
13	Ensuring discipline in house (elder siblings)
14	Can cook a simple meal like porridge, boil egg and/or make Tea ("Tell me what you can cook alone without anyone helping you!")
15	Button the shirt (stitch the button)
16	Can complete basic food preparation (e.g., make sandwich, heat soup)
17	Taking care of younger siblings
18	Buying edibles from the market (boys)
19	Taking care of household items
20	Helping the younger siblings to study / explaining the subject matter or taking tests
21	Checking doors and locks and keeping an eye on their younger siblings
22	Making time table for younger siblings to study and play
23	Washing dishes
24	Helping mother preparing in meal
25	What do you use to make bread
26	What would you do if your house is caught on fire and nobody was home but you?
27	Can Clean daal n rice independently
28	Carrying out responsibilities assigned at home.
29	Show picture of cooler, bed, comb/brush, candle and macth box and ask to name all.

1	Can do a forward roll
2	Folds paper two times on diagonal in imitation
3	Unscrews the lid of a bottle or jar
4	Can jump rope by self
5	Cuts a piece of paper with scissors
6	Hits ball with bat or stick
7	Picks up objects from ground while running
8	Rides bicycle
9	Uses pencil or crayon for drawing (draws with pencil or crayon and produces simple but recognizable forms such as man, house, tree, animal, landscape)
10	Stands on one foot eyes open
11	Stands on tiptoes with eyes closed for at least 5 seconds
12	Cuts a star out of a piece of paper with scissors following the drawn lines
13	Bears weight one knee - half kneeling position
14	Puts small objects in a box using thumb and index finger
15	Can jump with both feet into the air
16	Can walk for 15 minutes without pause ("How long does it take to walk to your house from school?"). *Uses skates, sled, wagon – (takes care of self unsupervised outside of own yard in use of skates, led, wagon, velocipede, skooter and similar play vehicles involving small hazard)
17	Can hop on one foot at least 3 time without losing his balance
18	Can draw a straight line with the use of a ruler
19	Can open and lock a padlock
20	Can fold a piece of paper and put it into an envelope
21	Can thread a needle with an average size opening
22	Walks backward on a line
23	Walks and bounces a ball
24	Can jump on a step or stone block alternating each foot at least 20 times
25	Can flip bottle caps so they fall on each other
26	Can trace a path in maze with a pencil without touching the borders
27	Manages kite
28	Can catch a small ball from 3 meters' distance

Detail of Items included in Each Factor

		Daily Living Skills (Factor 1)
1	Points to at least 5 body parts	
2	Points to 5 common objects	
3	How old are you	
4	Tells the names of familiar people	
5	Describes action in a picture	
6	After listening to a story answer questions	
7	Prints simple words by using pencil for writing	
8	Name something that you can eat; you can drink; you can ride ; you can eat	
9	Follows a series of three related instructions	
10	Makes telephone calls	
11	Name three kind of animals who have 4 legs	
12	Tells telephone number	
13	Points to 10 body parts in the test booklet	
14	Follows a sequence of three or more related instructions both verbal and written	
15	Names 20 well known objects	
16	Carry conversation with another person for 10 minutes using average vocabulary	
17	Describes events in a logical order	
18	Recognizes few letters and numbers	
19	Understands classifications	
20	Understands these prepositions before and after; above, and below; in and on	
21	Saying prayers or singing national anthem in school	
22	Greeting others by saying salam and shaking hands	
23	Is afraid of being caught doing something he's not supposed to	
24	Takes care of others belongings ("If you use some ones book, how do you treat it?")	
25	Makes sure not to loose his things ("When did you last loose something that belongs to you?	
26	Acts properly at public place without drawing negative attention.	
27	Reciting Bismillah before eating.	
28	Washes hands and face	
29	Uses correct utensils for food (Which one do you drink out of ; Which one do you eat custard with)	
30	Follows classroom rules	
31	Completes routine classroom tasks in the given amount of time	
32	Control anger or hurt feelings when denied his/her own way	
33	Avoiding fights when they are given responsibilities	
34	Apologizes for mistakes or errors in judgment	
35	Likes to make own decisions when allowed to	
36	What should you do if you lose your reading book	
37	Saying no to activities or things against their will	

38	Where could you find a doctor
39	Knows the timings of all prayers and knows the significance of religious festivals
40	Can accept criticisms and suggestions without becoming angry or annoyed
41	Asks to see School Nurse or other adult when ill or hurt
42	Conscious about interacting with strangers/ not taking something to eat from them
43	Avoiding physical contact with strangers
44	Plays with toys or other objects alone or with others
45	Invites a peer to join a game
46	Plays competitive active play of three or four of like age, e.g., tag, hide and seek.
47	Refuse to play with the friend who do not follow the rules of the game
48	Learns a new game, sport, or other activity easily
49	Can keep score when playing certain games
50	Participates in preadolescent plays – (Boy engages in group cooperative baseball, football
51	Which one do you use to hit the nail – Knife ; Hammer; Scissor
52	Regular and punctual in school
53	Cooperative with others
54	Work patiently
55	Works consistently
56	Correctly identify objects
57	Indicate the right number of objects up to 10 ("Show me 2,5,7, and 9 bottle caps!")
58	Can distinguish between "round" and "rectangular" objects
59	Understands the difference between yesterday, today and tomorrow
60	Can name all the days of the week in the correct order
61	Reads 3 simple words of 3 letters & identifies corresponding picture in booklet
62	Counts from 10 to 20
63	Reads own name
64	Can copy a word made up of four letters
65	Can order objects according to color
66	Names daytime and the corresponding activities (awakening, mealtimes,
67	Can read five simple printed words: "house", "school
68	Can respond correctly to the question: "What day and date do we have today?"
69	Writes simple sentences of three or four words (Ahmed goes to school
70	Show coins worth Rs. 1, 2 and 5, ask child to name each
71	Locates important dates on calendar
72	May be able to copy simple designs and shapes
73	Knows basic colors like red, yellow, blue, green, orange
74	Draws pictures that represent animals, people, and objects
75	Understands that Urdu books are read from right to left, English books are read from left to
76	Can place objects in order from shortest to tallest
77	Able to learn difference between left and right
78	Understands "more," "less," and "same"
79	Unscrews the lid of a bottle or jar
80	Can jump rope by self

81	Hits ball with bat or stick
82	Picks up objects from ground while running
83	Rides bicycle
84	Stands on one foot eyes open
85	Stands on tiptoes with eyes closed for at least 5 seconds
86	Cuts a star out of a piece of paper with scissors following the drawn lines
87	Puts small objects in a box using thumb and index finger
89	Can jump with both feet into the air
90	Can walk for 15 minutes without pause ("How long does it take to walk to your
91	Can hop on one foot at least 3 time without losing his balance
92	Can draw a straight line with the use of a ruler
93	Can open and lock a padlock
94	Can trace a path in maze with a pencil without touching the borders
95	Manages kite
96	Catch a small ball from 3 feet
97	Remaining silent in library
98	Keeping the things on their right place especially in library and shopping centre
99	Do not misbehave with others
100	Seek permission before entering class
101	Knows the correct price of at least 3 objects (matches .pencil ,orange)
102	Collects trash and disposes of on request (instruct and observe!)
103	Going to the Doctor and expressing problems
104	Crossing street /road carefully

	Total number of items	Item Numbers
Factor 1	104	C1, C4, C6, C7, C8, C9, C10, C12, C13, C15, C16, C19, C20, C21, C23, C26, C27,C31, C32, C33, C34, C35, S2, S6, S10, Sc1, Sc2, Sc3, Sd1, Sd2, Sd3, Sd5, Sd7, Sd8, Sd11, Sd13, Sd14, Sd18, Sd23 ,Cs4, Cs6, Cs7, Cs8, Cs10, Cs11, Cs13, Cs22, Hs3, Hs4, Hs9, W1, W 5, W 8, W 9, W 10, L1, L3, L6, L9, L10, L12, L16,FAS1, FAS2, FAS3, FAS4, FAS5, FAS6, FAS7, FAS8, FAS9, FAS11, FAS12, FAS13, FAS14,FAS15, FAS16, FAS18, FAS19, FAS21, FAS22, FAS23, FAS26, FAS27, M3, M4, M6, M7, M8, M10, M11, M12, M14, M15, M16, M17, M18, M19, M20, M26, M27, M28

**Social Skills
(Factor 2)**

1	Can write a paragraph to clearly convey an idea
2	Asks permission to use objects belonging to others
3	States feelings about self: mad, happy, love

4	Plays simple games – (Takes turns and observe rules and does so without undue dissensions.)
5	Says "please", "thank you" and "sorry"
6	Helps others if necessary ("Can u tell me when u last helped someone?
7	Can cooperate in a group without quarreling ("Do you often get into fights with other children when you are in a group?")
8	Follows school rules or other standards of conduct
9	Not overly dependent on others
10	Congratulates others when something good happens
11	Had number of emergency services 911, 1122 or family relatives to call in emergency
12	Expressing pain and discomfort
13	Is left to care for self and others – (Is sometimes left alone or on own responsibility for
14	Avoids dangers of electrical objects ("Show me how to pull put the plug!") (Child pulls
15	Avoids danger of sharp objects
16	Interested in magic and tricks
17	Making partners and carry leisure activity with them
18	Reading signs/ directions.
19	Can write important messages
20	Show rupees 20, 50 and 100, ask child to name each and identify which worth more
21	Reading warning signs on edibles, products and medicine
22	Tells time accurately. Show card and ask for time indicated
23	Folds paper two times on diagonal in imitation
24	Knows the value of coins
25	Ensures discipline
26	"I have 100 rupees and buy bread for 50. Please give me my change"
27	Waiting for turn in queue
28	Leaving seat for elders, greeting familiar people
29	Use of public transport with an elder member
30	Knowledge of public bathroom signs
31	If you move in new neighborhood name three things you could do to make new friends
32	folds paper n put it in envelope
33	Where do you get your car worked on
34	Name three games you can play with other children on the play ground
35	If you find a purse on floor
36	How old do you have to be to Vote ; Get a good Job ; Drive a car
37	Where should you go to post a letter or a parcel
38	Where should you go if you need to borrow a book for few days
39	Goes to local store to make small purchases (pays proper amount ,gets correct change)

	Total number of items	**Item Numbers**
Factor 2	39	C28, C36, S4, S5, S7, S11, S12, S13, S16, S17, S22, S24, Hs6, Hs8, Hs12, W 6, L7, L8, FAS24, FAS25, FAS30, FAS31, FAS32, HL12,HL13, Cs2, Cs3, Cs14, Cs17, Cs18, Cs19,Cs20, Cs21,Cs26, Cs27, Cs28, Cs29, Cs30, Cs32.

	Self Care (Factor 3)
1	Tells address
2	Knows the names of his area/ neighborhood, his city, his province, and the prime minister
3	Understands could get in trouble
4	Can identify when he is being put down or made fun of
5	What number do you dial to call rescue services
6	Gives borrowed objects back without being reminded
7	Bathes self except for back, neck and ears
8	Uses knife or spoon for spreading soft toppings on toast or rooti
9	Buckles and unbuckles belt on dress, pants or shoes
10	Dresses self completely, including all front fastenings except ties
11	Brushes teeth with tooth brush or maswaq
12	Hangs up cloths on hanger .
13	Why do you take bath/ shower
14	Serves self at table and passes serving dishes.
15	Prepares own sandwich
16	Peels and cuts Vegetables and fruits into portions.
17	Can toast chapatti or bread on tawa
18	Manners for eating not talking while eating, making noises,filling hands with food
19	What should you do if you get lost in (name child's home or nearest town)
20	Knows the method of WUZU fully.
21	Follows advice by elders
22	Can defend himself in calm way if unfairly treated
23	Proposes solution in group conflicts (such as sticking to rules of the game)
24	Discriminating between family, friends and strangers
25	Where could you buy cough medicine or prescription for medicine
26	Reads for own entertainment or information practical, such as sign boards, comic strips,
27	Putting things in right order at home
28	Uses utensils n tools
29	Taking care of baggage while travelling

30	Why do we need to have police.
31	Knowledge of traffic signals
32	Why grownups need to work.
33	Taking care of school tools
34	Follow the traffic rules while crossing the street

	Total number of items	**Item Numbers**
Factor 3	34	C18,C24, S14, S26, S27, Sc4, Sc5, Sc6, Sc7, Sc8, Sc9, Sc10, Sc11, Sc12, Sc13, Sc14, Sc15, Sd10, Sd15, Sd16, Sd20, Sd21,Sd24, Cs12, Cs16, Cs31, Hs7, Hs10, Hs11, Hs13, Hs14, W 3, L13, L15. HL25.

Home Living (Factor 4)

1	Helps at little household tasks (helping to set up or clear table, feeding pets, dusting, picking up things
2	Does routine household tasks (Helps effectively at simple tasks about house which recur routinely and for which some continuous responsibility is assumed
3	Capable of remembering phone numbers and address
4	Can make list of important items needed at home.
5	Can write down all the expenditure after shopping and make calculations
6	Can thread a needle with an average size opening
7	Does small errands in home surroundings
8	Takes care of guests in absence of adult family members
9	Helps in cleaning the house, dusting, washing clothes
10	Can light a candle and places it in a safe place
11	Makes his own bed and changes the sheets regularly
12	Can use a stove without danger for heating food or water
13	Washes and irons own clothing
14	Exchanges an amount of coins in another
15	Can complete basic food preparation (e.g., make sandwich, heat soup)
16	Taking care of younger siblings
17	Helping the younger siblings to study / explaining the subject matter or taking tests
18	Buying edibles from the market (boys)

19	Can cook a simple meal like porridge, boil egg and/or make Tea ("Tell me what you can cook
20	Making time table for younger siblings to study and play
21	Checking doors and locks and keeping an eye on their younger siblings
22	Helping mother preparing in meal.
23	Button the shirt (stitch the button).
24	Can Clean daal n rice independently
25	What would you do if your house is caught on fire and nobody was home but you?
26	Washing dishes
27	Taking care of household items
28	What do you use to make bread
29	Can you find your way home from school alone?

	Total number of items	**Item Numbers**
Factor 4	29	Cs1, W 2, W 4, HL3, HL4, HL5, HL6, HL7, HL8, HL9 ,HL10, HL14, HL15, HL17,HL18, HL 19, HL20, HL21, HL22, HL23, HL24, HL26, HL27, HL28, FAS17, FAS20, FAS28, FAS29, M21.

Children's Behavior Questionnaire-Teacher Form

<u>Instructions</u>: <u>Please read carefully before starting</u>:
On the next pages you will see a set of statements that describe children's reactions to a number of situations. We would like you to tell us what the above named child's reaction is likely to be in those situations. There are of course no "correct" ways of reacting; children differ widely in their reactions, and it is these differences we are trying to learn about. Please read each statement and decide whether it is a "<u>true</u>" or "<u>untrue</u>" description of the child's reaction <u>within the past six months</u>. Use the following scale to indicate how well a statement describes the child:

Circle #   If the statement is:

1	extremely untrue of this child	2 quite untrue of this child
3	slightly untrue of this child	4 neither true nor false of this child
5	slightly true of this child	6 quite true of this child
	7 extremely true of this child	

If you cannot answer one of the items because you have never seen the child in that situation, for example, if the statement is about the child's reaction to your singing and you have never sung to the child, then circle <u>NA</u> (not applicable).

Please be sure to circle a number or NA for <u>every</u> item.

1.   **Seems always in a big hurry to get from one place to another.**
   I   2   3   4   5   6   7   NA
2.   **Gets angry when told s/he has to remain still during rest time.**
   I   2   3   4   5   6   7   NA
3.   **Is not very bothered by pain.**
   I   2   3   4   5   6   7   NA
4.   **Likes going down high slides or other adventurous activities.**
   I   2   3   4   5   6   7   NA
5.   **Notices the smoothness or roughness of objects s/he touches.**
   I   2   3   4   5   6   7   NA
6.   **Gets so worked up before an exciting event that s/he has trouble sitting still.**
   I   2   3   4   5   6   7   NA
7.   **Usually rushes into an activity without thinking about it.**
   I   2   3   4   5   6   7   NA
8.   **Cries sadly when a toy he or she likes gets lost or broken.**
   I   2   3   4   5   6   7   NA
9.   **Becomes quite uncomfortable when cold and/or wet.**
   I   2   3   4   5   6   7   NA
10.   **Likes to play so wild and recklessly that s/he might get hurt.**
   I   2   3   4   5   6   7   NA
11.   **Seems to be at ease with almost any person.**

| I | 2 | 3 | 4 | 5 | 6 | 7 | NA |

12. Tends to run rather than walk from place to place.

| I | 2 | 3 | 4 | 5 | 6 | 7 | NA |

13. Notices it when others are wearing new clothing.

| I | 2 | 3 | 4 | 5 | 6 | 7 | NA |

14. Has temper tantrums when s/he doesn't get what s/he wants.

| I | 2 | 3 | 4 | 5 | 6 | 7 | NA |

15. Gets very enthusiastic about the things s/he does

| I | 2 | 3 | 4 | 5 | 6 | 7 | NA |

16. When practicing an activity, has a hard time keeping her/his mind on it.

| I | 2 | 3 | 4 | 5 | 6 | 7 | NA |

17. Is afraid when hearing about ideas such as "boogie man" or when hearing about "burglars" or others who pose a threat.

| I | 2 | 3 | 4 | 5 | 6 | 7 | NA |

18. When outside, often sits quietly.

| I | 2 | 3 | 4 | 5 | 6 | 7 | NA |

19. Enjoys funny stories but usually doesn't laugh at them.

| I | 2 | 3 | 4 | 5 | 6 | 7 | NA |

20. Tends to become sad if plans (for a special event or activity) don't work out.

| I | 2 | 3 | 4 | 5 | 6 | 7 | NA |

21. Will move from one task to another without completing any of them.

| I | 2 | 3 | 4 | 5 | 6 | 7 | NA |

22. Moves about actively (runs, climbs, jumps) when playing indoors.

| I | 2 | 3 | 4 | 5 | 6 | 7 | NA |

23. Is afraid of loud noises.

| I | 2 | 3 | 4 | 5 | 6 | 7 | NA |

24. Seems to listen to even quiet sounds.

| I | 2 | 3 | 4 | 5 | 6 | 7 | NA |

25. Has a hard time settling down after an exciting activity.

| I | 2 | 3 | 4 | 5 | 6 | 7 | NA |

26. Enjoys quiet, soothing activities.

| I | 2 | 3 | 4 | 5 | 6 | 7 | NA |

27. Seems to feel depressed when unable to accomplish some task.

| I | 2 | 3 | 4 | 5 | 6 | 7 | NA |

28. Often rushes into new situations.

| I | 2 | 3 | 4 | 5 | 6 | 7 | NA |

29. Is quite upset by a little cut or bruise.

| I | 2 | 3 | 4 | 5 | 6 | 7 | NA |

30. Gets quite frustrated when prevented from doing something s/he wants to do.

| I | 2 | 3 | 4 | 5 | 6 | 7 | NA |

31. Becomes upset when friends are getting ready to leave the classroom

| I | 2 | 3 | 4 | 5 | 6 | 7 | NA |

32.	Comments when someone (teacher, classmate) has changed his/her appearance.
		I	2	3	4	5	6	7	NA
33.	Enjoys activities such as being chased, spun around by the arms, etc.
		I	2	3	4	5	6	7	NA
34.	When angry about something, s/he tends to stay upset for ten minutes or longer.
		I	2	3	4	5	6	7	NA
35.	Is not afraid of the dark.
		I	2	3	4	5	6	7	NA
36.	Takes a long time in approaching new situations.
		I	2	3	4	5	6	7	NA
37.	Is sometimes shy even around people s/he has known a long time.
		I	2	3	4	5	6	7	NA
38.	Can wait before entering into new activities if s/he is asked to.
		I	2	3	4	5	6	7	NA
39.	Enjoys "snuggling up" next to an adult
		I	2	3	4	5	6	7	NA
40.	Gets angry when s/he can't find something s/he wants to play with.
		I	2	3	4	5	6	7	NA
41.	Is afraid of things such as fire or the loud noise of a fire drill
		I	2	3	4	5	6	7	NA
42.	Sometimes seems nervous when talking to adults s/he has just met.
		I	2	3	4	5	6	7	NA
43.	Is slow and unhurried in deciding what to do next.
		I	2	3	4	5	6	7	NA
44.	Changes from being upset to feeling much better within a few minutes.
		I	2	3	4	5	6	7	NA
45.	Plans for new activities or changes in routine to make sure s/he has what will be needed.
		I	2	3	4	5	6	7	NA
46.	Becomes very excited while planning for new activities such as field trips.
		I	2	3	4	5	6	7	NA
47.	Is quickly aware of some new item in the class room.
		I	2	3	4	5	6	7	NA
48.	Hardly ever laughs out loud during play with other children.
		I	2	3	4	5	6	7	NA
49.	Is not very upset at minor cuts or bruises.
		I	2	3	4	5	6	7	NA
50.	Prefers quiet activities to active games.
		I	2	3	4	5	6	7	NA
51.	Tends to say the first thing that comes to mind, without stopping to think about it.
		I	2	3	4	5	6	7	NA

52. Acts shy around new people.
I   2   3   4   5   6   7   NA
53. Has trouble sitting still when s/he is told to (story time, etc.).
I   2   3   4   5   6   7   NA
54. Rarely cries when s/he hears a sad story.
I   2   3   4   5   6   7   NA
55. Sometimes smiles or giggles playing by her/himself.
I   2   3   4   5   6   7   NA
56. Rarely becomes upset when listening to a sad story
I   2   3   4   5   6   7   NA
57. Enjoys just being talked to.
I   2   3   4   5   6   7   NA
58. Becomes very excited before a special class event (e.g., outing, picnic, party).
I   2   3   4   5   6   7   NA
59. If upset, cheers up quickly when s/he thinks about something else.
I   2   3   4   5   6   7   NA
60. Is comfortable asking other children to play.
I   2   3   4   5   6   7   NA
61. Rarely gets upset when told s/he has to remain quiet during rest times.
I   2   3   4   5   6   7   NA
62. When drawing or coloring in a book, shows strong concentration.
I   2   3   4   5   6   7   NA
63. Is afraid of the dark.
I   2   3   4   5   6   7   NA
64. Is likely to cry even if a little bit hurt.
I   2   3   4   5   6   7   NA
65. Enjoys looking at picture books.
I   2   3   4   5   6   7   NA
66. Is easy to soothe when s/he is upset.
I   2   3   4   5   6   7   NA
67. Is good at following instructions.
I   2   3   4   5   6   7   NA
68. Is rarely frightened by "monsters" in stories or films.
I   2   3   4   5   6   7   NA
69. Likes to go high and fast when pushed on a swing.
I   2   3   4   5   6   7   NA
70. Sometimes turns away shyly from new acquaintances.
I   2   3   4   5   6   7   NA
71. When building or putting something together, becomes very involved in what s/he is doing, and works for long periods.
I   2   3   4   5   6   7   NA
72. Likes being sung to.
I   2   3   4   5   6   7   NA

73.   Approaches places that s/he thinks might be "risky" slowly and cautiously.
        I   2   3   4   5   6   7   NA
74.   Rarely becomes discouraged when s/he has trouble making something work.
        I   2   3   4   5   6   7   NA
75.   Is very difficult to soothe when s/he has become upset.
        I   2   3   4   5   6   7   NA
76.   Likes the sound of words, such as nursery rhymes.
        I   2   3   4   5   6   7   NA
77.   Smiles a lot at people s/he likes.
        I   2   3   4   5   6   7   NA
78.   Dislikes rough and rowdy games.
        I   2   3   4   5   6   7   NA
79.   Often laughs out loud in play with other children.
        I   2   3   4   5   6   7   NA
80.   Rarely laughs aloud in the classroom.
        I   2   3   4   5   6   7   NA
81.   Can easily stop an activity when s/he is told "no."
        I   2   3   4   5   6   7   NA
82.   Is among the last children to try out a new activity.
        I   2   3   4   5   6   7   NA
83.   Doesn't usually notice odors such as perfume, smoke, cooking, etc.
        I   2   3   4   5   6   7   NA
84.   Is easily distracted when listening to a story.
        I   2   3   4   5   6   7   NA
85.   Is full of energy, even during quiet times.
        I   2   3   4   5   6   7   NA
86.   Enjoys sitting on adult's lap.
        I   2   3   4   5   6   7   NA
87.   Gets angry when called away from an activity or game before s/he is ready to quit.
        I   2   3   4   5   6   7   NA
88.   Enjoys riding a tricycle or bicycle fast and recklessly.
        I   2   3   4   5   6   7   NA
89.   Sometimes becomes absorbed in a picture book and looks at it for a long time.
        I   2   3   4   5   6   7   NA
90.   Remains pretty calm about upcoming desserts like ice cream.
        I   2   3   4   5   6   7   NA
91.   Hardly ever complains when ill with a cold.
        I   2   3   4   5   6   7   NA
92.   Looks forward to special class events, but does not get too excited about them.
        I   2   3   4   5   6   7   NA
93.   Likes to sit quietly and watch people do things.

	I	2	3	4	5	6	7	NA
94.	**Enjoys gentle rhythmic activities, such as rocking or swaying.**							
	I	2	3	4	5	6	7	NA

Please check back to make sure you have completed all the pages of the questionnaire. Thank you very much for your help!

Temperament in Middle childhood Questionnaire (version 3.0)

Instructions: Please read carefully before starting:

On the next pages you will see a set of statements that describe children's reactions to a number of situations. We would like you to tell us what <u>your</u> child's reaction is likely to be in those situations. There are of course no "correct" ways of reacting; children differ widely in their reactions, and it is these differences we are trying to learn about. Please read each statement and decide whether it is a "<u>true</u>" or "<u>untrue</u>" description of your child's reaction <u>within the past six months</u>. Use the following scale to indicate how well a statement describes your child:

<u>Circle #</u>	<u>If the statement is:</u>
1	Almost always untrue of your child
2	Usually untrue of your child
3	Sometimes true, sometimes untrue of your child
4	Usually true of your child
5	Almost always true of your child

If you cannot answer one of the items because you have never seen the child in that situation, for example, if the statement is about the child playing wildly and recklessly and you have never seen your child play that way, then circle <u>NA</u> (not applicable).

Please be sure to respond by circling a number or NA for <u>every</u> item. If you find an item objectionable or upsetting, you may make an exception to this instruction and skip the item.

My Child ...	Almost always <u>untrue</u>	Usually <u>untrue</u>	Sometimes <u>true, Sometimes untrue,</u>	Usually <u>true</u>	Almost always <u>true</u>	Does Not Apply
1. Likes poems.	1	2	3	4	5	NA
2. Likes to be physically active.	1	2	3	4	5	NA
3. Likes going down high slides or other	1	2	3	4	5	NA
4. Greatly enjoys playing games where s/he can win	1	2	3	4	5	NA
5. Is bothered by pain when s/he falls down.	1	2	3	4	5	NA
6. Can stop him/herself when s/he is told to stop.	1	2	3	4	5	NA
7. Is easily distracted when listening to a story.	1	2	3	4	5	NA

My Child ...	Almost always untrue	Usually untrue	Sometimes true, Sometimes untrue,	Usually true	Almost always true	Does Not Apply
8. Has a hard time settling down after an exciting activity.	1		3	4	5	NA
9. Likes rough and rowdy games.	1	2	3	4	5	NA
10. Likes the crunching sound of leaves in the fall.	1	2	3	4	5	NA
11. She/he is afraid of fire.	1	2	3	4	5	NA
12. Likes to think of new ideas.	1	2	3	4	5	NA
13. Is afraid of heights.	1	2	3	4	5	NA
14. Can't help touching things without getting permission.	1	2	3	4	5	NA
15. Is always on the move.	1	2	3	4	5	NA
16. Tends to say the first thing that comes to mind, without stopping to think about it.	1	2	3	4	5	NA
17. Looks around the room when doing homework.	1	2	3	4	5	NA
18. Would like to be friends with lots of people.	1	2	3	4	5	NA
19. Is very difficult to soothe when s/he has become upset.	1	2	3	4	5	NA
20 Can make him/herself do homework, even when s/he wants to play.	1	2	3	4	5	NA
21. Prefers playing outdoors to indoors when weather permits.	1	2	3	4	5	NA
22. Interrupts others when they are talking.	1	2	3	4	5	NA
23. Would rather play a sport than watch TV.	1	2	3	4	5	NA
24. Tends to become sad if plans don't work out.	1	2	3	4	5	NA
25. She/he says the first thing that comes to mind.	1	2	3	4	5	NA
26. Can say hello to a new child in class, even when feeling shy.	1	2	3	4	5	NA
27. Sometimes appears to be downcast for no reason.	1	2	3	4	5	NA
28. Has a hard time speaking when scared to answer a question.	1	2	3	4	5	NA
29. Cheers up quickly.	1	2	3	4	5	NA
30. Cries when given an injection.	1	2	3	4	5	NA
31. Becomes sad when told to do something s/he does not want to do.	1	2	3	4	5	NA

My Child ...	Almost always untrue	Usually untrue	Sometimes true, Sometimes untrue,	Usually true	Almost always true	Does Not Apply
32. Likes to play quiet games.	1	2	3	4	5	NA
33. Would like to spend time with a good friend every day.	1	2	3	4	5	NA
34. Likes the sound of poems.	1	2	3	4	5	NA

My Child …						
35. Cries sadly when a favorite toy gets lost or broken.	1	2	3	4	5	NA
36. Notices the color of people's eyes.	1	2	3	4	5	NA
37. Likes to get out of the house and do something physical.	1	2	3	4	5	NA
38. Becomes quite uncomfortable when cold or wet.	1	2	3	4	5	NA
39. Can take a Band-Aid® off when needed, even when painful.	1	2	3	4	5	NA
40. Can stop him/herself from doing things too quickly.	1	2	3	4	5	NA
41. Enjoys exciting and suspenseful TV shows.	1	2	3	4	5	NA
42. Usually stops and thinks things over before deciding to do something.	1	2	3	4	5	NA
43. Likes to run.	1	2	3	4	5	NA
44. Notices the sound of birds.	1	2	3	4	5	NA
45. Likes exploring new places.	1	2	3	4	5	NA
46. Can make him/herself run fast, even when tired.	1	2	3	4	5	NA
47. Becomes self conscious when around people.	1	2	3	4	5	NA
48. Likes to make up stories.	1	2	3	4	5	NA
49. Becomes tearful when tired.	1	2	3	4	5	NA
50. Enjoys making her/his own decisions.	1	2	3	4	5	NA
51. Is warm and friendly.	1	2	3	4	5	NA
52. Would find moving to a new, big city exciting.	1	2	3	4	5	NA
53. Gets very angry when another child takes his/her toy away.	1	2	3	4	5	NA
54. Likes reading or listening to make believe stories.	1	2	3	4	5	NA
58. Likes to make others feel good.	1	2	3	4	5	NA
59. Can generally think of something to say, even with strangers.	1	2	3	4	5	NA
60. Is followed by other children.	1	2	3	4	5	NA
61. Gets angry when called in from play before s/he is ready to quit.	1	2	3	4	5	NA
62. Can tell if another person is sad or angry by the look on their face.	1	2	3	4	5	NA
63. Is scared of injections by the doctor.	1	2	3	4	5	NA
64. When s/he cries, tends to cry for more than a couple of minutes at a time.	1	2	3	4	5	NA

My Child …	Almost always untrue	Usually untrue	Sometimes true, Sometimes untrue,	Usually true	Almost always true	Does Not Apply

	1	2	3	4	5	NA
65. Enjoys exciting places with big crowds.	1	2	3	4	5	NA
66. Is energetic.	1	2	3	4	5	NA
67. Likes listening to music.	1	2	3	4	5	NA
68. Remains upset for hours when someone hurts his/her feelings.	1	2	3	4	5	NA
69. Is bothered by loud or scratchy sounds.	1	2	3	4	5	NA
70. Has a hard time making him/herself clean own room	1	2	3	4	5	NA
71. Enjoys drawing pictures.	1	2	3	4	5	NA
72. Calls out answers before being called on by a teacher or group leader.	1		3	4	5	NA
73. Enjoys looking at books.	1	2	3	4	5	NA
74. Makes up mind suddenly.	1	2	3	4	5	NA
75. Is afraid of burglars or the "boogie man."	1	2	3	4	5	NA
76. When a child is left out, can ask that child to play.	1	2	3	4	5	NA
77. Touches fabric or other soft material.	1	2	3	4	5	
78. When working on an activity, has a hard time keeping her/his mind on it.	1	2	3	4	5	
79. Has a hard time waiting his/her turn to talk when excited.	1	2	3	4	5	NA
80. Has a hard time paying attention.	1	2	3	4	5	NA
81. Is bothered by light or color that is too bright.	1	2	3	4	5	NA
82. Needs to be told by teacher to pay attention.	1	2	3	4	5	NA
83. Often rushes into doing new things.	1	2	3	4	5	NA
84. Is first to speak up in a group.	1	2	3	4	5	NA
85. Is afraid of sleeping over at someone's house.	1	2	3	4	5	NA
86. Likes quiet reading time.	1	2	3	4	5	NA
87. Gets angry when s/he can't find something s/he is looking for.	1	2	3	4	5	NA
88. Is very careful and cautious when crossing the street.	1	2	3	4	5	NA
89. Has a hard time working on an assignment s/he finds boring.	1	2	3	4	5	NA
90. Is afraid of loud noises.	1	2	3	4	5	NA
91. Goes to school nurse's office for very minor complaints.	1	2	3	4	5	NA
92. Likes the feel of warm water in a bath or shower.	1	2	3	4	5	NA
93. Does a fun activity when s/he is supposed to do homework instead.	1	2	3	4	5	NA
94. Gets angry when s/he has trouble with a task.	1	2	3	4	5	NA
95. Likes to look at trees.	1	2	3	4	5	NA
96. Likes to play so wildly and recklessly that s/he might get hurt.	1	2	3	4	5	NA

My Child …	Almost always untrue	Usually untrue	Sometimes true, Sometimes untrue,	Usually true	Almost always true	Does Not Apply
97. Is told by others to "cheer up" and be happier.	1	2	3	4	5	NA
98. When with other children, is the one to choose activities or games.	1	2	3	4	5	NA
99. Gets angry when s/he makes a mistake.	1	2	3	4	5	NA
100. Her/his feelings are easily hurt.	1	2	3	4	5	NA
101. Can make her/himself get out of bed, even when tired.	1	2	3	4	5	NA
102. Likes active games.	1	2	3	4	5	NA
103. Can apologize or shake hands after a fight.	1	2	3	4	5	NA
104. Has a big imagination.	1		3	4	5	NA
105. When angry about something, s/he tends to stay upset for five minutes or longer.	1	2	3	4	5	NA
106. Places great importance on friends.	1	2	3	4	5	NA
107. Seems to feel down when unable to accomplish a task.	1	2	3	4	5	NA
108. Gets into trouble because s/he does things without thinking first.	1	2	3	4	5	NA
109. Notices small changes in the environment, like lights getting brighter in a room.	1	2	3	4	5	NA
110. Has temper tantrums when s/he doesn't get what s/he wants.	1	2	3	4	5	NA
111. Notices things others don't notice.	1	2	3	4	5	NA
112. Has a hard time going back to sleep after waking in the night.	1	2	3	4	5	NA
113. Likes to sit under a blanket.	1	2	3	4	5	NA
114. Notices even little specks of dirt on objects.	1	2	3	4	5	NA
115. Enjoys playing chase.	1	2	3	4	5	NA
116. Likes to pretend.	1	2	3	4	5	NA
117. Gets nervous about going to the dentist.	1	2	3	4	5	NA
118. Is shy.	1	2	3	4	5	NA
119. Likes to go high and fast on the swings.	1	2	3	4	5	NA
120. Needs to be told to pay attention.	1	2	3	4	5	NA
121. Would think that skiing or snowboarding fast sounds scary.	1	2	3	4	5	NA
122. Usually wins arguments with other children.	1	2	3	4	5	NA
123. Likes to run his/her hand over things to see if they are smooth or rough.	1	2	3	4	5	NA
124. Grabs what s/he wants.	1	2	3	4	5	NA
125. Becomes upset when hair is combed.	1	2	3	4	5	NA
126. Enjoys riding bicycle fast and recklessly.	1	2	3	4	5	NA

127. Likes to run around outside.	1	2	3	4	5	NA
128. Decides what s/he wants very quickly and then goes after it.	1	2	3	4	5	NA

My Child ...	Almost always untrue	Usually untrue	Sometimes true, Sometimes untrue,	Usually true	Almost always true	Does Not Apply
129. Would like to confide in others.	1	2	3	4	5	NA
130. Usually rushes into an activity without thinking about it.	1	2	3	4	5	NA
131. Likes to be in charge.	1	2	3	4	5	NA
132. Can make him/herself take medicine or eat food that s/he knows tastes bad.	1	2	3	4	5	NA
133. Feels sad often.	1	2	3	4	5	NA
134. Likes hugs and kisses.	1	2	3	4	5	NA
135. Likes to plan carefully before doing something.	1	2	3	4	5	NA
136. Acts insecure with others.	1		3	4	5	NA
137. Feels nervous for a long time after being scared.	1	2	3	4	5	NA
138. Is quite upset by a little cut or bruise.	1	2	3	4	5	NA
139. Can make him/herself pick up something dirty in order to throw it away.	1	2	3	4	5	NA
140. Is afraid of dark.	1	2	3	4	5	NA
141. Is able to keep secrets.	1	2	3	4	5	
142. Is bothered by bath water that is too hot or too cold.	1	2	3	4	5	
143. Has a hard time slowing down when rules say to walk.	1	2	3	4	5	NA
144. Tends to feel sad even when others are happy.	1	2	3	4	5	NA
145. Loves pets and other small animals.	1	2	3	4	5	NA
146. Gets mad when provoked by other children.	1	2	3	4	5	NA
147. When s/he sees a toy or a game s/he wants, is eager to have it right away.	1	2	3	4	5	NA
148. Likes to feel close to other people.	1	2	3	4	5	NA
149. Gets distracted when trying to pay attention in class.	1	2	3	4	5	NA
150. Notices when parents are wearing new clothing.	1	2	3	4	5	NA
151. Likes to make things.	1	2	3	4	5	NA
152. Has a hard time getting moving when tired.	1	2	3	4	5	NA
153. Is very frightened by nightmares.	1	2	3	4	5	NA
154. Is likely to cry when even a little bit hurt.	1	2	3	4	5	NA
155. Enjoys winning arguments.	1	2	3	4	5	NA
156. Likes just being with other people.	1	2	3	4	5	NA
157. Can make him/herself smile at someone, even when s/he dislikes them.	1	2	3	4	5	NA

Appendix

<u>Characteristics of Sample D of Study – II of Phase II</u>

Table S
Demographic Characteristics of the Sample D (N = 248)

	Girls *(n = 119)*	Boys *(n = 129)*
Age		
Mean	9.71	8.16
SD	2.33	1.27
Family System		
% Joint	64 %	56 %
% Nuclear	36 %	44 %
Marital Status of Parents		
% Married	90.70 %	88 %
% Divorced	9.30 %	10 %
% Widow		2 %
Family Income		
Mean	47000	40000
Mode	35000	31000

     The percentage of girls (48 %) in this group is lower compared to the boys (52 %). Majority of the boys were first born (mode = 1; percentage = 57.3), whereas most of the girls were second born (49.5 percent). Majority of the girls were students of grade 5, whereas most of the boys were in grade 4. Most of both girls and boys had 3 siblings. Majority of parents of both girls and boys were married. The mean age of fathers was observed to be 41.39 years and mean age of mothers was noted to be 32.67 years.

Characteristics of Sample Representing ID Group

Table T . 1
Demographic Characteristics of the ID Sample

	Girls (*n* =44)	Boys (*n* = 59)
Age		
Mean	8.69	9.25
SD	1.90	2.09
IQ		
Mean	43.26	42.24
SD	16.05	15.07
Family System		
% Joint	56.8	50.8
% Nuclear	43.2	49.2
Marital Status of Parents		
% Married	84.1	83.1
% Divorced	13.6	15.3
% Widow	2.3	1.7
Family Income		
Mean	30597.22	29531.91
Mode	30000	20000

The percentage of girls in this group is lower compared to the boys. Majority of the boys were first born (mode = 1; percentage = 45.6), whereas most of the girls were second born (32.6 percent). Most of both girls and boys had 3 siblings. The mean IQ of girls is slightly higher than boys in this group.

Other than the personal characteristics of children, significant demographic indicators of family characteristics were also assessed. The information is mentioned in the table below.

Table T . 2

Gender wise Family Characteristics of Sample

	Girls		Boys	
	Mother	Father	Mother	Father
Age				
Mean (*SD*)	37.27 (9.30)	41.45 (8.48)	34.25 (5.27)	39.40 (5.84)
Education				
Illiterate	27.9	20.6	29.3	18.4
Below Matric	18.6	20.6	22.4	16.3
Matric	27.9	20.6	19.0	24.5
Intermediate	11.6	11.8	13.8	18.4
Graduation	11.6	5.9	10.3	10.2
Masters	2.3	20.6	5.2	12.2
Post Masters				
Occupation				
Laborer	-	6.5	-	14.3
Domestic Helper	8.8	-	4.1	-
Skilled worker	-	25.8	2	16.7
Farmer	-	3.2	-	2.4
Banker	-	3.2	-	4.8
Engineer	-	-	-	9.5
Doctor	-	-	2	4.8
Teacher	2.9	6.5	16.3	7.1
Business	-	25.8	-	19
Lawyers	-	-	-	-
Job	-	29.0	-	21.4
Housewives	88.2	-	75.5	-

Table T.3

Mean and SD of Subscales of Temperament for ID Group

	Full Sample M (SD)		Girls (n = 46)		Boys (n = 59)	
			M	(SD)	M	(SD)
Activity Level	3.65	(1.28)	3.29	(1.27)	3.46	(1.25)
Activity Control	2.07	(1.49)	1.95	(1.53)	2.17	(1.49)
Anger/ Frustration	2.97	(1.62)	3.02	(1.70)	2.90	(1.57)
Attentional Focusing	3.04	(1.20)	3.29	(1.23)	2.87	(1.16)
Affiliation	2.34	(1.53)	2.13	(1.59)	2.50	(1.49)
Assertiveness	1.85	(1.34)	1.83	(1.48)	1.87	(1.25)
Discomfort	3.12	(1.67)	3.36	(1.73)	2.92	(1.63)
Falling Reactivity/ Soothability	2.61	(1.32)	2.59	(1.26)	2.59	(1.37)
Fantasy Openness	2.05	(1.33)	2.06	(1.42)	2.04	(1.28)
Fear	3.29	(1.73)	3.55	(1.71)	3.07	(1.74)
High Intensity Pleasure	3.72	(1.19)	3.42	(1.19)	3.96	(1.16)
Impulsivity	3.78	(1.21)	3.65	(1.29)	3.89	(1.16)
Inhibitory Control	3.18	(1.26)	3.33	(1.32)	3.09	(1.20)
Low Intensity Pleasure	3.51	(1.27)	3.81	(1.27)	3.31	(1.22)
Perceptual Sensitivity	3.37	(1.33)	3.70	(1.26)	3.14	(1.33)
Sadness	2.79	(1.47)	2.87	(1.38)	2.71	(1.53)
Shyness	4.03	(1.25)	4.22	(1.39)	3.92	(1.14)

On surgency domain the mean score for girls is 15.93 with standard deviation of 4.62, whereas, boys have mean of 17.39 and standard deviation of 5.64. The mean score of girls on Effortful control is 15.97 with standard deviation of 4.78, however, boys have mean of 14.29 with 4.52 standard deviation. The boys score 13.77 mean with standard deviation of 6.83 on negative affectivity when girls have 15.03 and 6.56 as mean and standard deviation.

Characteristics of Sample Representing ASD Group

Table U. 1

Demographic Characteristics of the ASD Sample

	Girls *(n =32/1)*	Boys *(n = 62)*
Age		
Mean	8.84	8.53
SD	1.88	1.86
IQ		
Mean	37.00	38.52
SD	8.48	8.86
Family System		
% Joint	56.3 %	50.8 %
% Nuclear	43.8 %	49.2 %
Marital Status of Parents		
% Married	68.8 %	72.1 %
% Divorced	21.9 %	18.0 %
% Widow	9.4 %	9.8 %
Family Income		
Mean	44560	54788.46
Mode	30000	15000

The percentage of girls in this group is lower compared to the boys. Majority of both girls (46.7%) and boys (40.4 %) were first born (mode = 2) and most of girls (34.5%) and boys (32.1%) had 2 siblings. The mean IQ of girls is slightly lower than boys in this group.

Other than the personal characteristics of children, significant demographic indicators of family characteristics were also assessed. The information is mentioned in the table below.

Table U. 2

Gender wise Family Characteristics of ASD Sample

	Girls		Boys	
	Mother	Father	Mother	Father
Age				
Mean (*SD*)	36.76 (2.69)	41.38 (5.58)	36.06 (5.86)	41.57 (7.24)
Education				
Illiterate	13.3 %	27.3 %	7.1 %	9.6 %
Below Matric	3.3 %	4.5 %	16.1 %	13.5 %
Matric	33.3 %	4.5 %	17.9 %	17.3 %
Intermediate	30.0 %	22.7 %	28.6 %	11.5 %
Graduation	13.3 %	27.3 %	14.3 %	25.0 %
Masters	6.7 %	13.6 %	14.3 %	23.1 %
Post Masters			1.8 %	
Occupation				
Laborer	-	5.3 %	-	8.3 %
Domestic Helper	13.6 %	-	4 %	2.1 %
Skilled worker	-	10.5 %	2 %	2.1 %
Farmer	-	5.3 %	-	-
Banker	-	5.3 %	-	10.4 %
Engineer	-	5.3 %	-	4.2 %
Doctor	4.5 %	5.3 %	6 %	6.3 %
Teacher	-	-	8 %	2.1 %
Business	-	5.3 %	4 %	37.5 %
Lawyers	-	-	-	-
Job	-	57.9 %	-	20.8 %
Housewives	81.8 %	-	76 %	-

Table U.3

Mean and SD of Subscales of Temperament for ASD Group

	Full Sample		Girls (n = 31)		Boys (n = 62)	
	M	*(SD)*	*M*	*(SD)*	*M*	*(SD)*
Activity Level	3.14	(1.29)	2.75	(1.24)	3.33	(1.28)
Activity Control	1.64	(1.29)	1.51	(1.17)	1.71	(1.35)
Anger/ Frustration	4.26	(3.52)	5.07	(5.70)	3.85	(1.43)
Attentional Focusing	2.84	(1.17)	2.69	(1.16)	2.90	(1.18)
Affiliation	1.89	(1.45)	1.86	(1.50)	1.92	(1.43)
Assertiveness	1.55	(1.29)	1.41	(1.25)	1.64	(1.32)
Discomfort	4.05	(1.28)	4.15	(1.18)	4.01	(1.33)
Falling Reactivity/ Soothability	3.55	(1.09)	3.39	(1.11)	3.64	(1.09)
Fantasy Openness	1.85	(1.41)	1.58	(1.28)	1.99	(1.44)
Fear	4.11	(1.39)	4.24	(1.22)	4.06	(1.46)
High Intensity Pleasure	3.50	(1.21)	3.21	(1.19)	3.64	(1.18)
Impulsivity	3.28	(1.29)	3.29	(1.27)	3.27	(1.31)
Inhibitory Control	2.87	(1.14)	2.91	(1.33)	2.83	(1.04)
Low Intensity Pleasure	3.42	(1.21)	3.29	(1.31)	3.45	(1.18)
Perceptual Sensitivity	3.42	(1.32)	3.58	(1.32)	3.31	(1.32)
Sadness	3.69	(1.35)	3.85	(1.33)	3.62	(1.35)
Shyness	3.49	(1.32)	3.44	(1.30)	3.50	(1.34)

On surgency domain the mean score for girls is 14.47 with standard deviation of 6.37, whereas, boys have mean of 15.71 and standard deviation of 6.79. The mean score of girls on effortful control is 12.53 with standard deviation of 3.88, however, boys have mean of 13.60 with 3.76 standard deviation. The boys score 18.83 mean with standard deviation of 5.78 on negative affectivity when girls have 19.49 and 5.10 as mean and standard deviation.

<u>Characteristics of Sample Representing Typically Developing Group</u>

Table V.1
Demographic Characteristics of the TD Sample

	Girls *(n = 103)*	Boys *(n = 136)*
Age		
Mean	8.03	7.88
SD	1.83	2.11
Family System		
% Joint	59.2 %	60.3 %
% Nuclear	40.8 %	39.7 %
Marital Status of Parents		
% Married	94.2 %	95.6 %
% Divorced	3.9 %	3.7 %
% Widow	1.9 %	.7 %
Family Income		
Mean	51044.94	42818.90
Mode	60000	50000

The percentage of girls in this group is lower compared to the boys. Majority of the boys were first born (mode = 1; percentage = 29), whereas most of the girls were second born (40.2 percent). Most of both girls and boys had 3 siblings.

Other than the personal characteristics of children, significant demographic indicators of family characteristics were also assessed. The information is mentioned in the table below.

Table V . 2

Gender wise Family Characteristics of TD Sample

	Girls		Boys	
	Mother	Father	Mother	Father
Age				
Mean (*SD*)	37.04 (4.53)	41.49 (4.37)	38.16 (4.68)	42.76(4.83)
Education				
Illiterate	9.6 %	8.6 %	9.2 %	11.3 %
Below Matric	8.5 %	5.4 %	7.2 %	7.1 %
Matric	13.8 %	9.7 %	15.3 %	11.7 %
Intermediate	19.1 %	17.7 %	21.9 %	15.6 %
Graduation	35.1 %	36 %	25.8 %	29.9 %
Masters	12.8 %	20.4 %	15.6 %	22.8 %
Post Masters	1.1 %	2.2 %	5 %	3.6 %
Occupation				
Laborer	-	1.5 %	-	15.8 %
Domestic Helper	-	-	.8 %	-
Skilled worker	-	3.3 %	-	3.1 %
Farmer	-	1.1 %	-	-
Banker	1.1 %	18.5 %	1.5 %	3.9 %
Engineer	-	1.6 %	-	1 %
Doctor	2.1 %	3.3 %	.8 %	2.8 %
Teacher	4.3 %	-	6.9 %	3.6 %
Business	-	50 %	.8 %	44.9 %
Lawyers	-	1.1 %	-	4 %
Job	-	19.6 %	-	29.3 %
Housewives	92.6 %	-	89.2 %	

Fathers of majority of participants are businessmen in both groups. Income of the families of girls is higher than the families of boys.

Table V. 3

Mean and SD of Subscales of Temperament for TD Group

	Girls (n = 103)		Boys (n = 136)	
	M	(SD)	M	(SD)
Activity Level	3.99	(1.04)	4.39	(1.33)
Activity Control	1.67	(0.76)	1.34	(1.60)
Anger/ Frustration	2.58	(0.20)	2.58	(1.22)
Attentional Focusing	3.68	(1.27)	3.44	(1.35)
Affiliation	1.87	(0.96)	1.52	(1.87)
Assertiveness	1.83	(0.95)	1.47	(1.82)
Discomfort	2.68	(0.27)	2.33	(1.16)
Falling Reactivity/ Soothability	2.70	(0.19)	2.51	(0.99)
Fantasy Openness	1.85	(0.93)	1.47	(1.80)
Fear	2.69	(0.34)	2.49	(1.24)
High Intensity Pleasure	4.01	(.89)	4.11	(0.97)
Impulsivity	3.60	(1.05)	3.79	(1.13)
Inhibitory Control	3.96	(1.03)	4.08	(1.83)
Low Intensity Pleasure	4.11	(1.15)	3.97	(1.26)
Perceptual Sensitivity	4.11	(1.22)	3.68	(1.25)
Sadness	2.42	(1.13)	2.34	(1.05)
Shyness	3.60	(1.29)	3.97	(1.27)

On surgency domain the mean score for girls is 19.53 with standard deviation of 5.99, whereas, boys have mean of 21.53and standard deviation of 7.01. The mean score of girls on effortful control is 17.51 with standard deviation of 2.87, however, boys have mean of 16.44 with 3.18 standard deviation. The boys score 12.24 mean with standard deviation of 4.95 on negative affectivity when girls have 13.16 and 6.18 as mean and standard deviation.